Creolization in the French Americas

Creolization in the French Americas

Edited by Jean-Marc Masseaut,
Jordan Kellman, and Michael Martin

University of Louisiana at Lafayette Press
2015

© 2015 by University of Louisiana at Lafayette Press
All rights reserved

Reprinted in 2025

ISBN 13 (paper): 978-1-935754-68-8

http://ulpress.org
University of Louisiana at Lafayette Press
P.O. Box 40831
Lafayette, LA 70504-0831

Library of Congress Cataloging-in-Publication Data

Creolization in the French Americas = Créolités aux Amériques françaises / edited by Jean-Marc Masseaut, Michael Martin, and Jordan Kellman. pages cm -- (Journal of the shackles of memory = Cahiers des Anneaux de la Mémoire ; no. 15)
Parallel title: Créolités aux Amériques françaises
Includes bibliographical references.
ISBN 978-1-935754-68-8 (paper : acid-free paper)
1. Creoles--America--History. 2. France--Colonies--America--History. 3. Creoles--America--Ethnic identity. 4. America--Ethnic relations--History. 5. America--Social life and customs. 6. Culture diffusion--America--History. 7. Acculturation--America--History. 8. Creole dialects--America--History. 9. Intercultural communication--America--History. I. Masseaut, Jean-Marc. II. Martin, Michael S., 1972- III. Kellman, Jordan, 1966- IV. Title: Créolités aux Amériques françaises.
E29.C73C74 2015
303.48'2097--dc23
2015016622

Journal of the Shackles of Memory N°15
Cahiers des Anneaux de la Mémoire N° 15

Creolization in the French Americas,
Créolités aux Amériques françaises,

c (copyright) Association les Anneaux de la Mémoire.
ISSN 1280-4215

Les Anneaux de la Mémoire
18 rue Scribe,
Nantes, France, 44 000

Table of Contents

Acknowledgments ix

Preface to the English Edition
Jordan Kellman xi

Foreword
Jean-Marc Masseaut xv

1. **Encounter and Environment in La France Equinoxiale: Franciscans and Tupinambá in Maranhão, Brazil, 1612-1613**
Jordan Kellman 1

2. **On the Origins of the First African Populations in Lower French Louisiana: The Early Eighteenth Century**
Jean-Marc Masseaut 15

Danse Gwoka, rythme Léwoz..*36*

3. **Creolized Frenchmen and Frenchified Amerindians in Louisiana**
Sophie White 45

Danse Gwoka, rythme menndé *54*

4. **Creole Identity in French Louisiana: From the Memoir of Dumont de Montigny**
Gordon Sayre 63

5. **Haydel Habitation (Whitney Plantation): History of a Plantation on the German Coast of Louisiana (1750-1860)**
Ibrahima Seck 71

6. **South Louisiana Creoles: Origins and Evolution of a Modern Cultural Identity**
Elista Istre 93

Danse Gwoka, rythme Woulé *124*

7.	Le Gwoka Mona Georgelin	**129**
8.	Bitasyon Gwotanbou, on The lands of Gwoka Max Diakok	**133**

Danse Gwoka, rythme Toumblak *134*

9.	A Linguistic Process: Creole in the Americas Josette Nonone	**139**
10.	Defense and Illustration of Haitian Creole in Frankétienne's Works Rafaël Lucas	**151**

Danse Gwoka, rythme Pajanbèl *166*

11.	Creole/ Creolism/ Creolization/Créolité Jacques De Cauna	**173**
12.	Images of Being, Places of the Imagination Edouard Glissant, with Comment by Olivier Douville	**177**
13.	Is Creolization a Philosophy of History? The Colonial History of the Antilles, Globalization and "Globality" Edelyn Dorismond	**191**
14.	Creolization: Some Observations Carlo Celius	**203**
15.	Theorizing About Caribbean Society: From Plantation Society to the Post-Colony, and Creolité Anthony Bogues	**221**

Danse Gwoka, rythme Kaladja *232*

16.	Creolization Metaphors in the Southeast Asian Context Bryce Beemer	**241**

17.	The Creole Origins of the Early New World Banjo James L. A.Webb	249

Danse Gwoka, rythme graj *262*

Memory, History, Oblivion: The Work of History
and/or of Memory: Hommage to Yolande Joseph (1933-2011)
Elisée Soumonni   279

In Memory of Hugues Liborel-Pochot
Jean- Marc Masseaut   281

About the Contributors   285

Acknowledgments

This volume would not have been conceivable without the strong collaboration between the Shackles of Memory Society in Nantes and the Center for Louisiana Studies at the University of Louisiana at Lafayette, a collaboration nurtured over the course of many discussions on both sides of the Atlantic. The editors from both institutions relied on the help of many individuals over the course of this project. Philippe Gustin, director of the Centre International de Lafayette, played a crucial role in laying the foundations of this volume by bringing its French and American editors together, as did Christine Renard, who introduced *The Shackles of Memory* to Louisiana. James L.A. Webb, Elista Istre, and Carlo Celius all made important contributions to the conceptual framework of the collection. Other key individuals who helped this project in a variety of ways include Olivier Douville, co-founder of the *Anneaux de la mémoire* journal; Sylvie Glissant, who generously authorized the publication of her husband's writings; Lucie Cassand and Mona Georgelin, heads of the Mamanthé Association, who permitted the inclusion of Azzedine Hsissou's photo essay of the Gwoka dance troupe Massilla Ka, and guest artists Max Diakok, Jan Mary Lurel, and Georges Janette; the French Foreign Minister for his confidence and financial support; Patricia Beauchamp Afade, Mathilde Bouclé Bossard, Manuel Rui Mascate, and Renaud Deschamp, who assured the association's cooperation and the production of the French edition. At the University of Louisiana at Lafayette, we thank Leslie Schilling, director of the Humanities Resource Center, and Mary Karnath Duhé, production assistant for the UL Press, for their invaluable work on the manuscript. We owe a special debt to our translator, Rachel Doherty, whose patience and keen eye were crucial to the success of the project. Finally, we thank the members and friends of *The Shackles of Memory* for their constant support of the journal, and its president and director of publication, Yvon Chotard, who maintains the interests and convictions of the association in his numerous activities, as well as the staff of the Center for Louisiana Studies at the University of Louisiana at Lafayette.

Preface to the English Edition

This volume is the English version of a collection of essays conceived from the beginning as a bilingual work. The essays and creative works gathered here were explicitly drawn from the distinct but related literatures emerging in the Francophone, Anglophone, African, and Caribbean scholarship on creolization and French colonial society. The aim of the editors was to place these strains of scholarship and creative production in conversation with one another. Thus the idea of bilingual publication, with a French edition published first—in 2014 as a special issue of the journal *Cahiers des Anneaux de la Mémoire* (n.15) entitled *La Créolité aux Amériques Françaises*—and now the present volume, with all French articles translated into English. Together, the editors believe, these nearly simultaneous publications allow a greater number of readers to see the variety of scholarship that bears on the question of Creole identity in the French Americas and the many interconnections among the perspectives offered.

The diversity of articles goes well beyond linguistic and national traditions. Disciplinary roots of the contributions include such divergent fields as early modern European colonial history, dance choreography, psychoanalysis, linguistics, literary study of new world travel narratives, American Studies, African Diaspora history, French literature, philosophy, art history, African studies, and museum studies. It is one of the features of the modern academy that these disciplines are not often seen in direct conversation with one another. Of course, there is more than academic territorialism at stake in this state of affairs: the question of who speaks for the social groups that make up colonial and post-colonial societies has long been and will continue to be contested. This volume rests on the firm conviction that, in order to be understood, complex phenomena like the emergence and evolution of Creole identity require perspectives that only such a diversity of disciplines and points of view can offer, and that those disciplines and perspectives can come together and progress toward knowledge and understanding.

The volume's title, *Creolization in the French Americas*, asserts the viability of two concepts that a few decades ago would have been almost unthinkable. First, the idea of creolization as a process that has important things to tell us about the historical and cultural developments of European expansion and the creation of modernity is relatively new. While the idea of a Creole language, cuisine, and identity as an important component of new world society has a long history, the claim that a process of creolization that was not controlled by any particular group and yet had a profound impact on all of the groups involved in the creation of new world societies, and that indeed those societies cannot be understood without it, has only been accepted in the past decade or two. Second, the assumption of a coherent, historical, and cultural French America that links colonial experiences from Quebec to Brazil, is distinct both from Spanish, English, Dutch, and other colonial societies, and forms an important and long overlooked aspect of French and Atlantic history, has also gained currency only in the past decade.

Changes over time in the meaning of the word Creole itself follow a telling historical path that in many ways mirrors broader interpretations of the European colonization of the New World and the development of societies there. Originally applied to those of European or African descent born in the new world beginning in the sixteenth century, it came to denote during the eighteenth century anyone of European ancestry living in the Americas or other colonial territories. During the nineteenth and early twentieth centuries, and depending on location, it came to refer to a variety of emergent communities that had shared African and European cultural and linguistic roots. During the late twentieth century, the term took on the broader meaning of the encounter and mixing of diverse cultures. Thus the process of creolization refers to the European and African diasporas in the Americas, to the various historical identities created by the process, and to the process of identity creation itself in a diverse population.

Recent scholarship on creolization has emphasized its special role in shaping and understanding power relations in post-colonial society. The assertion of Creole identity is now taken to be an explicit or implicit rebellion against the hegemony of European, white, and western culture and power in all of their forms. In this context, the linguistic non-conformity of Creole languages becomes symbolic of a broader refusal of externally imposed structures and norms, extending even to the rejection of western science as a guiding epistemology in favor of embracing local, traditional, and magical forces. On the social axis, *créolité* often stands in for the embrace of local community against the imposition of legally constituted metropolitan society. But neither could creolization ever be conceived as an elevation of one cultural tradition over another, because at the very heart of the concept, historically and conceptually, lies the mixture of cultures. Thus embracing and co-opting the symbols, traditions, and cultural currency of various groups has always been part of Creole society. Attitudes toward this feature have gone from disdain and fear, on the part of European colonial officials and their sympathizers, to embrace and celebration, on the part of modern commentators who see in it a local victory over the colonial discourse of command and control.

The essays in this volume seek to transcend this simplistic continuum by digging deeply into the dynamic of the process of creolization to tease out its often unspoken motives and patterns and situating them in broader historical and theoretical frameworks. While the collection is situated firmly in the newly popular category of Atlantic history and owes a great theoretical debt to the work done in the past two decades in that field, it also seeks to go beyond some of the limitations of Atlantic history as traditionally defined. Many of its authors dispense with the institutional history that has guided much of our understanding of the formation of the colonial Atlantic and Caribbean worlds and embrace instead personal and cultural experience—in particular the formation and negotiation of Creole identity, often on an individual or community level—as the core process guiding the formation of colonial Atlantic societies. Further, the structure of the collection eschews both linear chronological development and even a strict thematic approach in favor of an organization meant to highlight both problematics and harmonies in the study of Francophone creole society from a vast variety of different locations and time periods. Thus theoretical articles are placed in conversation with more focused case studies, and historical articles are paired with linguistic and philosophical essays. Photographic images of Gwoka dancers, symbols of the richness and unlikely strength and survival of Creole culture, form a leitmotif, punctuating the transitions and recalling the central theme of the collection.

The dynamic of the guiding conception behind this collection emerges from the scholarly commitments of the volume's editors and authors, but also from the genesis of the project itself. The fruit of countless conversations over the past five years in Nantes, Lafayette, Marseilles, New Orleans, Dakar, Fort de France, and elsewhere, this volume is the embodiment of a unique collaboration that the editors hope can serve scholars everywhere who are interested in reckoning with both the frightening power and the creative potential of the modern human diaspora.

Jordan Kellman

Foreword

Creolization is not inherently exotic. It has been a part of French identity ever since the French ventured from the motherland to discover the world, bringing to the nation not only riches and a presumption of domination, but also a consciousness of universality. This consciousness emerged slowly over the course of early modern history, and there is still much of it to be explored. But from this point forward, if today in the twenty-first century we understand the first explorers' interpretation of the foreigners they discovered as "exotic" at all, it appears to us to come from retrograde ignorance.

The results of the slave trade, that powerful mass phenomenon that spread across the Atlantic Ocean for four centuries, were as far from the eyes of the Old Worlds of Europe and Africa as they were an everyday reality in the New World. The influence and consequences of this trade persist across time in memories and in bodies, still plainly visible and identifiable in the populations and cultures of the Americas, even if it remains difficult to define them. The consequences of the slave trade are also visible in a variety of ways in the Old Worlds, which are experiencing a growing consciousness and return impact of this powerful historical phenomenon, even if it is even more difficult to define them there.

For several decades, poets and scholars of French literature in the Americas have been among those calling for a vast reflection on the pursuit of individual and collective identities based on an idea of *creolité* inspired by the heritage of the American slavery experience. This experience was defined by the humans who lived it, the distance between the civilizations concerned, the modernity of the system that was put into place, and the characteristics of absolute tragedy and modern racist ideology that justified it. Today the experience of slavery has become a point of reference for many because it demonstrates that, beyond all the oppressions and traumas of history, cultures cannot be eradicated—that they resist, that they reinvent themselves and mutually enrich each other thanks to the shared universal experience of which each culture shares a part.

The European Atlantic trade is now understood as the critical vehicle for taking account of the historical processes of slavery in the Mediterranean, in Africa, and in the Americas in the Early Modern period. The present volume hopes to contribute to the reflection on one of the major heritages of the history of the Atlantic world: creolization. It begins from the principle that to have an honest experiment in the work of memory, one must start with history. Prior to its theoretical development, however, creolization is first a multitude of human experiences that reveals a diversity of historical paths. This is why we have chosen to use the plural for the French title "*Créolités,*" which we have usually translated as creolization. Creolization is also an old, lived historical process that continues and that theory can only hope to account for *a posteriori*. This is why we have chosen the term "creolization" for the English title of this bilingual edition, which draws together researchers and artists from Europe, Africa, and the Americas.

Creolization is not simply the mixing of bodies. Today the word refers to a willingness to define the terms of meeting and exchange between cultures. In the past these meetings were essentially compelled by violence; today each individual can choose and find his place. The meeting of Europeans and Africans, disastrous as it was, also produced this concept, which attempts to define continually strengthening relationships between cultures. Many of these relationships have existed since long before the advent of the slave trade, and they have not ceased to develop over the course of history. The theory of creolization that we are building today strives not only to make sense of the introduction of Europeans and Africans in the Americas, but of all the introductions between cultures and individuals that make up the history of humanity, not all of which were tragic. If the tragic paroxysm of the slave trade and of slavery in the history of the Atlantic world can be reckoned with, then we have a starting point for understanding and believing in the future of the chaotic and yet inexorable development of relations between individuals and cultures in the Atlantic basin.

The choice of the French Americas as the focus of this collection permits the exploration of a diverse and yet coherent set of creole experiences that are human and artistic, individual and collective, and that exemplify the ideas that these experiences have inspired. Additionally, some examples from outside the French Americas demonstrate the universality of these creole experiences and the richness of the idea of creolization, while also suggesting its usefulness as a tool in grasping the difficulties of the globalization process.

In the first article, Jordan Kellman analyzes the viewpoint of exoticism held by the first religious arrivals from France to the New World. Kellman demonstrates how the lived experiences of the world outside of France and Europe—even before that world was economically influential—could also be culturally significant, and how perceptions of that world informed French thought beyond the colonial encounter itself. In the sixteenth century, the debate over the nature of indigenous societies was carried out in the context of religious, scientific, and popular perceptions, and these played out very differently in the diverse French colonial theaters, from New France to Fort Caroline to *La France Equinoxiale*. How did these indigenous societies perceive and interact with religious debates and other European ideas? Exploring the encounter between the Tupi and European understandings of nature as recorded and interpreted by the French Capuchin monks who organized the first French colonial settlement among them, Kellman uncovers both a unique analysis of nature and the natural history of Brazil and a critique of European society and its relationship to the environment that are far more subtle and complex than popular images of either the noble or ignorant savage suggest. Both are the unique result of the interactions between European and Tupi societies and create a kind of creole natural history that reflects the origins of both.

The pressures of ambition and progress in modern times, which for Africans, among others, resulted in the high price of deportation from Africa and working toward the development of the Americas and Europe, ultimately dominated the evolution of the Atlantic world and the relations between diverse societies. In this context Jean-Marc Masseaut describes one of the methods of populating French Louisiana with slaves. The deportation of African populations on slave ships navigated by European sailors was a formative experience, and it was one of the first stages in the history of encounters between Europeans and Africans. This phase was fundamental in the formation of the images of the self and the other that came to exemplify the Atlantic world.

Even at a time and place where creolization was imposed or coerced by brute force—near the Great Lakes in the Upper Louisiana Territory—Sophie White contends that there were experiences that might be classified as "chosen creole identity." While speaking of choice may appear audacious and problematic in this context, White's essay nevertheless offers a number of convincing arguments for its existence and an intriguing direction for further inquiry. Native Americans sometimes chose to marry Frenchmen, to "Frenchify" themselves, and to transform a part of their original identity. This was not always an alienation or a forced, opportunistic appropriation in response to the demands of the French colonizers; it was sometimes done in the spirit of native traditions. For the Native Americans of Illinois, White argues, "their attraction to novelty did not begin with the French incursion into North America," "the concept of creolization or malleability of identity" already had a place in these cultures. White further suggests that the French colonizers themselves equally experienced creolization of various kinds as they adapted to their environment and sought to make use of indigenous peoples to further their aims.

The question of European creolization at first contact with other civilizations has existed since the inception of their adventures outside of Europe, beginning with the Portuguese pioneers who invented the term *crioulio*, which developed in the languages of all the maritime and colonizing nations of the West. The first Creoles were Europeans born in the colonies. This fact called into question a certain idea of identity advocated in Europe, and Gordon Sayre analyzes the evolution and the diverse approaches to the notion of créolité in British, Latin, and French America. Beyond the differences, what these approaches had in common was their revelation of the difficulties that people in the French mainland had in considering their creole (born abroad) compatriots as equals. The conflicts that certain protagonists faced in the construction of the colony in Lower Louisiana, around New Orleans, offer a significant window into understanding the broader questions of creolization.

This part of French Louisiana, which received its African workers as slaves from the beginning of its existence, was also the theater of another creole experience: technology. Ibrahima Seck's research reveals the relationship between Senegambian slaves' knowledge and the beginning of indigo production on a plantation owned by German immigrants along the lower Mississippi River in the early days of the colony. The populations captured in war or by African slave raiders to be sent to the European Slave Coast consisted of young adults chosen for their strength

Foreword

and capacity to work. Others were chosen for other abilities. In the beginning of the eighteenth century, the French colonists of Saint Domingue learned to master sugar cane farming and sugar refinement, and they abandoned the less profitable production of indigo. This was an opportunity for the colonists in Louisiana who took over the industry, cultivating the plant and producing dye using the skills already possessed by their slaves.

The technological creolization of Europeans and Africans in Louisiana is one example of the creolization processes that unfolded through conflicts and convergences among Amerindian, French, African, Spanish, and finally American cultures. These processes are at the heart of what Elista Istre calls "modern cultural identity." Pointing to the great regional variance in the definition of the term "creole," she shows that Louisiana was and remains a laboratory of diversity and creativity of creole experiences. This region's first peopling of African workers during the early eighteenth century was renewed several decades later during the Spanish period, and then again in the American period. A consequence of this interruption of African peopling in Louisiana was the emergence of an original society of creole and francophone slaves who would develop a specific culture that did not disappear despite the other demographic and cultural additions that succeeded it over time. Today, those who claim this ancestral creole culture call themselves "creole", and affirm their identity especially in Zydeco music. They have maintained the existence of a specifically creole dialect of French, a topic treated elsewhere in this work. They also affirm their identity in such areas as cuisine. Finally, Istre echoes Sophie White's belief in the possibility of chosen creole identity. Today, as sometimes in the past, one can exercise some volition and choice in establishing one's identity, rather than simply inheriting it.

This idea is also affirmed by Mona Georgelin in her treatment of the Guadeloupian art of Gwoka dancing. The impact of this eminently creole popular art has not diminished with time. The dances and music that drive it are powerful illustrations of diverse creolities in the Americas that have not only completed the path of triangular trade by returning to Europe, but have spread all over the world. The powerful salesmanship of its promoters, however, is insufficient to explain its success. Here again, universality and popular talent, not uniquely subaltern qualities, are at the center of these different forms of musical art and dance, and herein lies their broad appeal.

Gwoka is certainly little known in Europe and the Americas, but it remains inspiring to the artists who practice it and the public that welcomes it. Max Diakok, dancer, musician, and poet, is one of the foremost contemporary artists shedding a modern light on this deeply creole poetry of the body.

"Creole" is also the term used for languages that are constructed during the creole experience and are one of its major legacies, and which remain one of the tools of affirmation for these diverse and complex identities. The Lesser Antilles were the theater of creolization processes prior to Louisiana, and Josette Nonone recalls the historical context in which this other region of French America produced, beginning in the sixteenth century, a popular language based on Spanish, Portuguese, and Native American languages. This Creole language preceded and partially influenced the francophone Creole language in these islands, which was itself the consequence of French colonization and the increasingly massive arrival of Africans beginning in the mid-seventeenth century for the development of sugar production. This historical approach also animates the perspective of the Martiniquan writer and linguist Jean Bernabé, who believes that "in order to understand the origin of creole languages, it is necessary to return to history, to have knowledge of present social groups and to put a linguistic framework in place with a view to establishing possible kinships." Languages play an essential role in the experimental work of memory, and contextualizing their historical development, Nonone shows, is the first step in unpacking their meaning.

Creole, as a language, is not just a testimony to the past, but also a "literary heritage in development," as writers such as Frankétienne claim, a proposition Rafaël Lucas explores in "Defense and Illustration of Haitian Creole." Lucas refers to a passage from another, more well-known and older defense and illustration by Joachim du Bellay concerning the French language in the sixteenth century, claiming that there are no inferior languages, just different ones. Languages are more than codes of communication in the vein of advertising discourse, because individuals at the center of their respective cultures are not content with communicating, but also aspire to express their identities, sensibilities, and creativities. The variety and the diversity of languages are not outmoded avatars from bygone eras, but expressions of the personality of each speaker and each culture that always resurface, even when we believe them to be eradicated. Like cultures, certain languages pursue their evolution in the continuity of their long histories, and others, in particular more recent ones, build themselves in the image of the original societies of their speakers.

It is not easy to construct a coherent theory of a process founded on such a diversity of human and historical experiences; the introduction of a modicum of method is necessary to achieve clarity. Thus Jacques de Cauna brings useful precision to the diverse neologisms that seek to define the movements of these collective and individual forms of creolization. Edouard Glissant likewise seeks to detangle some of the complexity of creolization processes in his exploration of what the movement reveals about our human condition. The experience of creolization calls into question the very notion of uniquely rooted identity, framed by borders. Glissant suggests that we abandon a certain idea of the universal that attempts to "abstract all the disagreements of the world into an absolute truth" in favor of an idea of relation that absorbs differences. The notion of relation imposes itself on the construction of each individual identity with all its intertwining roots, and on each collective culture, whether it be the product of a long history or a recent creation. This approach requires a process that is not only scientific but also poetic "to the extent that the poetic aspires to a knowledge of depth" and that admits that the world and individuals are inextricable and composite. And if we are not essentially identical, this does not mean that we could not make the choice of relation over the choice of rivalry.

This reflection brings to mind a popular Louisiana metaphor: is a culture or an individual a gumbo in which all the ingredients are mixed together in an indistinct mass? Or are they a salad, whose flavor comes from the combination of distinct ingredients and their respective textures? The idea of the universal "which is built upon a form of negating the other, and which executes a negation of the universal, precisely in the name of the universal" characterizes the European colonial and slave systems of the past. This idea has, however, been refuted ever since the era of violent slave insurgencies and the broad rejection of its underpinnings. Today the cause is taken up by what Oliver Douville calls, from a psychoanalytic perspective, strategies of "dodging or detour" on the part of societies "that have capitalized on hybrid input" and that participate in the permanent movement of identity quests that are constantly reactualized.

Edouard Glissant believes that Antillean societies do not have a history, since their history is only "the progression of neurosis," that is, from a psychoanalytic viewpoint, "the impossible advent of telling and narration." Edelyn Dorismond proposes another perspective on creolization, founded on history but also on histories. He takes up the idea of relation by applying it to all the diverse histories that converge and interlock and form the history of the world. However, a philosophy of history inspired by creolization calls upon a western vision, reduced to a linear historiography bent toward a unique and common objective that neglects differences, in favor of a transversal historiography made up of multiplicity and adventure. This is not a negation of history, but a recomposition of its philosophy for a better "understanding of the historical and cultural dynamic of globalization, understood as a flux of encounters and relationships" that is no less made up of a global history. The critique of one idea of the universal cannot consist in the reinvention of another, creole but "just as predatory" universalism.

This idea is also at the center of what Carlo Celius examines in his "remarks" on creolization. The question of creolization, which came into its own at the end of the twentieth century, had its origins at the end of the nineteenth century among Haitian researchers such as Louis Joseph Janvier. Anthénor Firmin also endeavored to deconstruct the thesis of racial inequality during this period, which saw the flourishing of racist ideology under the pretext of progressive science. During the 1950s, Anglophone Caribbean linguists and anthropologists pursued this reflection, which was then amplified by the Francophone Caribbean writers and researchers who followed them. The debate is far from over, and Carlo Celius contributes to it by bringing together current research that strives to identify the richness and the limits of the question of creolization. As Celius puts it, "It concerns the entire history of human societies and cultures. . . .," "It is ancient and current, but is not a global phenomenon, only one dynamic among others. . . .," and "It is neither an exception nor an outcome, it is a phase."

The choice of "French America" as the theme of this collection was not inspired by a vain claim of French exceptionalism, but more simply to propose a method to our readers based on one case among many, possibly a familiar one to those who share French culture. The *a priori* assumption is that the problematic of creolization effectively "concerns the entire history of human societies and cultures." This is surely the case in the

Anglophone Caribbean as well, where a theory of creolization processes developed independently of the Francophone tradition. Anthony Bogues recalls that, especially in the Anglophone tradition, culture is not "a body of intellectual and imaginative work," but is partially defined by "ways of life." Creolization is therefore a "set of practices" modeled both by power and rebellion against power, and this is why this theoretical approach is not inspired so much by Being as by a consciousness of the power of structures. The Anglo-Caribbean researchers of the 1960s thus approached the question of creolization from the reality of plantation society, from which the original Caribbean society emerged. For Bogues, "Here the question is not so much what culture/s have been produced but on *what basis* has this production occurred and how has it been sustained?" The comparative analysis of Anglophone and Francophone Caribbean theories that Anthony Bogues proposes—both anthropological and literary—mark the beginning of a new research program, not an end.

The question goes beyond the Caribbean, and even beyond the Atlantic World. Bryce Beemer focuses his research in Southeast Asia, where he applies his theory of creolization to certain aspects of the kingdom of Burma, influenced by artistic practices brought from the kingdom of Siam, Thailand, which was a reservoir of slaves for wealthy Burmese. Coincident with the pinnacle of Atlantic trade, when African populations were deported en masse for the construction of the New World, in 1767 the Burmese plundered the capital of Thailand in the tradition of slave raiding known in this part of the world. In the Atlantic system, Africans were enslaved to create a workforce, even if they were sometimes chosen for their talents. In the creole experience described by Beemer, those who were captured were separated according to their abilities: "The skills and talents of captured people were not necessarily diminished or degraded because they had origins among a defeated people." This was the case for dancers and musicians of the Thai royal court, who were integrated into the heart of the artistic elite in the Burmese royal palace. This fusion gave rise to new art forms of dance and music that came from each tradition, which can also be classified as creole through the invention of original artistic practices that are still alive today. It no longer applies solely to the Atlantic world, but rather to a relationship between domination and the integration of cultures in an ancestral, universal context of slavery. This continuity allows us to consider the importance of the idea of creolization as a tool for understanding exchange between people and to comprehend it beyond any particular geographic sphere where it appears.

The evolution of music often testifies to the reality and history of creolization processes. Musicians transported their instruments and their knowledge across the world and, with the confrontations and exchanges between their diverse artistic practices, they created other instruments. The banjo provides a telling example: is this instrument African, European, or American? James L. A. Webb's response, guided by historical research, is clear: this instrument is perfectly Atlantic creole, but may go beyond the Atlantic as well. The banjo belongs in the lute category, or instruments equipped with strings placed parallel to an acoustic chamber permitting the production of varied sounds by plucking of the strings. The origin of the word "lute" comes the Arabic *al'ud*, and West African lutes were introduced in this region during the period of Islamic expansion, while Western Europe was developing another long tradition of lute making and lute music. Webb also mentions a lute tradition from southern Asia that the Portuguese introduced to southern Africa at the beginning of maritime exploration. His careful examination of texts and iconography suggests that the plucked-string lutes that appeared in the Caribbean around the seventeenth century are the result of "an amalgam, with indefinite cultural influences from West Africa, Madagascar, and perhaps South Asia." And so the banjo was born as an expression of music, culture, and identity of slaves and more generally of the poor people in the New World, but also inextricably as the result of the vast network of cultural exchange that linked Europe, Asia, Africa, and the Americas.

The collection is punctuated with images of bodies in motion, inspired by the inimitable poetic quality of authentically creole music and dance. The cultural association Mamanthé of Marseille, a French city that is creole, Mediterranean and Atlantic, organized the troupe of dancers and musicians Massilia Ka, supported by guest artists, to contribute these original images to this volume.

Universalist though they may have been, the French thinkers of the Enlightenment were not unaware of the problematic of creolization in society. "So many men, so many different cries.... Such diverse chatter, such a host of discordant cries in that one forest which we call society ," wrote

Foreword

Denis Diderot, who in the eighteenth century produced the Encyclopedia, composed of the juxtaposition of contiguous territories, perhaps the first modern work to attempt to place all the categories, variety, and cacophony of human existence side-by-side, and force them into conversation with one another, and thus begin the dialogue that we continue today.[1]

Jean-Marc Masseaut

---

1. Jean Starobinski, *Diderot, un diable de ramage,* Editions NRF; Gallimard 2012, p.9, p..39.

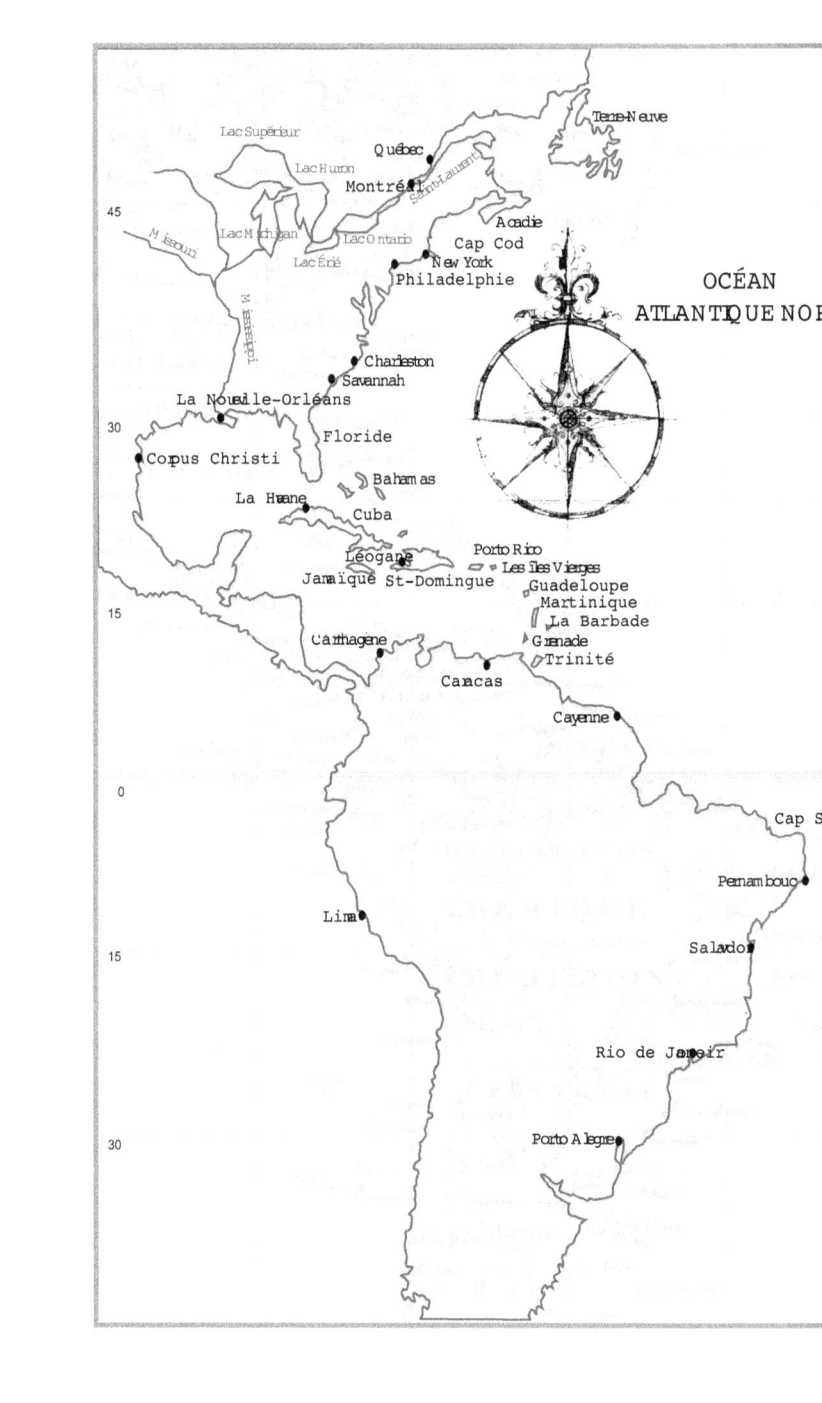

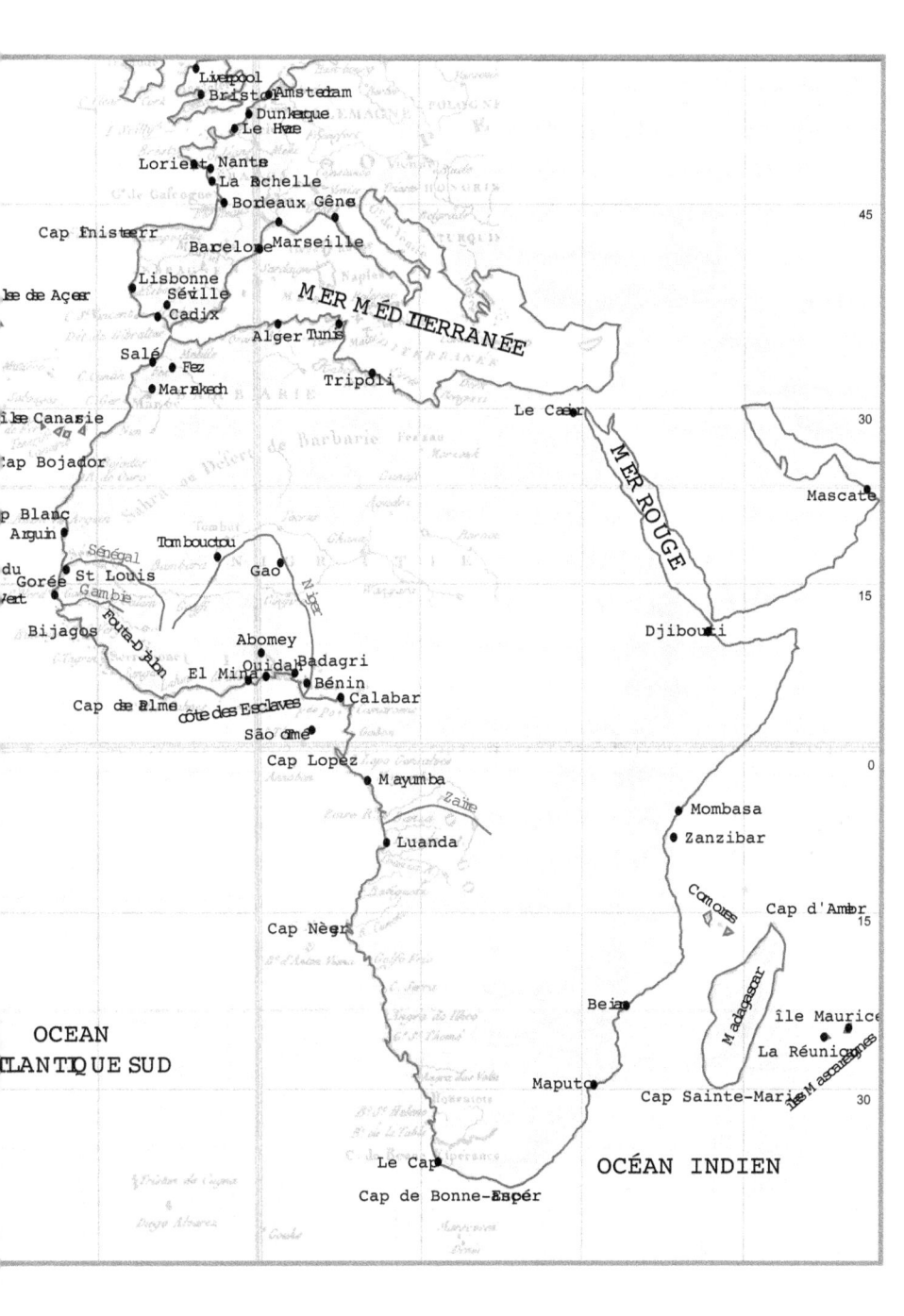

Claude D'Abbeville, *Histoire de la mission des peres capucins en l'isle de Maragnan et terres circonvoisines*, 1614, frontispico.

Encounter and Environment in La France Equinoxiale: Franciscans and Tupinambá in Early Modern Maranhão, Brazil

Jordan Kellman

Among the Early-modern European colonial encounters with peoples across the globe, the first wave of French missionary encounters in the New World hold a unique place.[1] From the Franciscan André Thevet and the Protestant Jean de Léry's first encounters with the Brazilian rain forest, to the failed Huguenot settlement at Fort Caroline and the Jesuit expeditions to New France, religious experience and royal ambition melded to form a set of expectations and parameters that revealed the dynamics and worldview of French society through their encounter with nature and peoples that were profoundly other. Among these the encounter between Jesuits and Montagnais and Iroquois natives in New France is unique in the ethnographic depth of experience and the extensive record in the form of letters later published as the *Jesuit Relations*. These accounts, while certainly steeped in the viewpoint of missionary zeal, formed a peculiar perspective as missionaries like Paul Lejeune and Jean de Brébeuf became more and more immersed in native society and impressed with its sophistication and adaptation to the harsh environment of the Canadian winter. These early encounters between native, nature, and monastic colonist are among the roots of the worldviews of the creole societies that grew up in the French colonial Americas in the centuries that followed.

1. Parts of this research were published in *Proceedings of the Western Society for French History* 38 (2011).

The far lesser-known travels of French Franciscans in Brazil pose a marked contrast to the Jesuit experience. First, the Franciscans departed Europe with a decidedly different monastic education and experience, one that gave them a particular perspective on nature, natives, and their relationship in the New World. Second, the nature and natives that they encountered were a world apart from the keen battle for survival of tribe against tribe and all against the elements experienced in New France. Third, the nature of their accounts was fundamentally different: while the Jesuit relations were written in the context of a long-term, coherent monastic mission undertaken as part of a close relationship between the order and the French crown in relatively uncontested territory as far as European colonial powers were concerned, the French Franciscans in Brazil had only a brief and superficial relationship to the crown, and quickly found themselves caught in a struggle with Spanish military forces for allegiance with and control over the last native independent Tupinambá population.

Out of this contrast emerged two very distinct encounters and two distinct images of the New World natural environment and the place of Native Amerindians in it. For the Jesuits, nature was a common enemy that natives and colonizers battled together. The fierceness of the New France winter and the exquisite adaptation of the Iroquois and Montaignais to these conditions made the Jesuits famously dependent on their native hosts. Whether frostbite or the scourge of disease unwittingly introduced by the colonists themselves, nature was an ever-present threat and evidence of the precariousness of mortal life and the power of God to challenge human hubris and mastery.[2] For the Franciscans in Brazil, nature in the New World, and its Tupinambá inhabitants, seemed instead overwhelming in hospitality and bounty, and forced a systematic rethinking of the relationship between God, humans, and the environment, one that appeared to throw the entire mission and its colonial context into question.

The case of Claude D'Abbeville illustrates the contrast between the Jesuit mission to New France and the Franciscan mission to Brazil. D'Abbeville was one of four Capuchin monks who spent four months as

---

2. Gordon Sayre, *Les Sauvages Amériquains: Representations of Native Americans in French and English Colonial Literature* (Chapel Hill: University of North Carolina Press, 1997): 248–304; Carole Blackburn, *Harvest of Souls: The Jesuit Missions and Colonialism in North America (1632–1650)* (Montréal and Kingston: McGill-Queen's University Press, 2000).

a missionary in the small peninsula now know as São Luís Island, in the Brazilian province of Maranhão during the autumn of 1612. D'Abbeville traveled to what the French then called 'Maragnan' as part of a colonial flotilla, supported first by Henry IV and then by Marie de Medicis during the regency, that brought over five hundred French colonists to establish a French colony to capitalize on local resources and counter the ever-expanding Portuguese and Spanish dominions in the equatorial Americas.[3] The French were expelled by the Portuguese in 1614, after only two years, and the traces of D'Abbeville's brief visit to *La France Equinoctiale* have been limited. D'Abbeville's account of the voyage, *Histoire de la mission des pères capuchins en l'isle de Maragnan et terres circonvoisines* (1614) is best known as one of the most detailed colonial-era sources on Tupi-Guarani society.[4] It was popular at the time—a second edition printed within a year—but in modern commentary it has almost always been read against the grain: the work of a simpleton amateur with little scientific training, blinded by his missionary agenda and Eurocentric zeal, but rich with uncomprehendingly recorded clues about Tupi culture. D'Abbeville's own perspective is considered an embarrassment or a tragedy, or both, symbolized by the six Tupinambá who returned to France with him and were paraded through the royal court and baptized in Franciscan robes, three of whom died within a month of their arrival, the other three returning to Brazil in 1614.[5] These striking symbols of physical and cultural captivity have evoked the dehumanizing quality of European colonial travel and of the early ethnographic encounter.[6]

3. "Maragnan" is now known as São Luís Island, in the Bay of Maranhão, and the city that grew from the French encampment is today São Luís do Maranhão, Maranhão province, in Northeastern Brazil.

4. Claude D'Abbeville, *Histoire des Pères Capucins en l'Isle de Maragnan et terres circonvoisines* (Paris: François Huby, 1614).

5. Claude D'Abbeville, *L'Arrivée des Pères Capucins en L'Inde Nouvelle, appelée Maragnon, avec la réception que leur ont faict les sauvages de ce pays, et la conversions d'iceux à nostre saincte foy* (Paris: A. Le Febvre, 1612), 11–15.

6. D'Abbeville, *L'Arrivée*,13–14. For D'Abbeville's discussion of the Tupi interpretation of the encounter, see D'Abbeville, *Histoire*, 74. See also John Hemming, *Red Gold: The Conquest of the Braziliian Indians* (Cambridge: Harvard University Press, 1978), 201–2; Sara Melzer, *Colonizer Or Colonized: The Hidden Stories of Early Modern French Culture* (Philadelphia: University of Pennsylvania Press, 2012), Chapter Four.

Claude D'Abbeville, *Histoire de la mission des peres capucins en l'isle de Maragnan et terres circonvoisines*, 1614: Louis Marie.

Recent literature on the exploration and exploitation of nature in early modern New World colonies has stressed the commercial networks that drove such exploration and the circulation of commodities as they acquired new meanings and values within different societies.[7] Much recent work on French missionary travel has focused on the Jesuit tradition, especially in New France, and offers an image where the natural environment of the New World was a backdrop to the drama of cultural encounter and conversion.[8] Even the literature on the early seventeenth-century Jesuit Relations stresses, as do the *Relations* themselves, the withering and antagonistic relationship between colonists and the New World environment.[9]

Read on its own terms, however, D'Abbeville's understanding of his Brazilian experience poses several challenges to the historiography of European colonialism and has the capacity to disclose a new root of European environmentalism, one that posits the value of the environment not on the basis of its fragility, but on the basis of its very robustness. For D'Abbeville, in spite of much sanctimonious and devout language and framing, the real story of the voyage was the natural environment of Maranhão: Clearly overshadowing both the missionary and ethnographic elements of

---

7. See, for example, Antonio Barrera-Osorio, *Experiencing Nature: The Spanish American Empire and the Early Scientific Revolution* (Austin: University of Texas Press, 2006), which stresses that the commercial and royal forces that drove Spanish colonial exploration and exploitation were paramount and undergirded the bulk of naturalist knowledge.

8. Miguel De Asúa and Roger French, *A New World of Animals: Early Modern Europeans on the Creatures of Iberian America* (Aldershot, England, Ashgate, 2005), 148–52. Le Père Fournier's account, while dismissive of the scientific quality of the missionaries' observations, nonetheless expresses admiration for what they were able to accomplish with little training. See Paul Fournier, *Voyages et découvertes scientifiques des missionaries naturalists français à travers le monde pendant cinq siècles: XVe à XXe siècles* (Paris: Lechavalier, 1932), 30–33. The most comprehensive study of the expedition is Andréa Daher, *Les Singularités de la France Équinoxiale, Histoire des pères capucins au Brésil (1612–1615)* (Paris, Honoré Champion, 2002). See also Maurice Pianzola, *Des Français à la conquête du Brésil (XVIIe siècle): les perroquets jaunes* (Paris: Harmattan, 1991), 91–116; Alfred Métraux and Jacques Lafaye, eds, *Histoire de la Mission des Pères Capucins en l'Isle de Maragnan et Terres Circonvoisins* (Graz: Akademische Druck und Verlagsanstalt, 1963), i–xlii.

9. See Guy Laflèche, "Les jésuites de la Nouvelle France et le mythe de leur martyrs," in *Les Jésuites parmi les hommes aux XVIe et XVIIe siècles*, ed. Guy Demerson (Clermont-Ferrand: Presses Universitaires de Clermont-Ferrand, 1987), 25–45; Pierre Berthiaume, "Les *Relations* des jésuites: nouvel avatar de la *Légende dorée*," in *Figures de l'Indien*, ed. Gilles Thérien (Montréal: L'Hexagone, 1995), 79–87.

the travel narrative, nature itself, as a complex and transcendent system that was in many ways beyond the comprehension of European or Tupi, was the subject of D'Abbeville's encounter story. Even his extensive account of the encounter between the French settlers and the indigenous Tupi—and his understanding of their strange customs—is cast in the context of the New World natural environment.

Like the Jesuit expeditions to New France, the Maranhão encounter falls between the first French naturalist explorations of Brazil, those of André Thevet and Jean de Léry, and the disciplined observation promoted by the Paris Academy of Sciences later in the century and culminating in the La Condamine expedition of the 1730s. In contrast to the Jesuit mission, D'Abbeville's account was structured by a theological framework unique to the early seventeenth-century Capuchin order and was also indebted to a particular natural philosophical worldview: a melding of Aristotelian, Renaissance natural philosophy with new currents in natural history characteristic of someone on the fringes of learned discourse in Europe at the end of the sixteenth-century. D'Abbeville's image of nature on the island of Maranhão offers an early glimpse of a European vision of nature as a self-regulating system that is at odds in important ways with its human inhabitants and with human development.

The relationship between the Tupi and the Franciscans and their fellow colonists is established immediately upon the arrival of the Frenchmen: The Tupi had fled Portuguese settlements and were eager to embrace the French as allies; for the French, the Tupi served as guides and ushers into the natural wonders of this new environment. For D'Abbeville, there was nothing linear or familiar about the nature of Maranhão. It was a kind of microcosm in which all the features of creation were seen in exaggerated form, European nature so intensified that it defied all accepted natural categories. For D'Abbeville, nature in the New World was super-productive and super-reproductive, and on a scale unimaginable in France. The darkness of night seemed deeper. Wind itself seemed in Brazil to only purify, while in France, the winds were "Putrid, sickening and corrosive. . . ."[10] Animal colorings were more vivid, animals were more lean and stealthy, insects were almost comically large and abundant. Even birds in this part

---

10. "*putride, maladif et extrêmement corrosive . . . ,*" D'Abbeville, *Histoire*, 198.

of the world seemed to exist in a profusion that indicated either spontaneous generation or a creator with heretofore unsuspected power. Trees appear literally covered with birds of every imaginable size and description. Oysters and mussels were twice the size of those D'Abbeville knew, sweeter and more delicate, and sometimes even found growing on trees.

This number and variety were for D'Abbeville the result of two factors: the climate itself, which causes the profusion of natural life in a seemingly infinite variety, and, directly by the hand of God, as yet another aspect and evidence of the special status of the region within creation itself. D'Abbeville may here be reviving a Thomistic argument concerning the variety and abundance of natural kinds. In *Summa contra Gentiles*, Aquinas reasons that since creation was a mirror of the infinity and splendor of God but was in itself incapable of equaling God, it strove to do so through profusion and variety of natural kinds. If this equation of God and natural creation is surprising, it is echoed elsewhere by D'Abbeville. "It seems that God and nature studied each other," he writes, "in order to populate this country with animals more admirable than in any other country."[11]

One of the first signs that D'Abbeville saw Maragnan as a place in which the action of God on nature was special is in his discussion of climate. After a long explanation of the traditional climate zones and the physics of the sun's heating power, he points out that by the logic of these factors Maragnan should be insupportably hot. But here, on the contrary, God has tempered the sun's heat with "a multitude of marvelous means." Chief among these is the purity and moderation of the air, which makes Brazil a "temperate and delicious place."[12] The elements themselves in Brazil appeared cleaner and purer than in France, and indeed, than of anywhere else he had been. Nor is this purity an accidental factor of geography; if there is any corruption of it, he assures us, it is an accident in the Aristotelian sense and must come from somewhere else. Maragnan is exempt from "all extreme contrarieties" of other places; the cold, gloomy fogs and violent storms of France are unknown here.[13]

---

11. "*il semble à voir que Dieu et Nature se soient estudiez particulièrement à peupler ce païs d'animaux admirables sur toutes les autres regions . . .*" D'Abbeville, *Histoire*, 231.

12. "*Je n'estime pas . . . qu'il y aye lieu plus tempèré et plus delicieux que ce païs là.*" Ibid., 192.

13. Ibid.

D'Abbeville's depiction of the natural environment in Brazil amounts to that of a self-sustaining ecological system, one in which natural forces balanced each other to create an explosion of life. In advance of the hottest part of the year comes a season of heavy rains, which "temper marvelously the sun's ardor, and render the earth extremely fecund."[14] The winds are perfectly balanced such that they moderate the effects of the sun, providing a kind of umbrella against its heat. Because of these moderating counterforces, and unlike in other equinoctial regions such as in Africa, the sun does not appear to have a permanent blackening effect, on humans or otherwise. The fertility of the entire Brazilian environment seems to D'Abbeville to have no limit: soil fertilizers are unknown here, where the ground is nourished by the air and the water, and the labors of man tend only to disrupt this natural fertility. The earth does not produce if one works it, D'Abbeville notes, but it does produce abundantly if one does not; all one has to do is throw seeds on the ground and things grow. Tidal and rain pools seem to spawn an infinity of delicious fish that the Tupi carefully harvest. When these pools dry out and subsequently refill, a whole new crop of fish wondrously appears.

The image of France that emerges by way of contrast is striking and suggests the dawning of a certain perspective on European society that would be shared by New World Creoles of different races and backgrounds. Throughout the account, France provides a foil for Brazil's brilliance and splendor. Its landscape is covered with infected vapors and putrid smoke, which fill the corrupted air.[15] The clean, pure air of Brazil is not merely a pleasant feature: For D'Abbeville, it determines the quality of everything in it. For example, he notes many insects that are similar to those found in France, but due to the purity of the air, the ones in Brazil are found to be without venom and incapable of harm to humans. Similarly the pristine water, in countless enormous rivers, lakes and natural fountains, sprinkles the earth and animates all its plants and animals with its fertile purity. It also moderates the air and the heat given off by the sun.[16] Each morning,

---

14. ". . . tempère merveilleusement l'air et l'ardeur du soleil, et rend la terre extrèmement féconde." Ibid., 195.

15. Ibid., 193.

16. Ibid., 194.

Encounter and Environment in *La France Equinoxiale*

cool dew is deposited in abundance on all the vegetation, allowing it to prosper in the full sunlight of day. During the Atlantic crossing, the French water became putrid and black, upon exposure to the heat and elements, before becoming blue and still more putrid. By the time they got to the Canaries it was completely undrinkable. The water from Maragnan, however, apparently did not change at all on the return journey, remaining "delicious and healthy" for over three months.[17]

Influenced though it was by his Brazilian surroundings, D'Abbeville's natural theology draws on early Franciscan traditions that were the centerpiece of the Capuchin movement. The first Franciscan orders were devoted to a conception of nature as a vehicle for God's wisdom and creativity. This is usually taken to apply to animals, but in many ways it went beyond even individual natural bodies, focusing on whole natural systems.[18] The Capuchin order was founded with the purpose of restoring the pure, original form of Franciscan monastic observation, from which the Franciscans themselves were felt to have fallen. D'Abbeville's account is not primarily focused on the rigors and limits of direct observation, as European scientific travel writing would be within a few decades. Rather, it is rooted in the assumption that perception is divinely guided and that apprehension and discernment are fundamentally internal processes guided by God, not external analytical reductions of the world. Confronted with the intense profusion of natural productions, the Franciscan ideal of perception was a kind of divinely guided ecstatic appreciation of the natural world, in striking contrast to the Jesuit approach of disciplined and analytical rigor deployed toward spreading faith irrespective of the environment. D'Abbeville's analysis of nature in Brazil amounts to an almost literal transposition of Francis's *Canticle of the Sun*, whose line "through Brothers Wind and Air, and clouds and storms, and all the weather, through which you give your creatures sustenance" coincides precisely with D'Abbeville's proposed relationship between climate and the cycle of natural production. The seasons have completely different characters in Brazil, where even the winter is fecund—there is perpetual verdure, trees and plants flower all the time, and the entire countryside

---

17. Ibid., 205.

18. James Long, "Aquinas and Franciscan Nature Mysticism," *Logos* 8:2 (Spring 2005), 56–64.

resembles for him Virgil's ideal garden, where the odors waft in blissful harmony.[19] During summer in France, one becomes feeble, heavy, sleepy, and disgusted, but in Brazil, one is lively, strong and refreshed and hungry. This climate itself causes fertility, in contrast to the *"infeconde et affreuse"* winters of France.

***

In many ways D'Abbeville's perspective mirrors that of his Tupi hosts. He is known among anthropologists for offering one of the first detailed accounts of the Tupi-Guarani "journey to the land without evil," their own vision of leaving their troubled home world for one that promises eternal bliss through the bounty of nature, much like D'Abbeville's journey to Brazil.[20] First forced into migration by other Amerindians before European colonization, the Tupi-Guarani developed an elaborate mythology surrounding large communal journeys taken under the leadership of an especially powerful shaman. The physical hardship and depravation of the journey were matched only by the bliss of arrival: the land with no evil was a place of infinite bounty and fertility, where human intervention in nature was unnecessary because nature provided everything on its own. Later Jesuit missionaries documented these journeys, focusing on the illusion of the Shaman's spiritual power. Modern anthropologists have traced the contours and meaning of this highly structured ritual, which continues into the modern era, but have focused almost entirely on its human dimension—the social status of the shaman and the social structures and mythology of the community that evolves during the journey. D'Abbeville focuses instead on the natural surroundings of the destination, a mountain that takes four hours to climb, and offers deep forests with bubbling streams, delectable fish, and birds. But the two journeys have a surprising degree of commonality, one that clearly fits the perspective of deracinated social travelers, and that would have a lasting resonance among creole populations in the Americas.

19. Ibid., 200.

20. The classic anthropological treatment of the Tupi, drawing heavily on D'Abbeville and D'Evreux, is Alfred Métraux, *La Civilisation Matérielle des Tupi-Guarani* (Paris: Paul Geuthner, 1928); Alfred Métraux, *La religion des Tupinamba* (Paris, Anthropos, 1929).

Encounter and Environment in *La France Equinoxiale*

Claude D'Abbeville, *Histoire de la mission des peres capucins en l'isle de Maragnan et terres circonvoisines*, 1614: Anthoine Manen.

When D'Abbeville comes to discuss the Tupinambá in their own right, his tone and language change dramatically. In superficial physical characteristics they are nourished by the same climate and natural fertility: they live to an extremely old age (120–140 by his reckoning), and disease is very rare among them. But he perceives the Tupi as short, stubborn, violent, and quarrelsome. The volume's engravings of the Tupi are unlike many contemporary depictions that present natives as exotic and set off against civilized Europeans. Based on the six individuals who were brought back to France, paraded through towns and baptized in Franciscan robes, these Tupi, whose many barbarous customs are described in some detail in the text, are likewise depicted as domesticated, Europeanized, and completely removed from their environment. Even the three who died of exposure to disease shortly after their arrival are cast in classical poses, only their leaf garments distinguishing them from Greek statues. Did they ever partake of the vigor of the natural environment of Maranhão by which D'Abbeville was so enthralled? Not fully, the images suggest. D'Abbeville explains their customs of polygamy, warfare, and ritual cannibalism, already made popular by Hans Staden's account, as the natural result of the balance of forces and power in the rainforest. Where other missionaries saw moral failings and evidence of a benighted branch of humanity, and authors such as Montaigne saw signs of a more brave, pure, and noble humanity, D'Abbeville saw nature at work: a balance of inexorable forces in the rain forest that led to a natural social equilibrium very different from, but no less divine, than the European one.

Though far less known than other missionary accounts, this vision of new world nature as a self-sustaining, self-regulating system would have profound echoes in the modern period as the ideas of humans as part of an ecological system developed.[21] In the end, D'Abbeville's Brazil is not Eden, or even *an* Eden. He considers the idea that the Tupi represent a lost tribe of Israel, benighted by a long separation and in need only of reconnection to their former knowledge of God, but promptly rejects it. Although

---

21. Richard Grove, *Green Imperialism: Colonial Expansion, Tropical Island Edens and the Origins of Environmentalism, 1600–1860* (Cambridge, U.K.: Cambridge University Press, 1995), 47–53. For Grove, Western environmentalism emerged from the intersection of a pastoral ideal with a systematic understanding of natural processes and the ability of humans to disrupt them.

entirely reflective of his Capuchin natural theology, ultimately his interpretation of Brazil can not be readily absorbed into its biblical scheme: Maragnan is fundamentally different from the rest of creation, from its smallest insects to its people. For D'Abbeville, Brazilian nature represents a complete, robust, interwoven, interdependent and self-regulating system, an early-modern proto-ecology of which the Tupi and the French were only a small part. Though inspired by European monastic tradition, it was a fundamentally New World vision of nature that would influence the experiences of colonial settlers and natives and their descendents well into the modern era.

Exploration of the Mississippi and foundation of Louisiana

On the Origins of the First African Populations in Lower French Louisiana: The Early Eighteenth Century

JEAN-MARC MASSEAUT,
SHACKLES OF MEMORY PROJECT

Those who were sold and deported to the New World broke through the interior frontiers within which the Old World developed. They crossed the oceans and were the pioneers of new societies built upon other territories. Extraterritoriality was a singularity that identified those born outside of lands with a long western historical identity as being Creoles "raised, so to speak, in the middle of savages and knowing little of the kingdom's customs and government."[1] The Creoles were not foreigners to the Europeans, but neither were they compatriots sharing the same land.

It was not only extraterritoriality, however, that made the new worlds unique; it was also the experiences of the populations that built them in a process of creolization between communities that came from Europe and Africa. The Europeans had emancipated themselves from their feudal societies in the development of new American societies, and the Africans "arrived naked . . . , skinned of everything in the belly of the slave ship."[2] Creolization is not only a recognition through language of those who, although of European origin and for better or worse recreate the mother culture that they would nevertheless reside outside of, but it is also a recognition of foreign peoples who share the construction of a common destiny

1. See essay by Gordon Sayre below.
2. See essay by Edouard Glissant below.

with the memory of tragedy, of affront, and of domination. From the viewpoint of the old worlds the creole experience can appear exotic, but for the new worlds it is a powerful foundation for new societies.

Charles Le Moyne Père

Charles le Moyne de Longueuil et de Châteauguay crossed the Atlantic at the age of fifteen to immigrate to New France in 1641. He came from the port of Dieppe on France's Norman coast where his father was an innkeeper. He was much like other pioneers of French colonization in the Americas, many of whom were "indentured servants" who embarked primarily at La Rochelle, but also at Le Havre and Dieppe.[3] New France, in the north of the Americas, was essentially the destination for all these young people, who also supplied labor in the Caribbean islands at the center of the Americas. On these tropical latitudes the French rivaled other European powers in their quest to develop societies of colonial production. These preindustrial agricultural implantations would amplify the important economic progress of Europe in the eighteenth century, especially sugar, which required more and more labor, always provided by slaves, who were usually deported off the African coasts.

Charles le Moyne did not live in slavery on the plantation, but he knew another kind of temporary servitude under the Jesuits, to whom he was "given" for five years. This practice, put into place in the seventeenth century, allowed the missionaries to make use of unsalaried servants who accompanied them on their missions to evangelize the Indian populations of Canada. Through this experience he learned the customs and languages of the Indians, most notably the Hurons, who were allied with the French, and their adversaries the Iroquois, allied with the English. After this period in service of the Jesuits, he became a soldier and was noted for his talents in combat, as well as interpretation and negotiation with Indian peoples. He settled in the village that would become Montreal, where he had a prosperous career as a military officer and an ambassador and negotiator to the Indians.

At the age of twenty-eight he married a young Frenchwoman fourteen years his junior, Catherine Thierry. She was also born in Normandy, was an orphan, and had immigrated to New France at the age of eleven. They had fourteen children, two girls and twelve boys—all of the boys had careers

---

3. Gabriel Debien, *Les Engagés pour les Antilles, 1634–1715* (Abbeville: Imprimerie F.Paillart, 1951), 39. "Indentured servants" at the time were young people who would reimburse the cost of their voyage and earn the right-to-settle in the Americas through several years' work without salary, profiting the New World colony. They were at the bottom of the social scale among European immigrants.

in the French royal navy. The majority of them followed the example of their father in learning about Indian cultures, and they knew how to be effective interpreters and diplomats. They were also enemies of the English and their Indian allies, and six of them died in combat. From among these Canadian creole siblings—creoles in the sense that they were born outside of the mainland—were recruited the leaders of the maritime expeditions that brought to the kingdom of France the colonies of lower Louisiana on the shores of the Gulf of Mexico.

Robert Cavelier De La Salle 1670 1687

Another Norman, René-Robert Cavelier de La Salle, who had spent time with the Jesuits in the novitiate of Rouen at the age of fifteen, left the priesthood for adventure in New France in 1667, when he was twenty-four. Departing the St. Lawrence Valley, he explored the Great Lakes in 1678

Origins of the First African Populations in Lower French Louisiana

from where he reached the Illinois River and founded Fort Crèvecoeur.[4] While the English were establishing themselves more and more solidly on the Atlantic coast of North America, from Boston in New England to Savannah on the border of the Spanish territory in Florida, the French struggled to penetrate the interior of the vast continent. Cavelier de La Salle's exploration added upper Louisiana, or Illinois country, to New France and Acadie. He then descended the Mississippi from the North to the South and reached the Gulf of Mexico in 1682. He did not have the opportunity to profit from his explorations because he was killed in Texas during a return trip from France a short time later. But he had delineated the new territories of French Louisiana along the Mississippi, which extended from upper Louisiana near the Great Lakes to lower Louisiana along the Gulf of Mexico and which the French would endeavor to colonize in the south. This is what the Le Moyne brothers, born in Montreal, would do, commanding French fleets to conquer these lands.

The eldest, Pierre Le Moyne d'Iberville, went to Brest in October 1698 to lead an armada that would reach the Bay of Mobile (today in the state of Alabama) in January 1699. He followed his route westward along the coast and established a fort on the sandy Bay of Biloxi after having explored Lake Ponchartrain and the swamps of the Mississippi delta. This fort became one of the trading posts for the new Company of the Indies founded by John Law, who had taken control of the Company of the West or the Company of the Mississippi.

Pierre La Moyne D'Iberville

---

4. See essay by Sophie White below.

John Law's Company of the Indies Camp at Biloxi 1720

With his brother Joseph Le Moyne de Sérigny he established another fort at the eastern mouth of the Mississippi on a site thereafter identified as Cavelier de La Salle.[5] The fort La Balize became the landing point for incoming ships and a control station for captains charged with guiding them up the Mississippi to New Orleans and beyond. This strategic location allowed controlled access to the river and debarkation of prisoners from Africa, who were brought out of the hellish slave ship holds before being sent to the slave markets in New Orleans on river barges.[6] The island

---

5. Despite the technical progress in wind propulsion on ships, Louis XIV and his strategic advisors remained attached to oar propulsion on military galleys, which had the advantage of being maneuverable no matter the direction or strength of the wind. In short, these required oarsmen. There were some Africans deported from Senegambia on the Royal Company of Senegal's ships in 1680 who would eventually embark on the galleys of Marseille. There were also some Iroquois who were kidnapped in Quebec in 1687 at the request of the state for this purpose. Joseph Le Moyne d'Iberville's knowledge of the language gave him the opportunity to escort these deported Iroquois. Although they represented only 20 percent of the galley men, who were mainly condemned or volunteers, slaves of Mediterranean origin were present in the French Mediterranean territory at the end of the seventeenth century.

6. Biloxi was the first port in French Louisiana to receive transoceanic ships prior to the foundation of New Orleans. Beginning in 1723, the Company of the Indies' ships stopped regularly at La Balize.

Origins of the First African Populations in Lower French Louisiana

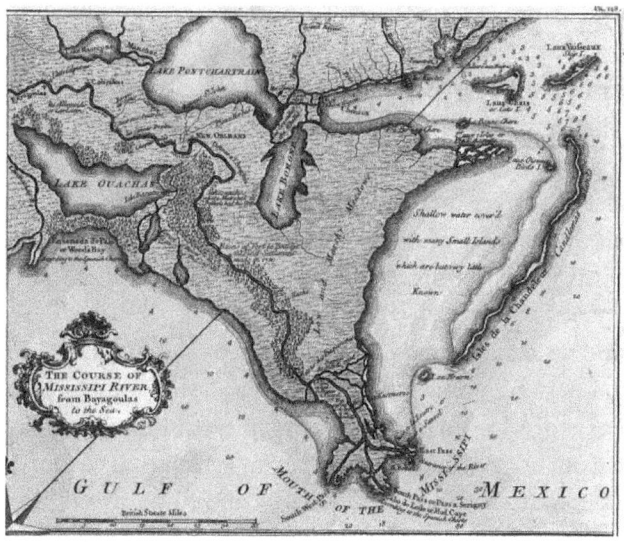

La Balize Channel east of the entrance to the Mississippi

and the wooden fort were destroyed by hurricanes several times, and the command station was thereafter situated upstream at Pilottown. This was also a port of call for the Company of the Indies' ships.

Finally, Jean-Baptiste Le Moyne de Bienville, the youngest of the three brothers and known as Sieur de Bienville, also participated in the founding of the fort of Biloxi. He succeeded his elder brother Pierre as governor of Louisiana in 1702. In 1718, he led the French expedition that went up the Mississippi to found the city of New Orleans. He was the governor of Louisiana several more times until he resigned in 1743.[7]

These French Creoles from New France were deeply involved in the extension of the French Americas along the Mississippi valley and to the Caribbean Sea on the Gulf of Mexico. This was the beginning of the settlement of this region by people from all over the Atlantic world, including Africa, who participated in the development of new French colonies voluntarily, under coercion or by deportation.

---

7. See essay by Gordon Sayre below.

The Sugar Islands

The era of conquest in French Louisiana was also an era of a rise in power for the colonial economies in the Caribbean, which no longer solley depended on the work of immigrants who became colonists, but rather depended more and more on the work of deported Africans who had become slaves. The organization of the system of trade and slaving that developed with Africa to grow the production of the "sugar islands" also extended into Louisiana.

The production of tobacco, indigo, cacao, and especially sugar in the islands fed a new economy that satisfied the tastes and appetites not only of the elite aristocracy but also the bourgeoisie of Europe. Today, we know the nutritive qualities of sugar that were only suspected at the time, but the preservative quality for foods like fruit was well known. This is why the use of sugar would spark an alimentary revolution capable of satisfying growing mass consumption which proved to be a market in permanent progression. Sugar allowed the development of a powerful economy that also satisfied a collective demand.[8] Europe's maritime nations, which had conquered the Atlantic, would rival each other, often to the point of war, for a place in that economy.

Long before the expansion of economic liberalism allowed private ship owners to invest in sugar using the exploitation of American plantations for cane production, slaves from the African coasts for labor, and the development of refineries in Europe for consumption, the French royal state stimulated the creation and development of this new economy. It was through a succession of monopolies organized in the form of varied investment societies, in which private capital investments matched those of the state, that the modern slave trade was instituted in the seventeenth century before reaching its height in the eighteenth century. The state was always financially present, if not the majority shareholder. It also held the power to regulate this commerce and the military strength to impose regulation.

The list of these companies is long and includes the various Companies of Senegal, of the Indies, East and West, the Comapny of the West, and

---

8. Sidney W. Mintz, *Sweetness and Power: The Place of Sugar in Modern History* (New York: Penguin, 1985). The author develops his analysis based on the example of England, but it is perfectly comparable to France.

others. The history of their evolution and financial twists and turns is well known.[9] Beginning in 1626, the Norman Company was founded by Richelieu with merchants in Dieppe and Rouen for the exploitation of Senegal and Gambia in Africa. In 1658, it was replaced by the Company of Cap-Vert and Senegal, created by Louis XIV's Minister of State Jean-Baptiste Colbert, which monopolized the slave trade. In 1627, Colbert also created the Company of New France in the north and acquired a monopoly on commerce in its new territories. In 1635, the Company of the American Islands was founded for the development of Martinique, Guadeloupe, and Tortuga, which included the introduction of deported African slaves. This company succeeded another one founded ten years earlier by two Norman pirates, again supported by Cardinal Richelieu, considered the founder of the modern French state. Louis XIV created the Company of Guinea in 1684 to stimulate the production of sugar and its byproduct: the ever more massive deportation of African labor reduced to slavery on the islands.

At a time when Saint-Domingue was still only a buccaneers' landmark and Louisiana had only just been explored, Martinique and Guadeloupe were the laboratories for this new economy.[10] Yet the bases of French globalization around the Atlantic, between Europe, Africa, and the Americas, were in place for a long time. When the French state undertook the development of the Louisiana territories at the beginning of the eighteenth century, the organization of this "world economy" (following Fernand Braudel's model) was already well advanced. It was the new Company of the Indies this time, founded in 1718 by John Law, that took over the Company of Louisiana, which earlier had become the Company of the West or the Mississippi Company, and was charged with the development of these new territories in liaison with the African continent. The sugar island model was applied to Louisiana, which was the new destination for the deported African labor source and the continuity of another experience of creolization between not only European and Native American peoples and cultures, but African ones too. Into this irreversible historical process, African men and women were brought.

---

9. Abdoulaye Ly, *La Compagnie du Sénégal*, (Khartala, 1993).

10. See essay by Josette Nonone below.

The Coasts of Africa

In 1984, Jean Mettas and Serge Daget, research pioneers of French Atlantic trade, published a directory of French slaving expeditions that shows the inventories for voyages of twenty slaving ships known for having transported 3,500 persons from the African coast to Louisiana between 1718 and 1729. After crossing the Atlantic, these Africans disembarked and were immediately enslaved.[11] In the summer of 1718 two of the Company of the West's ships[12] left Saint-Malo for the coast of Ouidah, in the present Republic of Benin, where they stayed for nearly five months. There, they took on 200 and 250 prisoners respectively, who were delivered to Pensacola, in present-day Florida, after a two month long crossing.

The West African coastal Xwéda people, led by the king of Savi, had sold slaves to the Portuguese since their exploration of the coast beginning in the fifteenth century. At the end of the seventeenth century, the growth of European demand at the harbor of Ouidah increased the prosperity of this coastal kingdom, as well as violence and raids on neighboring populations. The powerful kingdom of the Dahomeys, in the interior of the continent, conquered the coast in 1727 to seize the blossoming slave commerce and spread slave wars and raids further north. The African populations thrown into this Atlantic world also came from the interior of the continent, far from the ocean.[13]

---

11. Jean Mettas, *Répertoire des expéditions négrières françaises au XVIII° siècle,* vol. 2 (Serge et Michelle Daget Editions, 1984).

12. Ibid. These ships, *Le Duc du Maine* and *L'Aurore*, had a 200 and 250 cask capacity at about twenty-five meters long. They sailed together and returned to Saint-Malo the same day in October 1719. They had already completed the triangular voyage from Saint-Malo to Judah. After a few months, they crossed the Atlantic as far as Granada, which at the time was a port of call for ships near the end of their voyage. They then went to Pensacola in June 1729 before going back to Saint-Malo.

13. Elisée Soumoni, "De l'intérieur à la côte," *Les Cahiers des Anneaux de la Mémoire* 1 (1999), 207–16. Elisée Soumoni, "Impact de la traite transatlantique sur l'évolution de l'Afrique" *Mémoire de révolution d'esclaves à Saint Domingue* (Editions du Cidihca, Montréal, sous la direction de Franklin Midy), 27–40; Félix Iroko, *La côte des esclaves et la traite atlantique* (Nouvelle Presse Publication, Cotonou, 2003). Brigitte Kowalski, "Badagri, un comptoir de la traite sur la côte des esclaves" *Les Cahiers des Anneaux de la Mémoire* 11 (2007), 235–47.

There was yet another expedition from Saint-Malo to Ouidah in 1719 and one from Lorient in 1720. Thereafter, it was the French Company of the Indies, strengthened by all their experience accumulated in France, on the African coast and in the Americas, but also in the Indian Ocean, that armed the ships. Those who left the two ports in Brittany went on to Biloxi to supply 182 and 349 slaves, respectively. Cabinda was also a significant slave trafficking port and a contemporary with Ouidah. In 1720, another of the Company of the Indies' ships left La Rochelle for Cabinda, where it stayed for five months before embarking with 294 prisoners, this time from Central Africa, whom it delivered to Biloxi. From the beginning of the Atlantic trade partnership with the coastal populations of Senegambia and the Gulf of Benin, other slaving ports developed on the southern Atlantic coasts of central Africa.[14] The populations of this vast region contributed substantially to the construction of the Atlantic world.

Apart from these instances, the African populations deported on French ships early in the colonization of Louisiana left, for the most part, from the coast of Senegambia, and especially the port of St. Louis at the mouth of the Senegal River and Goree Island. This strategic place allowed control of traffic on the Petite Côte, in Rufisque Bay, and all the way to Bissau, situated on a more southern estuary than the Gambia and Casamance river estuaries. There were three departures from Le Havre to Senegambia in 1719, 1720, and 1722, under the Company of the Indies, but it was at Lorient that the Company settled definitively, and from here all the following slaving expeditions that they organized departed.

---

14. The great provision centers of Atlantic trade were already in place at the beginning of the eighteenth century. The discovery of the Atlantic African coasts, from Cap-Blanc in Mauritania to Cap-Negre in Angola, developed over the course of the fifteenth century, three centuries earlier. The great ports (in terms of the number of prisoners shipped) acquired important experience over the course of this first long, marginal but nevertheless influential period of commercial slave trade. The massive demand in the eighteenth century developed sites in Senegambia, the coasts of the Gulf of Benin, and Angola after several centuries of business relations of little importance but long in tradition. The European and African slavers had known each other a long time.

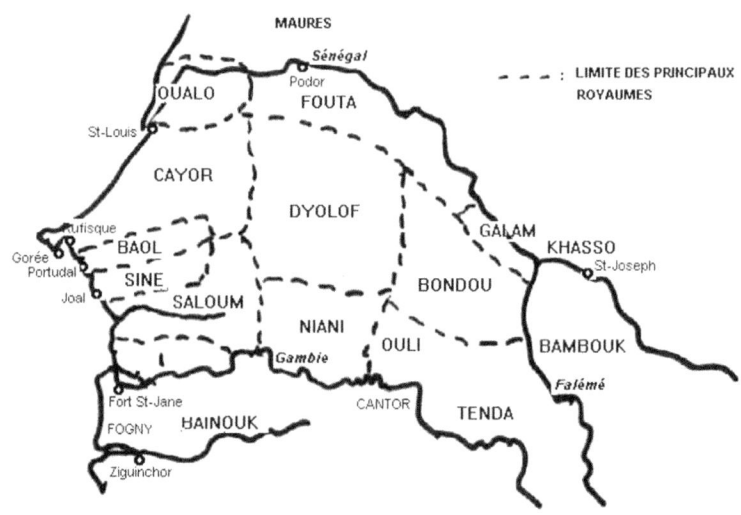

Kingdoms of Senegal

By the eighteenth century, the sites permitting the acquisition of prisoners over thousands of kilometers of the Senegambian coast were no longer to be found, and the India Company's slave ship captains did not venture forth. They went to Portendick[15] on the present-day coast of Mauritania, south of the Banc d'Arguin, and to Bissau, in present-day Guinea-Bissau, where the Company availed themselves of concessions both permanent and temporary in Saint-Louis, Goree, Rufisque, Joal, or Albréda at the mouth of the Gambia River.[16] There they met directors, deputy directors, storekeepers and French civil servants. They managed and developed commercial relations inherited from previous companies from half a century before, along with African or Creole—in the sense that they were descendants of African and European

---

15. Jean Mettas, *op. cit.* The ships *Saint-Louis* and *La Néréide* stayed at this harbor for several weeks at the end of 1729 and circulated from one port to another for a year.

16. Puilippe Haudrere, *La Compagnie des Indes françaises au XVIII° siècle,* vol. 1 (Les Indes savantes Edition, 2005), 198–99.

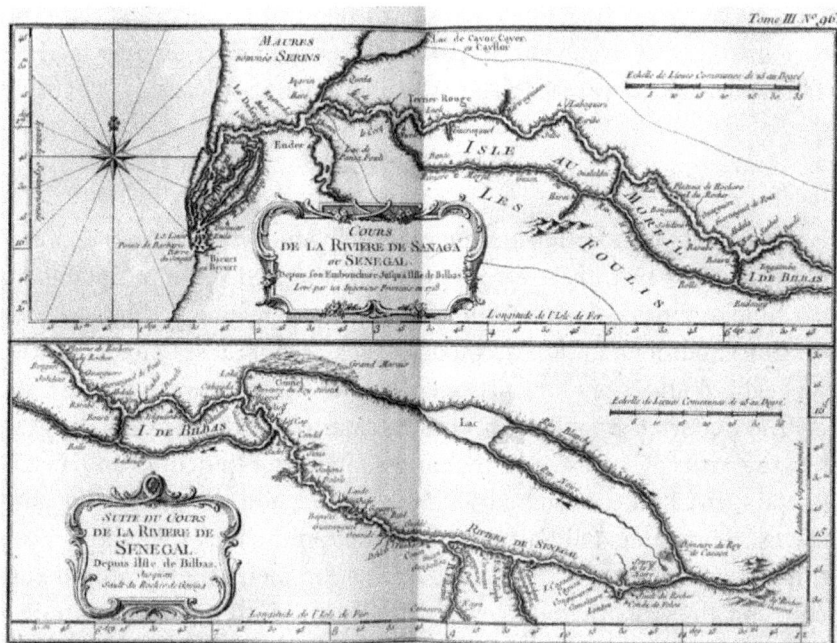

Senegal River map

parents—spokespersons.[17] The prisoners deported from this coast did not just come from the coastline frequented by long-distance courier ships, however. The Senegal River provided a means of penetrating the interior of the continent and further spreading the slave trade.

A brown-water navy sailed the river a thousand kilometers into the interior from Saint-Louis, the maritime port on the coast. The African sailors on these river ships worked and travelled by the hundreds and on river canoes by the thousands, from one port to another. The Company of the Indies used corvettes adapted for river navigation and chartered others. They made an effort to recruit competent sailors, known as *laptots*, for these sophisticated ships. They were chosen from among the best river canoe pilots.[18] The trade

---

17. James F.Searing, *West African Slavery and Atlantic Commerce: The Senegal River Valley, 1700–1860* (Cambridge University Press, 2003).

18. Ibid.; Touré Fall, "Les auviliaires de la traite des esclaves sur le fleuve Sénégal, 1664–1848" (Mémoire de Maîtrise de l'Unversite de Dakar, 2010); Company of the Indies Naval Archives. The comparative study of naval archive documents as well as data and analyses

world had a far-reaching influence over the land as its sailors and canoe pilots joined with caravanners. The Atlantic coast's influence on river societies of the Senegal River reached as far as Mali's western borders.

The Deportation

Practically no accounts on the part of anyone who survived deportation exist. However, there are documents produced by ship captains for maritime authorities of the time that can be supplemented by studying working conditions and the accounts of slaver sailors at sea. In this way we can begin to understand the prisoners' world within the slave ships' holds.

The deported populations were threatened by three major dangers: the same risks of sea travel as the sailors faced; the epidemics and deadly illnesses that they also shared with the sailors; and the prison-like conditions, repression, and murder inflicted upon them by the sailors. Even if these conditions of transoceanic navigation along the equatorial currents and the Atlantic loop were relatively easy[19] to manage, running a ship required competent and qualified sailors. Only the professionals running highly developed and well-constructed ships could execute such a massive deportation over such distances and for such a long period. A long-distance voyage on a slave ship could not be improvised; one not only had to know how to navigate over long distances but also how to control an inherently hostile, incarcerated population. These slaver sailors were not vagabonds without rule of law but people selected for their competence in their trade.[20] The same can be said for the ships that

---

gathered by James F. Searing and Touré Fall allow consideration that, although the salaries can only be estimated, the Senegalese sailors were basically equivalent to sailors from the Loire and its estuary at around the same time period. The salaries of the Senegalese sailors in the Senegal River's Saint-Louis estuary were comparable to those of seamen, sailors, and even naval officers who were captains of small river boats.

19. These are meteorological phenomena characteristic of the Atlantic in which the dominant winds in the Northern and Southern hemispheres form two inverse loops that blow over the three continents of the Old World and the New. The maritime routes of Atlantic trade were traced by the circulation of these dominant winds.

20. Marcus Rediker, *The Slave Ship, a Human History* (New York: Viking-Penguin Group, 2007), 227. "The 'white slaves' who served on his ship were the 'very dregs of the community.'" As far as the French slaving sailors who embarked on ships from Nantes,

Origins of the First African Populations in Lower French Louisiana 29

by twenty-first century standards seem primitive, yet were nonetheless well-constructed and state-of-the-art.

This was particularly the case for the Company of the Indies, and there were no shipwrecks and few victims of accidents on these ships destined for Louisiana. This was also true on the whole for Atlantic trade ships; shipwrecks were rare considering the mass of vessels, the distances travelled, and the quantity of passengers. There were, however, accidental drownings—not many, yet they occurred with regularity among the sailors and the prisoners when they revolted.

These were fearsome voyages. The sea is not the realm of man, especially for those who suffer it in fear and terror. On the slave ships, the prison-like holds were overcrowded and wretched, similar to the jails, fortresses, pontoons, and galleys of Europe, where innumerable prisoners were still dying. In this hostile universe of ocean crossing, the floating prisons sometimes transformed into floating death traps for the African prisoners awaiting slavery in the Americas.[21] Heavily laden with people and cargo, the ships took one to two months to cross the Atlantic. Even though the departure from the Senegambian coast was the shortest part of the voyage, the ships did not stay there, at least not until the captains had embarked the expected number of prisoners.[22] As the ships lingered along the coasts, going from one site to another in search of human cargo, ever-larger numbers of people piled up in them. Before travelling across the ocean, the prisoners were placed in the holds for months, sometimes for the year it often took to fill a Company of the Indies vessel.[23] These long

---

this is false. We have studied over 8,000 cases of the more than 50,000 sailors who armed the 1,400 slaving expeditions from Nantes. It is likely that it was similar for the 320,000 English slaving sailors, whom we have not studied, but who were also all professionals like their French counterparts who belonged to French society and were not marginalized. This controversy reveals the difficulty that lies in understanding historical processes and practices that offend today's moral conscience.

21. André Zysberg, *Les Galériens* (Le Seuil, 1987).

22. The journey from Goree to La Balize was made in three weeks in 1729 by *La Venus* of Lorient, which deported over 350 people.

23. The ship *Saint Louis* wandered for thirteen months over the years 1729 and 1730 between Portendick, Saint Louis, and Goree waiting for a total of 350 prisoners. A dispute between a representative for the Company of the Indies and the authorities in Galam in upper Senegal, 1,000 kilometers from the coast, delayed provisions and prisoners from reaching the ship.

Slave ship in harbor

months of enclosure resulted in sickness, by far the main cause of death on slave ships, especially in the various types of long-distance courier ships.

At the beginning of the eighteenth century bacteria, parasites, and viruses were unknown, and the cause of numerous maladies was attributed to the quality of the air.[24] Nutrition and hygiene on the ships were as poor as bodies on board were numerous. Warships with hundreds of soldiers and pontoons with prisoners of war or Africans were theaters of sanitary disaster due to many causes other than the bad quality of the air. It took time and devastation before epidemics could be identified and prevented. Naval sailors, plus those who worked in commerce and the slave trade and the deported Africans, were all beneficiaries of medical discoveries that effectively limited the death toll.

The length of time during which all these populations were coerced into the wretchedness of the ships and subjected to insufficient nutrition was one of the primary causes of epidemics. In 1730, the ship

---

24. James L.A.Webb Jr, *Humanity's Burden: A Global History of Malaria* (Cambridge, U.K.: Cambridge University Press, 2009), 3. The word malaria comes from the Italian "*mala aria*" (impure air). See the preceding article by Jordan Kellman. "The clean, pure air . . . determines the quality of everything in it."

La Néréïde remained on the Petite Côte, from Goree to the Gambia River, for ten months; the captain, seventeen sailors and thirty-nine crew members died during this time. Afterwards, the Atlantic crossing was quick (one month) and twenty of the two hundred prisoners who had embarked at the end of those ten months died.[25] Malaria, yellow fever, typhoid, dysentery, and scurvy were the deadliest illnesses for all aboard, sailors and prisoners alike.[26] No one knew how to treat or prevent these diseases.[27]

The parasite malaria, or paludism, ravaged tropical and equatorial Africa and, like yellow fever, originated on land.[28] Conversely, the ravages of typhoid, dysentery, and scurvy, though not unknown on land, became much deadlier onboard ships, which were veritable breeding grounds for these diseases. Such maladies were not characteristic of filthy conditions in tropical regions, as was the common belief of the time, but were caused mainly by the absence of hygiene and nutritional deficiencies on board the wretched vessels. They could decimate dozens among those who were enclosed or incarcerated on a slave ship in the middle of the ocean. It took many deaths at sea, usually of sickness, before the 3,500 survivors of these voyages arrived in Louisiana. The ocean was a shroud for those who died at sea with no tomb. Along with the fear and constant threat of death by disease in the middle of the ocean came the unending repression of the prison-like environment.

25. Jean Mettas, *op. cit.*

26. Scurvy is often cited as the principal cause of fatal epidemics observed on these ships destined for Louisiana. From a scientific point of view, the diagnostics of the time were approximative, and certain epidemics recorded over the course of these crossings probably had other origins.

27. In 1727 onboard *Le Duc de Noailles*, with a 250 barrel capacity at less than thirty meters long, the captain was astonished by the outbreak of scurvy in 410 people, both sailors and prisoners, "because fresh meat was never lacking." Remember that the discovery of vitamin C in the twentieth century eradicated scurvy.

28. James L.A.Webb Jr, *op. cit.* After a lengthy period of research on the history of malaria, the author demonstrates that European sailors or American colonists were more susceptible to the malaria parasite contracted in tropical latitudes than Africans, even though they were more or less immune to the malaria of European swamps. The malaria parasite in temperate zones is not the same as in the tropics. The difference in resistance between Europeans and Africans lead to a belief that Africans were more resistant to "tropical fevers" and therefore were sent to work in the tropical colonies of the Americas.

The long-distance ships required well-developed and competent crews. The warships of Europe's maritime nations that were at the forefront of naval techniques also created a large number of commercial sailors whose work organization was based on military methods.[29] Warship discipline was at work on merchant vessels so the crews would be cohesive and obedient during the voyages. Whips that bruised without breaking bones were the weapons of authority on all the ships, and the African prisoners endured these as well. The right to restrain the crews and prisoners gave the commanders and their officers the right to grant their inferiors life or death. On all warships one knew to shoot the mutineers as an example, or hang them in the yard. The principal instigator of a revolt in 1723 met just such a fate on *le Courrier de Bourbon* destined for La Balize. The revolt failed, and the participants were severely punished. Six were hung in the yard and one—considered the leader—was shot at the edge of the yard in front of all the prisoners "as an example."[30]

What most characterized the Atlantic trade, and the expeditions to Louisiana are a fine example, was the constant threat of rebellion, escape, and revolt of the prisoners. This necessitated a prison system forged by the experiences of war prisoners, political prisoners and galley men. It was powerful and effective, but it was not without fault in the face of the prisoners' refusal to be deported, which was endless. They submitted to force, but were constantly ready to revolt. Conflicts between sailors and prisoners were merciless. The rebels could only die or surrender. No one could flee these prisons in the middle of the ocean. Suicides were rare but regular over the entirety of Atlantic trade.

Departing the estuary of Gambia on May 26, 1729, the ship *l'Hannibal* was a theater of violent conflict between prisoners and sailors. The revolt was put down only after forty-five rebels and four sailors died. The spirit of sedition among the survivors was not subdued for long. Upon arriving

---

29. From the end of the seventeenth century, in 1685, Colbert promulgated a disciplinary code for registered commercial sailors as well as the Code Noir, which dictated the discipline and repression of slaves. Every registered commercial sailor who could receive sick leave theoretically had to serve one year on a warship every three years. Many commercial sailors went beyond these requirements over the course of the many naval wars of the eighteenth century.

30. Jean Mettas, *op. cit.*

Origins of the First African Populations in Lower French Louisiana 33

in the Americas, the boat had to stop at Saint Louis du Sud, a Company of the Indies trading post near Cayes in Saint-Domingue, for the crew put an end to the "continual mutiny." This revolt did not succeed in putting an end to the Africans' captivity, as did a few rare revolts over the entire course of Atlantic trade in the eighteenth century, but it was relatively detrimental to the interests of this slaving expedition. The prisoners destined for Louisiana were finally sold at Saint Domingue, to avoid the risk of another uprising before their arrival at La Balize or Biloxi.

The prisoners lived in fear of constant repression or assassination by their jailers, and the sailors also lived in fear of vengeance or revolt. This is why we note that the archives from the 3,500 French slaving expeditions reveal no case of solidarity between sailors and prisoners on board the ships.[31] The same can be said of the ships that first brought Africans to Louisiana. These ships were ideal prisons. From the depths of the hold, one can only escape by the bridge. They were so strong that the hulls that defended against powerful waves had only a few openings, which were narrow and easily closed to protect their impermeability. The many hundreds of people enclosed beneath the bridge were easy to watch through the tiny openings. A crew of about thirty sailors could attend to these duties while incarcerating and deporting hundreds of people. Only a few sentinels, armed and posted at the small openings, were required to maintain order. The bridge was an impenetrable frontier for the prisoners. The experiences lived by the Africans and Europeans on the slave ships that provided the first African peopling of Louisiana were also the founding stages in the race relations that inspired the scientific racism that developed at the end of the eighteenth century.

The main bridge, horizontal and capable of resisting the most powerful breaking waves, was the wall that enforced these divisive relations. The vertical guard rail raised in the middle of the bridge protected control of

---

31. Marcus Rediker, *op. cit.*, 221. "Clearly there were angles of both sailors' and slaves' protests against authority that could and did converge." As far as French slaving is concerned, this is false. There were certainly proletariat solidarities among European sailors and the African sailors, canoe pilots, carpenters, and porters at trade sites. But these numerous African workers who were indispensable to the function of Atlantic trade were not slaves. They benefitted from the slave trade. The outlook we should have today is not one of inventing hypotheticals and fantasies of proletariat solidarity between sailors and prisoners, but one of an effort to understand the absence of solidarity.

the ship, as well as its arms and munitions, against revolts, and it separated the sailors from the general staff on the back side and the subordinates on the front side. This marked the class relations of those in authority and those in subordination, which was true of the entire crew. The whites on each side of the guard rail over the main bridge were in solidarity. The others, the blacks, were piled below. The bridge was the horizontal border under which the African prisoners were gathered, exclusively black, and above which lived their jailers, mainly white. In the amazing overcrowding of hundreds of prisoners crammed on a ship of less than thirty meters in length, there was total horizontal racial separation, a powerful metaphor for the whole process.

The whites were on the bridge, ever vigilant facing the threat of the ocean despite the confidence they had in their technology, and always felt superior and mistrustful of their menacing prisoners despite the faith they had in the strength of their weapons. The blacks were under the bridge, ten times more numerous, with fear and rage in their bellies, losing all points of reference and on the verge of despair in the hold of a ship on an ocean they did not know. They were barely kept alive and dispossessed of all freedom, except the freedom to die. These experiences, in which each had his immutable place, were shared on the thousands of ships by men and women who suffered their respective destinies and who were usually young. The average age of the seamen was twenty-four and the prisoners were often even younger.

The slave ships are not only the historic place of an old crime from a bygone era that can be forgotten, they are a place of memory for the development of the image of self and other from the very beginning of the Atlantic trade process, and it concerns not only those who lived through it. It is this memory built upon the fear of the other—the sentiment most commonly shared by those aboard the slave ships—that is the heritage of the crossings and Atlantic trade, not fantastical racial fraternities or class solidarities. Yet the slave ships were not just hells of discrimination, suffering, and tears. They were also the theater of struggles for liberty, in the most literal sense of the word.

No beneficiary of the slave trade or of slavery, from the deepest areas of the African countryside to the Atlantic ships or the American plantations, could be unaware that the prisoners who became slaves rejected the fate inflicted upon them. They had to watch them, bind them, chain them, beat them, kill them, and terrorize them to obtain their submission. The will to retain their identity and to defend their liberty, sometimes to the point of group combat, never weakened, even if this will was often broken. This was also the creole experience among African populations confronted by the same oppression.

This was the first creole experience between Europeans and Africans, one of humiliation and fear, brutality and revolt "in the belly of the slave ships."[32] These encounters set the scene for a long process about which it is difficult to imagine that there remains no memory, not even a symbolic memory that still lurks. However, mass deportation in the service of a modern understanding of humanity, where individual values must disappear and which was among the first to have used superior technologies for the gains and prosperity of some at the price of oppressing others, nevertheless showed that human beings are more than cannon fodder when they are soldiers, and they are more than merchandise and anonymous labor when they are prisoners and slaves. Individuals resist, and they know to do it collectively if necessary.

The slave ships were another site of the encounter between Europeans and Africans, following but distinct from the partnership on the coast, that allowed Europeans to take human cargo. This encounter, which continued on the ocean, became a paroxysm of oppression that nevertheless proved that cultural and individual values can resist terror and surmount it. The origin of one of these creole experiences we have inherited today is absolute tragedy, not literary, imaginary, or virtual, but experienced by the suffering of bodies to the point of death. It cannot be forgotten, and it can be overcome.

---

32. See essay by Edouard Glissant below.

Mona Georgelin. *Association Mamanthé, troupe Massilia Ka.*

Danse Gwoka rythme Léwoz

Photographer : Azedine Hsissou

Mona Georgelin. *Association Mamanthé, troupe Massilia Ka.*

Mélinée Magen. *Association Mamanthé, troupe Massilia Ka.*

Mélinée Magen. *Association Mamanthé, troupe Massilia Ka.*

Mélinée Magen. *Association Mamanthé, troupe Massilia Ka.*

Mélinée Magen. *Association Mamanthé, troupe Massilia Ka.*

Artiste invité : Max Diakok. *Association Mamanthé, troupe Massilia Ka.*

Danse Gwoka, rythme Léwoz

Artiste invité : Max Diakok. *Association Mamanthé, troupe Massilia Ka.*

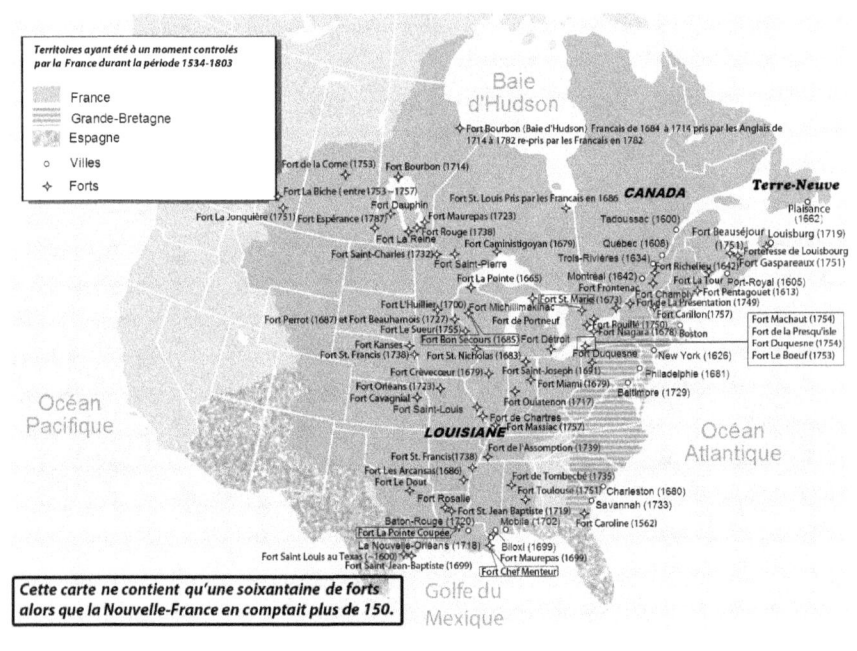

Map of New France before 1763

Creolized Frenchmen and Frenchified Amerindians in Louisiana

Sophie White

In 1680, deserters from René-Robert Cavelier de la Salle's expedition to the Illinois Country left a message for him after they had destroyed and deserted their own Fort Crevecoeur. Shortly before retreating into the wilderness to take refuge among Amerindians, one of the deserters scribbled on the ruins of the fort: "NOUS SOMMES TOUS SAUVAGES, CE 15 A[vril] 1680."[1] His choice of the word "sauvage" to describe French men was a charged one that went beyond the particular circumstances of French engagés' mass desertion from a colonial and military outpost. The word *sauvage* was the term for Amerindian. This definition derived from the original meaning of the word as wild or untamed, so, like a plant, with the potential to be domesticated—just as Frenchmen had the potential to lose their Frenchness and return to the wild as a result of their physical presence in the New World. As such, it embodied French beliefs—somewhat incredible to us in the twenty-first century—that the differences between French and Indians were not stable or biological. In other words, the inscription was not a simple message about *voyageurs* gone wild. Instead, it conveyed the state of mind of French soldiers trapped in Amerindian territory in the New World, who felt that they were not only slipping into Amerindian mores as they took refuge among them, but that they were in fact also at risk of metamorphosing into Amerindians. As such, this inscription, or graffito, is suggestive of the fundamental instability that Frenchmen felt as they colonized North America. And this possibility of transformation

---

1. Robert Cavelier de La Salle, *Relation of the Discoveries and Voyages of Cavelier La Salle from 1679 to 1681*, 232–33.

Portrait of Robert Cavelier De Lassalle

resulting from their presence in the New World can be directly linked to colonists' anxieties about creolization.

In the eighteenth-century sense of the word, "creole" referred to Old World populations (whether European or African) who were born in the colonies. As Joyce Chaplin explains, the term was intrinsic to the way that Europeans theorized the differences that they observed in others and the anxieties that these theories caused them to feel about their own identity.

If racism insists that human physical differences are essential, the term "creole" identified human differences that were in flux, that changed as people changed their customs and climate. Indeed, the usual assumption among early modern Europeans was that physical place created individual and national differences—France made humans into French people, and America made them into Indians. But the perceived malleability of humans was precisely what troubled English colonists. That their customs and very bodies might metamorphose in the new world was deeply revolting to them.[2] Chaplin's point is specific to the English colonies but was not exclusive to them, for the theory of monogenesis (that all mankind shared a common origin) framed all Europeans' early encounters with Amerindians, with its premise that identity, including skin color, was not fixed but malleable.[3]

---

2. Joyce E. Chaplin, "Creoles in British America: From Denial to Acceptance," in Charles Stewart, ed., *Creolization: History, Ethnography, Theory* (Walnut Creek, Ca.: Left Coast Press, 2006): quotation p. 47. On the concept of creolization in the eighteenth century, see also Charles Stewart "Creolization: History, Ethnography, Theory," in Stewart, ed., *Creolization: History, Ethnography, Theory*, 1–25; Ralph Bauer and José Antonio Mazzotti, "Introduction: Creole Subjects in the Colonial Americas," in *Creole Subjects in the Colonial Americas: Empires, Texts, Identities*, ed. Bauer and Mazzotti (Chapel Hill, N.C., 2009), 1–57; David Buisseret, et al., *Creolization in the Americas* (College Station: Texas A&M University Press, 2000).

3. Karen Ordahl Kupperman, "Fear of Hot Climates in the Anglo-American Colonial Experience," *William and Mary Quarterly*, 3^d Series, 41 (1984): 213–40; also Nancy

There was a corollary to this belief in the mutability of colonists' identity, namely that Amerindians also had the potential to be transformed as they changed their customs, metamorphosing from *sauvage* to *cultivé*. But only the French enshrined this belief—this reverse creolization—in official policies that were promulgated in New France and later in Louisiana. Policies of *francisation* help illuminate how the French could even contemplate Amerindians' potential for transformation into French subjects. But it was not only the French who conceived of identity as fluid and mutable: so did Amerindians. And for both groups, material culture and rituals centered on dress were key to enabling and controlling transformation. In this essay, I present a case-study that draws upon the archival research and interpretive scheme of my publications on Frenchification and creolization in Louisiana to show how one group of Amerindians, the Illinois, navigated themes of acculturation and metamorphosis.[4] In doing so, I signal one way in which the parallels with creolization can be used to frame questions about *Amerindian* beliefs in the mutability of their own identity.

***

In 1627, the charter for a Company of New France was composed. Among the preoccupations expressed by the document was the question of the Amerindians that the French planned to colonize. One clause of that charter touched directly on those Amerindians who would convert:

Shoemaker, *A Strange Likeness: Becoming Red and White in Eighteenth-Century North America*, (New York: Oxford University Press, 2004); Joyce E. Chaplin, *Subject Matter: Technology, the Body, and Science on the Anglo-American Frontier, 1500–1676* (Cambridge, Mass.: Harvard University Press, 2003); Kathleen M. Brown, "Native Americans and Early Modern Concepts of Race," in *Empire and Others: British Encounters with Indigenous Peoples, 1600–1850*, ed. by Martin Daunton and Rick Halpern (Philadelphia: University of Pennsylvania Press, 1999), 79–100; on Louisiana, see note 4, below.

4. Sophie White, *Wild Frenchmen and Frenchified Indians: Material Culture and Race in Colonial Louisiana* (Philadelphia: University of Pennsylvania Press, 2012); White, "'To ensure that he not give himself over to the *Sauvages*': Cleanliness, Frenchification, and Whiteness," *Journal of Early American History* 2 (2012): 111–49. On French colonists' fears of becoming sauvage, see White, "Massacre, *Mardi Gras*, and Torture in Early New Orleans" *The William and Mary Quarterly*, 3rd series, 70:3 (July 2013): 497–538.

XVII. Ordonnera Sa Majesté que les descendants des François qui s'habitueront au dit pays, ensemble les sauvages qui seront amenés à la connoissance de la foi et en feront profession, seront censés et réputés naturels françois, et comme tels pourront venir habiter en France quand bon leur semblera, et y acquérir, tester, succéder et accepter donations et légats, tout ainsi que les vrais regnicoles et originaires françois, sans être tenus de prendre aucunes lettres de déclaration ni de naturalité.[5]

The intent behind this assimilationist policy was to literally turn Amerindians into French subjects of the King: not only Catholic but also linguistically and culturally French. But the clause also alluded to French anxieties about creolization and seasoning that they feared was a consequence of their being born in, or becoming physically acclimated to, the New World (the "François qui *s'habitueront* au dit pays"). And in combining French colonists and Amerindian converts in the same clause, the document conflated their rights, privileges, and identities, as if they were one and the same.

Frenchification policies were tied both to Catholicism and to the development of French nationalism over regional and provincial affiliation.[6] The 1627 Charter would usher in a sequence of failed policies in New France aimed at frenchifying ("franciser") Amerindians, often, though not always, linked to the promotion of French-Amerindian intermarriage. By the time the French established the Illinois Country (site of the deserters' graffito) in the late seventeenth century, frenchification policies in New France had been deemed a failure. Yet it would be in this precise place that missionaries and officials began to claim that women converts married to Frenchmen, and their progeny, had achieved Frenchness, with some

---

5. See "Acte pour l'établissement de la Compagnie des Cent Associés pour le Commerce du Canada, contenant les articles accordés à la dite Compagnie par M. Le Cardinal de Richelieu, le 29 Avril 1627," transcribed in *Edits, ordonnances royaux, et arréts du Conseil d'Etat du Roi concernant le Canada*, I (Quebec, 1854), 10.

6. On frenchification, see for example White, *Wild Frenchmen*; Guillaume Aubert, "'The Blood Of France:' Race And Purity of Blood in The French Atlantic World," *The William and Mary Quarterly*, 3rd ser., 61 (2004): 439–78; Belmessous; "Être français en Nouvelle-France: Identité française et identité coloniale aux dix-septième et six-huitième siècles," *French Historical Studies* 27 (2004): 507–40. On the formation of French national identity in this period, see David Bell, "Recent Works on Early Modern French National Identity," *The Journal of Modern History* 68 (1996): 84–113; Peter Sahlins, "Fictions of a Catholic France: The Naturalization of Foreigners, 1685–1787," *Representations* 47 (1994): 85–100.

asserting, as late as 1732, "*quil ny avoit point de différence entre un sauvage Chrestien et un Blanc.*"[7]

Indeed, the Illinois Country *was* exceptional in its widespread pattern of conversion, intermarriage (beginning in 1694), and frenchification. Amerindian women and Frenchmen married according to French religious and civilian rites, and they had their children baptized (this is in stark contrast to the more usual pattern of French-Amerindian *mariages à la façon du pays* in the Great Lakes). By 1719 they lived not in Amerindian villages but in segregated French agrarian settlements farmed according to French methods using French equipment and tools.[8] Probate records of French-Amerindian households reveal that lodgings and outbuildings were built colonial-style, usually surrounded by mulberry picket fences. The dwellings were furnished with French-style furniture, textiles, cookware, and household goods, some of which, like armchairs, copper coffee pots or crystal glassware, hinted at a degree of refinement. But if the analysis of household goods is open to interpretation, since the end user cannot always be presumed, clothing, which was personal to one wearer, provides a more precise means of evaluating the degree to which individual women adhered to French material culture. And when the personal garb of these Amerindian wives, and that of their daughters, was inventoried, the records reveal their ownership of jackets, gowns, and petticoats, worn over shifts and bodices, the whole invariably accented with a cape and linen caps. In other words, there was no visual differentiation between their wardrobe contents and those of French female colonists settled in the Illinois Country. Notaries and appraisers were obviously underreporting indigenous features, whether of dress or other items. Many of these were necessarily retained by native women though they were also present in French-only households. What I am suggesting is that it is not so much the exclusion in probate records of references to Amerindian forms

---

7. The missionaries' words were reported in Centre des Archives d'Outre Mer C13A 15, 166v: 17 July 1732, Salmon to minister.

8. On the separation of the villages, see Joseph Zitomersky, "The Form and Function of French-Indian Relations in Early Eighteenth-Century French Colonial Louisiana," *Proceedings of the Fifteenth Meeting of the French Colonial Historical Society Martinique and Guadeloupe, May 1989*, ed. by Patricia Galloway and Philip P. Boucher (Lanham: University Press of America, 1992), 154–77.

of attire that is significant. Rather, what is pertinent is the *inclusion* of all the necessary components of full European dress among the belongings of Amerindian women and their children—i.e., that they had the ability to dress in the French style and to live in the French manner.[9]

And this seems to get us into some difficulty, because the trend has been to be wary of evidence of acculturation, focusing instead on recovering instances of cultural retention. Rather than interpreting this evidence of cultural frenchification as an example of assimilation into the hegemonic colonial and religious order, I argue that it should be seen as a sophisticated response to the arrival of the French, one that in fact demonstrates the *persistence* of Illinois belief systems.

Illinois Amerindians had a history of openness to new cross-cultural exchanges and alliances. Their cultural borrowings and taste for novelty goods did not begin with the incursion of the French in North America, since these Amerindians had traded goods and absorbed aesthetic influences, directly and indirectly, from other nations as far away as the Southwest. And marital alliances between Illinois women and French men were extensions of pre-existing practices.

We need to explore what it meant for Amerindian women to marry out and live with Frenchmen, and how that experience might resonate with indigenous rituals that deployed material culture, including dress, to achieve metamorphosis into a new identity. Read in the context of marital alliance, captive adoption, and other native practices premised, like the concept of creolization, on the malleability of identity, cultural frenchification begs the tricky question of whether Amerindian wives of Frenchmen saw themselves as having actually become French upon entering into Catholic marriage with Frenchmen, in the same way that the deserters might have understood their creolization and their transformation into *sauvages*.

By showing how Amerindian women in the Illinois Country lived with French possessions, inhabited them, and used them as a part of their daily activities, we can grasp the nonverbal ways in which these women channeled objects to convey their identity and to define community. As such, this analysis reveals less obvious ways of using objects to retain aspects of tribal culture and suggests reasons why Illinois Indian women converts

---

9. This chapter is a very brief summary of my research in *Wild Frenchmen and Frenchified Indians,* ch. 1.

married to French men might want to frenchify, in the same way that we need to probe why the French deserters of Fort Crevecoeur might have found it appealing to give in to creolization in order to become *sauvage*.

In this context of precedents for metamorphosis rituals, it pays to reconsider, through a material culture lens, the practice of deploying women to secure cross-cultural marital alliances among the Illinois. Upon marriage, the women would be required to permanently take on the clothing of their new tribe to signal the renunciation of their past identity and their assumption of a new one; just as in Europe, where foreign brides marrying into the French royal family were stripped of their national fashion and changed into French dress upon crossing the border into France and into their new French identity.[10] The tradition of cross-cultural alliances suggests that Illinois women were raised with the understanding that they would need to transgress their own (individual or collective) identities upon marriage to someone from outside of their tribe.

Beyond the example of intermarriage, there were other rituals that relied on transfers of clothing to accomplish and signal the transformation to a new identity. Among these was the gender re-assignment of the *berdaches*. Berdaches (as the French called them) were boys raised as girls, in a practice familiar from accounts of seventeenth-century Illinois Indians but not unique to this nation. According to these French eyewitnesses, the process of becoming a berdache was twofold. A boy who showed an affinity for female occupations (in leisure and work) was first veered toward female activities; next he was forbidden access to male privileges and status. Then he was dressed in women's clothing and, given that a metamorphosis lay at the heart of this change of clothing, we can expect that there was a ritual centered on stripping and redressing. The redirecting of the boy's gender identification was confirmed on reaching adolescence as a result of a religious vision quest that also conferred a role as shaman or manitou onto the berdache. The sources are unclear as to any link to homosexuality or intersexuality; they do specify that berdaches could have sexual relations with both males and females. While occupational and even linguistic factors

---

10. Caroline Weber, *Queen of Fashion: What Marie Antoinette Wore to the Revolution* (New York: Henry Holt, 2006), 25–32. This was the custom throughout Europe; see, for example Evelyn Welch, "Art on the Edge: Hair and Hands in Renaissance Italy," *Renaissance Studies* 23 (2009): 247–49.

played their part in the transformation, it was dress and appearance that were essential to constructing and marking the berdache identity, incorporating feminine clothing, hairstyles, and tattoo patterns.[11]

Captive adoption was another such practice, in essence a mourning ritual aimed at replenishing depleted populations. In this ritual, some enemies, whether men, women, or children, who had been seized in raids, were selected for adoption as replacements for the deceased, to re-quicken or "cover the dead." For those spared torture and death, through the process of adoption, the captives' previous identities were literally stripped from their bodies, and a new name conferred after the washing of the body, the cutting or re-styling of hair, and the putting on of new articles of dress. Permanent markers such as mutilated body parts or tattoos remained as signs of a past life but were not impediments to the assumption of a new identity. Through the process of captivity and adoption, the identity and even the clan affiliation of the captive were reinvented, and any children born to him or her thereafter were considered free; this kind of captivity was not hereditary, in contrast to French slave codes.[12]

While the Illinois Country was characterized by its pattern of church-sanctioned and/or legal intermarriages between French men and exogamous Amerindian women who lived in their husbands' households, not all of the women were Illinois. Some were former captives, and the actual degree of agency of former captives who converted to Catholicism, were manumitted, and then married Frenchmen in the Illinois Country, presents a distinct set of questions about hybridity to which material culture offers some fresh perspectives. There were at least four free Padoka women married in the church to Frenchmen in the area. Suzanne Keramy married three Frenchmen in total. The 1726 inventory of the property

---

11. White, *Wild Frenchmen*, 102-3, 129; Hauser, "The Berdache and the Illinois Indian Tribe;" Richard C. Trexler, *Sex and Conquest: Gendered Violence, Political Order, and the European Conquest of the Americas* (Ithaca: Cornell University Press, 1995), ch. 4.

12. White, *Wild Frenchmen*, 103-8. On captivity and captivity rituals in French America, see Roland Viau, *Enfants du néant et mangeurs d'âmes: Guerre, culture et societé en Iroquoisie ancienne* (Montréal: Boréal, 1997), 137-60; William A. Starna and Ralph Watkins, "Northern Iroquoian Slavery," *Ethnohistory* 38 (1991): 34-57; Brett Rushforth, "'A Little Flesh We Offer You': The Origins of Indian Slavery in New France," *William and Mary Quarterly*, 3rd Series, 60 (2003): 777-808, and Starna and Watkins, "Northern Iroquoian Slavery;" also Daniel Richter, *Ordeal of the Longhouse: The Peoples of the Iroquois League in the Era of European Colonization* (Chapel Hill: University of North Carolina Press, 1992), 66-74.

owned with her first late husband included a colonial-house furnished with a bed with bedding; a sideboard; two chairs and a walnut table with a red linen tablecloth; buckets; kettles; cauldrons; candlesticks; and an earthenware terrine.[13] Upon her death in 1747, the furniture and furnishings had grown by three beds with bedding; a sideboard; a table and six chairs; a large and a small tablecloth; eleven napkins; assorted copper or brass kettles; and pans, grill, terrines, pewter tableware, and basins.[14] Her dress similarly left no doubt as to its French character and identification: multiple shifts, jackets, and skirts, all cut and constructed from French-imported fabric into French styles. Her heirs paid for the French medicine with which she had been treated in her final illness, and they bought a wooden casket for her burial, capping her life with a final Catholic rite.[15]

In evaluating the material culture of former captives like Keramy who were married to Frenchmen, it is important to recognize that they came from tribes that also practiced covering the dead, as did the Illinois. As such, both former captives and Illinois Amerindian women might even have benefited from this practice, centered on metamorphosis, when their villages incorporated new slave laborers or when one of their own relatives had been resuscitated through captive adoption. And they anticipated it as a fate that might befall themselves or their own kin. This intimate familiarity with captivity as a way of life (and death) forces us to reconsider how former captives understood the implications for their own lives of the premise underlying captive adoption, that identity could be re-programmed through rituals and culture. Here then, in Amerindian societies was evidence of the mutability of identity, whether signaled by and achieved through the shift to new ways of dressing as a result of cross-cultural clan marriage alliances in patrilineal societies; exchanges of children and ritual exchanges of clothing at councils; the stripping and re-dressing of adopted captives; the re-gendering of transvestite *berdaches* through dress. All of these examples drew upon indigenous beliefs in the fluidity of tribal and gender identity, closely paralleling how Europeans understood identity as mutable and their own potential for creolization.

---

13. Kaskaskia Manuscripts, Rudoph County Courthouse, Chester, Illinois: 26:5:2:1, 26:5:2:1, 26:5:10:1, 28:6:7:1.

14. Kaskaskia Manuscripts, Rudoph County Courthouse, Chester, Illinois: 47:10:31:3.

15. Kaskaskia Manuscripts, Rudoph County Courthouse, Chester, Illinois: 47:10:31:3.

Artiste invité : Max Diakok. *Association Mamanthé, troupe Massilia Ka.*

Danse Gwoka
rythme menndé

Photographer : Azedine Hsissou

Artiste invité : Max Diakok. *Association Mamanthé, troupe Massilia Ka.*

Artiste invité : Max Diakok.   *Association Mamanthé, troupe Massilia Ka.*

Danse Gwoka, rythme menndé

Nathanaël Magen. *Association Mamanthé, troupe Massilia Ka.*

Mona Georgelin. *Association Mamanthé, troupe Massilia Ka.*

Mona Georgelin. *Association Mamanthé, troupe Massilia Ka.*

Artiste invité : Jan-Mary Lurel. *Association Mamanthé, troupe Massilia Ka.*

Mélinée Magen. *Association Mamanthé, troupe Massilia Ka.*

Creole Identity in French Louisiana: From the Memoir of Dumont de Montigny

Gordon Sayre

"Creole" is a word that shifted in meaning across time and space, the French *créole* even more than the English *creole*, Spanish *criollo*, or Portuguese *crioulo* (the earliest coinage, from which the others derive). The significance of créole in the francophone Caribbean, such as in the work of Aimé Césaire, Edouard Glissant, Rafael Confiant, Patrick Chamoiseau, Maryse Condé, and others, is the most dynamic and topical in contemporary cultural studies, but it has greatly evolved and diverged from the seventeenth and eighteenth-century meanings I will examine here.

Criollo first appeared in print in 1570 in Juan Lópes de Velasco's *Geografía y descripción universal de las Indias* as a term for those born in the American colonies of European, in this case Spanish, parents.[1] In the Spanish colonies, tension between criollos and European-born Iberian *peninsulares* was pervasive because the Spanish crown generally refused to appoint criollos to top posts in the colonial civil administration, church, or military. A reactionary anti-peninsular prejudice on the part of creole patriots was decisive in the Bolivarian revolutions of the early nineteenth century, and one consequence of this may be an over-emphasis on criollo identity in colonial historiography. Nonetheless, the tension between criollos and the *gachupins* or *chapetons* (the term "peninsulares"

---

1. See Ralph Bauer and José Antonio Mazzotti, eds., *Creole Subjects in the Colonial Americas* (Chapel Hill, 2009), 4. The first appearance of créole in French dictionaries came much later: the *dictionaire de l'academie française* of 1762 (Paris: B. Brunet, 1762), 439 provides the definition: "Nom qu'on donne à un Européen d'origine qui est né en Amérique Un créole, une créole," Dictionnaire de l'academie française (Paris: B. Brunet, 1762), 439.

was less often used before the nineteenth century) was strong in the colonial period.

In this short essay I wish to explore the tension and conflict between the créoles of eighteenth-century New France and Louisiana, and the French-born colonists who might be called "hexagonals" or "metropolitan French." My major source will be the autobiographical narrative by Jean-François Benjamin Dumont de Montigny (1695–1760), an officer in the colonial military who wrote a 443-page manuscript memoir, held at the Newberry Library in Chicago. I translated the memoir into English and and co-edited with Carla Zecher the first publication of the narrative in French.[2]

Dumont was the youngest son of an avocat in the *parlement de Paris*, whose family obtained for him a commission as a lieutenant in the *troupes de la marine*, the corps that provided nearly all French military forces serving in America. In 1719 Dumont sailed for Louisiana, and shortly after he landed the Governor and supreme commandant of the colony, Jean-Baptiste Le Moyne de Bienville, reviewed the newly-arrived officers:

> . . . one day when we were passing in revue before the commandant, he wanted to know who were the parents, the mothers and fathers, of the officers. He had his secretary next to him, who was writing down what each man said. But I was offended by this maneuver, and as I was young, I imagined that there might be some malice behind it. Given that I was an officer with a commission that the Company of the Indies had awarded to me, it was no business of his who I was or upon whom I was dependent. So when he came to question me about my father, I replied that he was a farmer.
>
> "What, a tax farmer?"
>
> "No," I said to him, "a farm laborer."[3]

2. Jean-François-Benjamin Dumont de Montigny, *Regards sur le monde atlantique, 1715–1747* (Sillery, Québec: 2008), and *The Memoir of Lieutenant Dumont, 1715–1747: A Sojourner in the French Atlantic* (Chapel Hill, 2012).

3. Montigny, *Regards*, 65.
> . . . un jour qu'on passoit en revue devant le commendant, il voulut sçavoir qui étoit les pères et mères des officiers, leurs parents. Il avoit son secrétaire à côté de lui, qui écrivoit ce que chacun lui disoit. Mais je me trouvé scandalizé de cette manœuvre et comme j'étois jeune, je m'imaginay qu'il y avoit quelque serpent caché là-dessous, puis- qu'étant officier avec brevet, la Compagnie des Indes m'en ayant honoré, il ne lui faisoit rien de sçavoir de qui j'étois et de qui je dépen- dois. Étant venu donc à

Jean Baptiste De Bienville

In writing of several confrontations during the ensuing seventeen years that he spent in Louisiana, Dumont dramatized his struggle with Bienville, who served as governor of the colony for four separate periods between 1701 and 1743, and whose heroic bronze statue stands near Jackson Square in New Orleans with an inscription that identifies him as the founder of the city. Bienville was a créole. He was born into a family of adventurers and soldiers, and he arrived in Louisiana as a teenager with the expedition of his older brother Pierre LeMoyne d'Iberville. Their father, Charles LeMoyne de Longueuil et de Châteauguay, had been born to modest social status, the son of an innkeeper in Dieppe, but after emigrating to Canada in 1641 had lifted himself and his sons into the colony's elite through military valor and the acquisition of seigneurial

---

moy pour me questioné qui étoit mon père, je lui répondis qu'il étoit fermier.
— *Comment, fermier général?*
— *non, lui dis-je, fermier laboureur.*

titles to Canadian land. The Le Moyne family exemplified the power and prestige achievable by creole colonists through military service and a nascent system of *noblesse d'epée* in New France.

But Dumont de Montigny did not wish to recognize Bienville's status, either as a decorated officer or as the head of the civil administration. The scene of Bienville's review of the genealogies of French officers may or may not have actually occurred, but it epitomizes the conflicting status registers of noble birth and military rank, of descent and consent, of the privileged son versus the self-made man. Dumont evidently felt offended by Bienville, whose family had no distinguished lineage in France. In principle, only a man of noble parentage, or whose father had been an officer, could receive an officer's commission in the French military. Bienville and his brother were examples of the rare instances when commoners did rise into the officers' ranks by valor in battle and leadership in the garrisons. Dumont himself met neither criterion; his initial enlistment in the *gardes marines* (an officer training corps for sons of privilege) and his commission as a lieutenant had been secured through the influence of his father and older brothers, who had connections with Louis-Claude Le Blanc, the *secrétaire d'état de la guerre* from 1718 to 1723. This period of the Orléans regency was also the period when the Scottish financier John Law was promoting shares in the Compagnie de l'Ouest and land along the Mississippi as an investment with the implicit backing of the French crown. Le Blanc and three partners, including Charles-Louis-Auguste, Fouquet de Belle-Isle, invested in four separate concessions in Louisiana and outfitted supplies and companies of soldiers and officers to develop and fortify these plantations. Dumont was among these companies, and his manuscript narrative was dedicated to Belle-Isle.

Dumont's sarcastic comment about a "fermier" further ironizes the status regimes in France during the time of John Law. A "fermier general" or tax farmer had much greater opportunities for enrichment than a landowner or farmer, and many used this wealth to purchase offices that conferred upon their descendants a title of nobility. Dumont's own family was not of the landed aristocracy, and of his large family only he and one of his nieces used the name "Dumont de Montigny," which implied that his family owned an estate at a place called Montigny.

In a subsequent encounter, Dumont insulted Bienville's kin. After Bienville learned that Dumont had spent a year in Québec before sailing for Louisiana, the governor insinuated that he had done so in the capacity of an indentured servant, and Dumont retaliated:

> ... he asked me if I had not been sent there for a period of thirty-six months? I was a bit shocked, but since this was my superior officer, what could I do? I let it pass [64] silently, but he went on the offensive again, asking me if I had not known a man named Le M****.
> I replied that yes I had known him, but that it was neither a great pleasure nor honor for me.
> — "And why not?" he said.
> — "Because he is a drunkard and a person unworthy of the society of honest men."[4]

Dumont concealed the name, although he expected his reader to decipher it as "Le Moyne." Bienville's response was: *"je vous suis bien obligé des bonnes qualités que vous donnez à mon parent"* ("I am much obliged for the good qualities that you have ascribed to my relative"). Dumont's sarcastic, provocative outbursts (if in fact he did utter them to Bienville) were fearless and self-destructive—no one in Paris, not even his powerful protector Belle-Isle, could prevent Bienville or other officers from punishing him for this sort of behavior. Still, these confrontations reflected the attitudes of other Frenchmen in Louisiana toward the creoles (who were nearly all Canadians, given that the Louisiana colony had been founded only twenty years before Dumont's arrival). This resentment and hostility among hexagonals was not confined to the military. The Capucin priest Father Raphaël wrote in the 1720s that the creoles had been *"élevés, pour ainsi dire, au milieu des sauvages, et ne connaissent que peu de choses des coutumes et gouvernement du royaume"* ("brought up, so to speak among savages, and know little of the customs

---

4. Montigny, *Regards*, 63–64.
   ... *il me demanda si ce n'étoit pas en qualité de trente-six mois? Cela me choqua un peu, mais c'étoit mon supérieur, que faire? Je passay cela sous silence mais luy, revenant à la charge, il me demanda si je n'avois pas connu un nomé Le M****
   Je lui répondis que je l'avois connu, mais que ce n'étoit pas un grand bonheur et honneur pour moy.*
   — *et pourquoy ? dit-il.*
   — *C'est que c'est un ivrogne et une personne indigne de la société de touttes les honnestes gens.*

and mode of government of the kingdom").⁵ The association of creoles with Amerindians was common and extended to the Spanish colonies as well. Near the end of his memoir Dumont wrote of learning in 1742 that Bienville had been replaced as governor:

> I have learned, since I left that country, that the King had recalled the first Canadian and had handed over the leadership of the people there to the son of M. de Vaudreuil. I do not doubt for a moment that his command is far better than that of his compatriot, who had learned all he knew from the Choctaw Indians. . . .⁶

Manners, dress, and perhaps language differentiated the French-born officers from the creoles or Canadians, who themselves looked down upon the French as cowardly in battle and ridiculously inept at woodcraft and survival in the New World. Bienville's success as governor lay in his skillful manipulation of alliances with Native tribes including the Choctaw (spelled "Chactas" in French), but the tensions existed all the same. However, whereas in New Spain the criollos complained that they were denied appointments to important posts in the church or military, in New France and Louisiana no such "glass ceiling" applied to the *créoles*, at least not in a systematic way.⁷ I see several reasons why *créole* identity did not develop in the French colonies as it did in the Spanish empire.

The most significant difference is that, following the English conquest of Canada and the subsequent Spanish cession of Louisiana in 1759–1763, the identity of French creoles was defined against the new rulers and administrators, who spoke a different language and hailed not from France but from a competing imperial power. There were brief acts of rebellion

---

5. "Lettre de Père Raphaël" 12 Mars 1726, Archives Nationales Françaises, Archives Coloniales, Correspondance générale, C13a, vol. 10, fol. 41.

6. Montigny, *Regards*, 441:
   J'ay appris depuis que j'ay quitté le pays que le Roy avoit rappellé le premier Canadien et avoit donné la conduitte de ce peuple au fils de Monsieur de Vaudreuil. Je ne doutte pas un seul moment qu'il y commende beaucoup mieux que son compatriotte, qui n'avoit appris que ce qu'il sçavoit parmy les Chactas sauvages, au lieu que celui-cy. . . .

7. A valuable discussion of the creole generation in French Louisiana may be found in Shannon Dawdy, *Building the Devil's Empire: French Colonial New Orleans* (Chicago, 2008), 6–11.

and resistance on the part of the French to colonial rule by Spain and England, such as the 1768 revolt in Louisiana, and the Patriot Rebellions in Canada in 1837–38. But those rebellions were unsuccessful, and in each case it was not a question of creoles versus hexagonals. The only place in the French Atlantic colonies where that kind of conflict developed was in the Caribbean, especially St. Domingue/Haiti, beginning after 1789 with conflicts between the free creoles of color, the French creole plantation owners, and the new Republican administration from France. Thus the rebellions in Saint Domingue/Haiti fit the pattern of the Bolivarian Creole revolutions in Spanish America better than they fit the pattern of the French American colonies of Canada and Louisiana.

If we look at the period prior to the Seven Years War, *créole* identity was forestalled by other factors. Most important of these was the policy in New France of *françisation*, an assimilation process that Sophie White describes as an effort "to turn Indian converts into Frenchified convert subjects of the king—not only Catholic but also linguistically, culturally, and legally French." New France was not a privately chartered colony as Virginia or New England were, it was an extension of the realm. The colonists of New France were French subjects just as much as the peoples of peripheral regions of metropolitan France, such as Brittany. And at the time the policy was articulated, in the 1630s, there was no modern racial ideology to prevent Indians from being accepted as French. White documents how françisation succeeded in the small settlements of the Illinois Country better than it did in either Canada or Louisiana, and the measure of its success was that Native women who married French men acquired French clothes and furnishings consistent with their social status and if widowed were legally accepted as heirs to their husbands' estates.[8]

In Anglophone America African ancestry of any degree generally has marked a person as "black" and most mixed-blood Natives were (and are) classified as "American Indians." In Spanish colonial America mixed-blood *castas* were scrupulously calculated down to the fourth or fifth generation (as in casta paintings made to represent the appearance of such people), even as many mixed-bloods with sufficient wealth and

8. Sophie White, *Wild Frenchmen and Frenchified Indians: Material Culture and Race in Colonial Louisiana* (Philadelphia, 2012), and "Trading Looks" *Common-place* 13:4 (Summer 2013) at common-place.org.

status recuperated an identity as Spanish criollos. This is the contrast between the "frontier of exclusion" in British America and the "frontier of inclusion" in Latin America.[9]

In New France many métis (mixed-blood Indian-French) developed a distinct social identity in the Great Lakes region but generally retained the legal rights of other francophones under both French and British régimes. In Louisiana "*créole*" did eventually operate in much the same manner as criollo in New Spain, to make "white" the mixed-race mestizos or *castas* who had sufficient wealth and status that they needed to be regarded as white. Anthropologist Virginia Dominguez has studied this process in detail.[10]

Finally, creole identity as a matter of social prestige, defined by education, ancestry, and cultural refinement that matched that in the home country, was much less relevant in New France and Louisiana, which had much smaller populations than New Spain or Peru and did not develop the universities, literary salons, periodicals, or publishers that existed in México and Lima. What's more, the neo-feudal social structure of the *encomienda* in New Spain, although it had a partial equivalent in New France in the land-grants called *seigneuries*, did not feature the reduction of Native peoples to serfs laboring without wages on what had been their own lands.

Given the relatively greater independence of Native nations, and their diplomatic relations to the French officials, it was more difficult in the French than in the Spanish American colonies to imagine a full feudal social structure where creoles could be lords.

---

9. See Bauer and Mazzotti, 34–42.

10. Virginia Dominguez, *White by Definition: Social Classification in Creole Louisiana* (New Brunswick, N.J., 1986).

Haydel Habitation (Whitney Plantation): History of a Plantation on the German Coast of Louisiana (1750–1860)[1]

Ibrahima Seck

Haydel Habitation, today called Whitney Plantation, is in St. John the Baptist Parish on River Road, the famous route that skirts the Mississippi between New Orleans and Baton Rouge, and creates a sort of artery that connects the richest and most famous pre-Civil War plantations in Louisiana.[2] This particular plantation was founded by Ambroise Haydel, a German immigrant who arrived in Louisiana in 1721 with his mother and his young brothers and sisters. At the end of the eighteenth century, following successive enlargements, the plantation came under the control of Jean-Jacques Haydel, the second oldest child of Ambroise. In 1820, succumbing to old age, Jean-Jacques ceded the plantation to his sons, Marcellin and Jean-Jacques Jr. In 1840, after the premature death of Marcellin Haydel, the plantation was sold to his widow, Marie Azélie Haydel. By the time of her death in 1860, the plantation had become one of the jewels of the southern sugar economy.

Beyond the presentation of this historic place to the scholarly community, our objective is simple: to show trends in the slave trade in and around Louisiana through the plantation's inventory of slave personnel;

---

1. Maitre-Assistant au département d'Histoire, Faculté des Lettres et Sciences Humaines, Cheikh Anta Diop University, Dakar, Sénégal.

2. Parishes, administrative divisions that correspond to counties in the other U.S. states, are a hold-over from the days of French governance.

during a time when European science had not yet invented the notion of "ethnicity," the slaves born in Africa were identified by their "nation." We will additionally show that the slave trade also produced a transfer of technologies and of knowledge long tested in Africa, and which the European colonists needed to showcase in their lands in America. The sources used in this study are mostly from the archives of parish courthouses. During the period preceding the Civil War, the documents were drafted in French, and to a lesser extent, in Spanish, between 1769 and 1803. Official documents also had to be produced in English after Louisiana was passed into American hands. Starting in 1869, the politics of Americanization led to a ban on the use of French.[3] These archives are generally well organized and preserved in good conditions. Through them the history of slavery can be easily read, notably in cases involving slaves that were being considered for emancipation or who were being judged for various reasons (marooning, murder, etc.). They consist, above all, of real estate succession records and the slaves that were attached to them, harvested stores and crops, the master's house and his outbuildings, furniture, workshops, tools, animals, and the "negro cabins."

Before approaching the history of Haydel Habitation proper, it is necessary to study the problems in the workforce that drove the mass importation of slaves into the colony.

Louisiana: From the Penal Colony to German Laborers

The history of French Louisiana begins in 1699 when Pierre le Moyne, Sieur d'Iberville established the colony of Biloxi on the shores of the Gulf of Mexico. The development of the colony was quite slow because many the colonists were decimated at once by the rigors of Atlantic crossing. The survivors had to face previously unknown hardships like yellow fever, hunger, and Native American attacks. On top of all this, French officials established an instable and corrupt administration. Starting in 1717, the king of France thought that he would find the true means of

---

3. A century later, Francophone Louisianans and defenders of cultural diversity in the United States would create the Comité de Défense du Français en Louisiane (CODOFIL), which today is known as the Comité de Développement du Français en Louisiane and is headquartered in Lafayette.

improving the colony in John Law's Company of the West.[4] In August of that year, a twenty-five-year edict was passed that extended the Company of the West outside of Louisiana and into the Canadian castor trade and into tobacco farms. The Company acquired Senegal on December 15, 1718, that is to say, trafficking on the African coast from Cap Blanc to Sierra Leone.[5]

While waiting for the first shipments of human cargo from the African coast, the Company found very few volunteers to come to the distant colony. They therefore had to resort to creating what can suitably be called a penal colony, a policy favored by the resurgence of salt and tobacco smuggling (in theory royal monopolies) along with increased rates of begging, prostitution, and vagabondage in the Paris region.[6] The mass deportation of dishonest salt vendors, tax evading tobacconists, vagrants, military deserters, and women of ill repute, however, created more problems than it resolved in the American colony. Numerous abuses were committed. Brawls between citizens and police and prison mutinies increased, and numerous members of the forces of law and order were killed or wounded by furious mobs.[7] Louisiana's reputation was compromised, and John Law himself took a land grant there for which he recruited thousands of German artisans and laborers with aggressive advertising.[8]

Between 1719 and 1721, the first wave of Germanic immigrants originating from German principalities, Switzerland, Bohemia, and Hungary brought to Louisiana family names such as Schexneider, Edelmeier,

---

4. For more information on the beginning of French colonization in Louisiana, see Chapter One of Gwendolyn Midlo-Hall, *Africans in Colonial Louisiana: The Development of Afro-Creole Culture in the Eighteenth Century* (Baton Rouge: Louisiana State University Press, 1992). Also see Marcel Giraud, *Histoire de la Louisiane Francaise*, vol. 2, Le Regne de Louis XIV, 1698–1715 (Paris: Presses universitaires de France, 1973).

5. André Delcourt, "La France et les Etablissements Français au Sénégal entre 1713 et 1763" (Dakar: Mémoires IFAN, 1952), 65.

6. Marcel Giraud, *Histoire de la Louisiane Française*, vol. 3, "L'Epoque John Law, 1717–1720" (Paris: Presses universitaires de France, 1966), 252–76.

7. Pierre Heinrich, *La Louisiane sous la Compagnie des Indes (1717–1731)* (New York: Burt Franklin, 1970), 47–48.

8. Ibid., 30.

Zweig, Heidel, and Himmel.⁹ These workers were decimated by the sickness, misery, and confusion that were born out of John Law's and the Company's bankruptcy. The survivors formed a community upstream from New Orleans, along the Mississippi river, on lands that had originally been cleared by Taensa Indians. The designated German areas of this region today comprise St. Charles, St. John the Baptist, and St. James parishes. These Germanic populations had to acclimate themselves to the French language and indeed to the culture. French officials would transcribe their names as best as they could; so Heidel became Aidele or Aydelle, and more recently Haydel. Certain surnames were simply translated. In this way the Zweig family (branch in German) became the Labranche family, whereas people from Baden-Baden, a German city in

Map of the Mississippi Debut of French Colonization

---

9. Glenn R. Conrad, *Saint-Jean-Baptiste des Allemands: Abstracts of the Civil Records of St. John the Baptist Parish with Genealogy and Index (1753–1803)* (Lafayette: Center for Louisiana Studies, 1972), ix–x.

Baden-Württemberg, became known as Badeau.[10] The first (May 1722) description of the "German Coast" is found in the work of Diron d'Artaguette, inspector general of the Louisiana command.

> The German families that number nearly 330 persons of both sexes and all ages are placed twelve leagues above New Orleans, on the left side going up river, on a very good site where formerly there were wild fields that are easily cleared, these Germans have divided themselves into three burgs, the terrain of which is expansive and has never flooded. As these people are very hardworking, there is reason to hope that this year they will have an abundant harvest and that they will succeed in making good establishments in the colony in the future.[11]

This French high commissioner's prediction was accurate, and the German Coast, then limited to St. Charles Parish, became the bread basket of New Orleans. In addition to the habitual requests for slaves to work the land and soldiers to protect the colonists, official reports also solicited new German colonists, whose qualities they extolled. This explains the arrival of the second wave of German immigrants in the 1750s, which included family names like Krammer, Jacob, Conrad, and many others.[12]

Ambroise Heidel, ancestor of all the Haydels in Louisiana, arrived in the colony on March 1, 1721, aboard the ship *Les Deux Frères*. He was then officially identified as being Ambroise Aidle, along with his brother Mathieu and sisters Barbe and Catherine. They were among the forty survivors out of two hundred passengers who embarked in Lorient, the port of France's India Company, on November 14, 1720.[13] Originally from Neunkirchen, close to Miltenberg in the Catholic diocese of Wurzburg,

---

10. For more information, see Conrad *Saint-Jean-Baptiste des Allemands* and Albert J. Robichaux, *German Coast Families: European Origins and Settlement in Colonial Louisiana* (Rayne, La.: Hebert Publications, 1997).

11. Early Census tables of Louisiana, Hill Memorial Library, Louisiana State University, Baton Rouge, 19–20.

12. Ellen C. Merrill, *Germans of Louisiana* (Gretna, La.: Pelican Publishing Company, 2005), 31. Also see Robichaux, *German Coast Families*, 59, and Conrad, *Saint-Jean-Baptiste des Allemands*, x.

13. John Hanno Deiler, *The Settlements of the German Coast of Louisiana and the Creoles of German Descent* (Philadelphia: Americana Germanicana Press, 1909), 28.

where he was born in 1702, Ambroise was the son of Johann Adam Heidel and Eva Schonberg.[14] The father died in Lorient before disembarking and the mother soon after arriving in the colony where the son, a baker, married Marguerite Schoff.[15] In August of 1752, a short time after a murderous Indian raid on the left bank of the Mississippi, an official document reports Ambroise Haydel as being among the German community in the village of Hoffen, on the right bank, on a six arpent farm facing the river, between (Christophe) Houbre and Albert (Schexnayder).[16] Ambroise died in 1767 or 1768, leaving behind a twelve arpent plantation and around twenty slaves.[17]

Slave Labor and the Development of the German Coast

The Company of the West, which became the Perpetual Company of the Indies in May 1719 when it incorporated the domains of the China Company and the French East India Company, focused a special attention to the advancement of the colony with slaves that were primarily taken from the closest African coast, Senegal. The directors, in a council meeting on April 30, 1723, decided to bring three thousand African slaves to America from then until April of the next year, two thousand of which were to come from the Senegalese concession. Of the three thousand slaves, 570 of them, nearly twenty percent, were destined for Louisiana. Among those 570, around a hundred were to be distributed to the most productive agricultural inhabitants of the colony, seventy of them were deemed necessary for the Company's work, and the remaining four hundred slaves had to be distributed among the proprietors of land grants who lived in Paris.[18]

14. Robichaux, *German Coast Families*, 197–200.

15. Deiler, *The Settlements of the German Coast*, 28.

16. Saint Charles Parish Tribunal Archives, Hahnville, La., SC-1752-34-125. An arpent is roughly the equivalent of 183 linear feet or 56 meters.

17. According to Robichaux, *German Coast Families*, 201, the last official document featuring Ambroise Haydel was dated March 20, 1767. He served as a witness to the property inventory of a certain Pierre Pommie (Pommier?).

18. *Décision du Conseil des Indes concernant le commerce d'Asie, d'Afrique et d'Amérique. 30 Avril 1723*; in Elizabeth Donnan, ed, Documents Illustrative of the History of the Slave Trade to America.(London: Octagon, 1969), 641–42.

The favor accorded to the latter group was due to the fact that the colonists, including German laborers, were generally insolvent. Between 1719 and 1731, the India Company convoyed twenty-two shipments of slaves from the African coast to Louisiana. Twelve slave ships arrived between 1726 and 1731, eleven of which came from Senegal.[19] The first slaves on the German Coast were reported during this period.

In 1731, the Company of the Indies resolved to give Louisiana back to the king of France for multiple reasons, the most serious one being Native American hostility, and one of the most tragic examples of which is the 1729 massacre of French colonists at Natchez. The consequences of the Company's withdrawal can be seen through the evolution of the servile population on the German Coast, where there were no more than two hundred slaves in 1746.[20] The Seven Years' War (1756–1763) resulted in the placing of the French colony under Spanish authority and in the arrival of the francophone Acadians who were expelled from Canada, which was thereafter under English control. The refugees settled upriver from the Germans' settlements at what became known as the Acadian Coast. The problem of the servile workforce would not begin to be truly resolved until 1777, when the Spanish opened slave commerce with the French Antilles, and especially after 1782, when the same authorities approved the free importation of slaves from neutral or ally countries.[21] In 1795, the German Coast contained 233 land grants and 2,797 slaves, or 12.5 slaves per concession.[22] The slave population greatly increased during the American period (after 1803) despite the ban on importing slaves to America that began in January 1808. With the Haitian Revolution, Louisiana received 5,000 slaves from Saint-Domingue, many of whom were skilled sugar workers. Between 1785 and 1850, the number of slaves in St. Charles Parish more than tripled. In St. John the Baptist Parish, the population grew eightfold.

19. Jean Mettas, *Répertoire des Expéditions Négrières Françaises au XVIIIe siècle*, vol. 2, *Ports Autres que Nantes*, Serge Daget and Michèle Daget, eds. (Paris: Société française d'histoire d'outre-mer, Bibliothèque d'histoire d'outre-mer, Nouvelle série, Instruments de travail II, 1984).

20. Helmut Blume, *The German Coast During the Colonial Era, 1722–1803* (Destrehan, La.: German-Acadian Coast Historical and Genealogical Society, 1990), 68.

21. Hall, *Africans in Colonial Louisiana*, 279.

22. Blume, *The German Coast During the Colonial Era*, 87.

In both parishes, slaves were imported from all the slaving ports of Africa, mainly from Senegambia, the Gulf of Benin, and central Africa. Up to the nineteenth century, the Senegambians appear most frequently in official documents. The "Congolese" took the reins in the American period. The German population had also augmented during this period, especially in the 1850s, following political events that jarred France and the German princely states in 1848.[23]

Farms were established on the Mississippi, along a narrow band of levees that are naturally formed by the silt that is brought by the river's rising water levels. The German colonists had also spread to the bayous of the

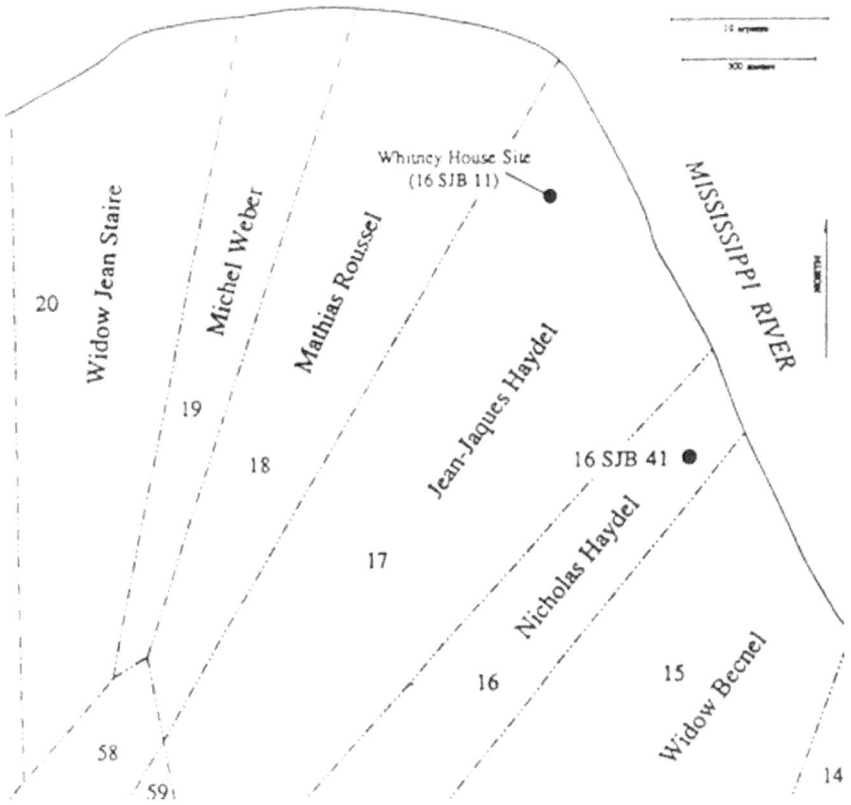

Configuration of Plantations along the Mississippi

23. Merrill, *Germans of Louisiana*, 62–67.

Mississippi, notably the Bayou Teche. All the plantation structures had to be elevated to protect them from flooding. Wide galleries—covered balconies to be more precise—protected the inhabitants from intense summer heat. Each colonist had a dock available for loading and unloading the pirogues that transported goods between farm and town.[24] The locality of a plantation was determined by its distance in *lieue* from New Orleans, its position in relation to the river (left or right bank), and the neighboring properties.[25] This last position was indicated by being on the "high side" (upstream) or the "low side" (downstream) of the property subject to inventory or sale at auction. The land was divided in arpents, often six arpents wide (face on), on the river. The properties were spread out in longitudinal bands, forty arpents long and of "ordinary depth," ending in the lowest, marshiest areas where cypress, fan palms or palmettos abounded. Where the natural levees were sufficiently large, Spanish authorities afforded "doubly wide" grants eighty arpents in width to the most industrious farmers.

The most difficult tasks were the clearing of land, the construction of artificial levees (dykes) to protect goods and people from flooding, and the channeling of land drainage through canals that guided overflows toward the shallows of a lake appropriately called "Des Allemands." Each farmer was legally obligated to build the portion of the levee on the frontal, river-facing side of his property. This was particularly difficult on concave banks of river bends, where any breach or crack could bring on a catastrophic flood. The most famous of these breaches was the one called "Bonnet Carré," or "Bonnet Crevasse," as Anglophones called it.[26]

The German farmers cultivated maize, rice, and beans. Maize did not require painstaking zoning because it could be planted on roughly cleared land, amid tree stumps and in holes made with hoes. Rice required more care, from the preparation of the land to water control. Husking the grain was another headache that, until the beginning of the twentieth century,

---

24. Jay Edwards et al., *A Creole Lexicon, Architecture, Landscape, People* (Baton Rouge: Louisiana State University Press, 2004), 124; Blume, *The German Coast During the Colonial Era*, 76–78.

25. Blume, *The German Coast During the Colonial Era*, 107; Edwards et al., *A Creole Lexicon*, 124. A *lieue* is 2.8 miles.

26. Joseph K. Menn, *The Large Slaveholders of Louisiana–1860* (Gretna, La.: Pelican Publishing, 1964), 359.

was achieved with the rudimentary, African-imported technique of the wooden mortar and pestle. The history of the Atlantic slave trade was more than the American importation of a robust people who were also accustomed to a tropical climate. It also consisted of a transfer of technologies and knowledge that had been tested over centuries, indeed millennia, on African soil.[27] Outside of food crops, the large scale of Haydel plantation is a window onto the slaves' incalculable contribution to the production of industrial crops: indigo and sugar cane.

Haydel Habitation:
From Indigo Farming to Masters of Sugar Production

At the beginning of the 1730s, the experiment showed that the lands of the lower Mississippi lent themselves poorly to tobacco cultivation. When the planters of the French Antilles turned toward sugar cultivation on a massive scale, those in Louisiana took advantage of the open indigo market. The transition did not happen quickly because although indigo grew easily in this area, it was lacking in slaves, and the natives and the colonists, to an even lesser extent, had not mastered the industry. Indigo farming had begun in 1721 in Louisiana, two years after the first share of slaves arrived directly from the African coast. Joseph Dubreuil, a Dijon native who had arrived in the colony in 1718, was the initiator. He was then the richest man in Louisiana, and his fortune was built on his ability to exploit the knowledge of African slaves.[28]

In Senegambia, indigo, called *boru* by the Fulbe, still grew wild, notably on *fonde* lands (unsinkable levees) in the Senegal river valley. The old generation of West African dyers use a mortar and pestle to make indigo cakes that are dried before they are soaked in *canaris* (large water jugs) where the indigo, mixed with potash, ferments for a few days. The color of a cotton fabric, ranging from light blue to dark blue, depends on the number of times the dyer submerges it in the *canari*, on the number of indigo cakes used, or even on the age of the dye. A mixture is generally renewed at the end of fifteen days.[29] This craft

---

27. For further reading, see Hall, *Africans in Colonial Louisiana,* Chapter Five.

28. Hall, *Africans in Colonial Louisiana*, 124, 137.

29. B. Appiat-Dabit, "Quelques artisans d'Afrique Noire," *Bulletin IFAN* 3 (January–October 1941), 2.

Indigoterie Simple

was generally women's work and was not restricted to any particular caste. All the African women (as well as men) from indigo-producing regions were predisposed to knowing the rudiments of the craft. Documentation collected by Helmut Blume shows that indigo became the principal crop exported from Louisiana beginning in 1743, the same year that *Le Saint-Ursin*, a ship chartered by Debreuil and his associate, returned from Gorée Island with 190 slaves.[30] At the time of Debreuil's death, many Senegambian women appeared in his plantation's inventory: Comba (Kumba), the wife of François; Ongué, the wife of Joly Coeur; Marie Gaolo (Marie-lagriotte in the Wolof language), Bouqui, the wife of Nomaque; Déla (Ndeela), the wife of Louis-Guiguia (Jijaak?), for instance.[31]

The methods of indigo extraction used in Louisiana and in the French Antilles were different from those just described. They were imported from India and had a reputation for being harmful to human health due to the

---

30. Blume, *The German Coast During the Colonial Era*, 51–57; Hall, *Africans in Colonial Louisiana*, 60.

31. *Liquidation de la propriété de Joseph Dubreuil*, in Henry P. Dart, "The Career of Dubreuil in French Louisiana," *Louisiana Historical Quarterly* XVIII (1935), 291–331.

effect of fumes that emanated from putrefying leaves and to the use of quicklime, which accelerates the precipitation reaction of indigo particles. Incidentally, in India, women do not work in indigo production because of infertility risks, even though in West Africa the same product was considered both a symbol of purity and a factor in fertility.[32] In Africa, men were involved in the production of indigo cakes but very rarely in the craft of dyeing. In America, one notes a role reversal with women working solely in the cultivation of indigo plants and men slaving over the nauseating vats.

After the 1770s, indigo colonized the agrarian countryside of the German Coast. On March 31, 1774, Ambroise Haydel's widow and her children sold a farm equipped with an "indigoterie" to a certain Antoine Albert.[33] On May 1, 1776, the asset inventory of Mathias Haydel, oldest son of Ambroise Haydel, and of his late wife Magdelaine Ouvre (Huber), mentioned more than four barrels of rice, one barrel of beans, one of maize, some indigo drums and an indigo seed drill. Marguerite Schoff died in 1778. We do not know the precise date of her death, or the exact birth dates of her ten children, three girls and seven boys, with the exceptions of Jean Jacques Haydel, the youngest. He married Marie Magdelaine Bozonnier de Marmillon, a New Orleans resident, on February 7, 1774.[34] His longevity permitted the youngest son of Ambroise Haydel to know two very different economic periods. When he married, the indigo industry was at its peak, but by the time of his death, he had enjoyed the benefits of the surging sugar economy.[35] The indigo industry was totally destroyed in the 1790s by a parasitic insect that steered planters to limit themselves to maize and sweet potato production and to exporting wood to the Antilles. Cotton, and above all, sugar cane were soon adopted as sources of revenue.[36]

32. Judith A. Byfield, *The Bluest Hands: A Social and Economic History of Women Dyers in Abeokuta (Nigeria), 1890–1940* (Portsmouth, N.H.: Heinemann, 2002), 11.

33. *Vente d'habitation; Veuve Ambroise Haydel et héritiers à Antoine Albert.* Louisiana State Archives, Saint John the Baptist Parish, Colonial Period, Baton-Rouge, Louisiana, SJB-BR-19-1776.

34. *Marriage Contract of Haidel, Jacques and Madalaine Bosonier,* in *L'Heritage,* 11:44 (October 1988), 297–99.

35. Blume, *The German Coast During the Colonial Era,* 99–100.

36. Richard Follett, *The Sugar Masters: Planters and Slaves in Louisiana's Cane World, 1820–1860* (Baton Rouge: Louisiana State University Press, 2005), 21–22.

When Louisiana became a state in 1812, sugar cane was already the principal cash crop in the lower Mississippi Valley. The first steam boats made their appearance that same year, and the port of New Orleans soon became the second most commercially active port in the United States, after New York. This new sugar kingdom was organized along the river, between New Orleans and Baton Rouge, before expanding toward Bayou Lafourche, Bayou Teche, Bayou Sara, Point Coupée, and the parishes in the northern part of the state in the 1830s and 1840s. This expansion was made despite the risk of wintertime freezes in these areas that were vulnerable to polar winds blowing from Canada. To overcome this ecological obstacle, the farmers put the mowed cane between the furrows, covering them with leaves while waiting to replant them or take them to the refineries. These were known as "windrowed canes," "*canes emmatelassées*," or "canes in *matelas*." This process was progressively abandoned after 1817 with the introduction of Javanese, or ribbon cane from Indonesia, alongside the creole cane used up to that point. The new variety was more resistant to winter ice, but its tougher skin required the use of steam mills instead of the old, animal powered grinders.[37]

The "cane stumps" were planted in January and February. While waiting for the *roulaison*, or harvest, which took place from mid-October through December, the slaves devoted themselves to such varied tasks as corn cultivation, gathering wood and maintenance of artificial levees and drainage canals. Sugar production began at the beginning of November. Raw sugar was consumed locally, but the majority of the product was transported to refineries in the northern states in wooden casks, called hogsheads, that had an average capacity of 550 kilograms. The mechanization of the entire production chain was not achieved until the twentieth century, and slaves were forced into an infernal work rhythm in a very dangerous environment, involving the manipulation of boiling liquids contained in open cauldrons, heated by wood fires. Norbert Rillieux (1806–1894), the African American son of a French farmer and a black slave, invented a steam boiler in 1846, a revolutionary process that

---

37. Follett, *The Sugar Masters*, 23–24, and Edward King, *The Great South; A Record of Journeys in Louisiana, Texas, the Indian Territory, Missouri, Arkansas, Mississippi, Alabama, Georgia, Florida, South Carolina, North Carolina, Kentucky, Tennessee, Virginia, West Virginia, and Maryland* (Hartford, Conn.: American Publishing Co,1875), 79.

allowed planters to achieve substantial gains in time and money and that saved human lives.[38]

Jean Jacques Haydel Sr. and Jean Christophe Haydel were the most fortunate among the children of Ambroise Haydel. Both brothers imparted two superb houses to posterity, each of which is an example of the highest order of heritage tourism and of local architecture. The property of Jean Jacques Haydel Sr. was the subject of an inventory in 1819, seven years after the death of his wife. The combined value of his possessions was estimated to be 112,383 piastres, which included two habitations estimated at 65,000 piastres, around sixty slaves at 44,000 piastres, as well as tools, furniture, decorations, and animals.

Aerial View of Witney Plantation

---

38. The River Road African American Museum: http://www.africanamericanmuseum.org/exhibits.html.

The principal habitation, estimated at 30,000 piastres, was described as being "established in sugar farming, facing the tract it is 17 arpents long, and doubly wide, situated in Saint John the Baptist Parish, on the right bank of the river, bordered on the upper side by the widow Mrs. Mathias Roussel's property, and on the lower side by that of Sir Jacques Haydel and sons; on the latter can be found a superb master's house, a kitchen, store houses, rice mills, a chicken house, slave cabins, and other structures, with sufficient windrowed canes to plant around 40 arpents. . . ." The second habitation, also an established sugar farm, was estimated at 35,500 piastres.[39] At the time of the auction, the two plantations had produced 190

Maison Witney Plantation

39. *Inventaire de la communauté d'entre Sr. Jn Jques haydel père et ses enfants héritiers de la Dame Marie Madelaine Bosonnier. 7 décembre 1819*, Saint John the Baptist Parish Tribunal Archives, Original Acts, Edgard, Louisiana, hereafter noted as SJB, SJB-116-1819.

Slave cabins Witney Plantation

hogsheads of sugar and 110 hogsheads of molasses.[40] This placed them among the highest producers of the German Coast.

Among the sixty-one inventoried slaves, nineteen were born in Africa (31 percent)—twelve from Senegambia, four from the Bight of Benin, and three from central Africa. Two slaves were originally from the Greater Antilles, more precisely from the sugar-producing isles of Saint-Domingue and Jamaica, and three were from the eastern coast of the United States. The rest were Creoles, meaning natives of Louisiana. The two sugar workers on the plantation were of the Bambara nation: Alexis and Barnabé, fifty and thirty years old respectively. Jean Jacques Haydel Jr. and Marcellin

---

40. *Vente des meubles et immeubles de la communauté d'entre le Sr. Jn Jacques haydel père et la feue dame Marie Madelaine Bozonnier son épouse. 13–14 janvier 1820*, SJB-1-1820.

Haydel, who inherited the main plantation, also personally bought these two slaves, the qualifications of whom they had meticulously researched. Alexis was also described as "sire long" and a "good negro servant."[41]

The estimated price of each slave was tied to his or her age, sex, and qualifications. François, a "griffin creole," or half Amerindian and black, was estimated at 900 piastres, despite his age of 50. More than being just a "carpenter of various duties on the plantation," he was also a "cooper" (barrel maker), an essential occupation for a sugar plantation, especially when it came to the fabrication of *boucauds*. The majority of the slaves were "cart drivers and laborers," some being more than "domestic servants" or "skilled in herding." Women and children had a relatively lower cost. The children younger than ten were by law sold with their mothers, since the Code Noir, passed in 1724, forbade selling them separately. Twenty-one women (34%) were listed with their nine children (14%). It is difficult, indeed impossible, to determine natural movements in the servile population based on inventories, as they were rare, isolated acts, most often associated with the death of the master or his wife. However, these data, combined with those that can be found in the registries of the Archdiocese of New Orleans holy sacraments, allow for some interesting conclusions. This approach firstly reveals maternal precociousness among female slaves (generally between thirteen and sixteen years of age) and a very high infant mortality rate. Thirty-nine children died on the plantation between 1823 and 1863, and only six among them reached the age of five. In other words, one child died every year on this plantation.[42]

In the group of African males, eleven (57.9 percent) of them were between twenty and thirty-five years old. Marguerite, a sixty-six-year-old Creole, was the plantation's doyenne. She was married to Sam, of the Sozo (Susu) nation, a sixty-year-old blind man. Two slaves suffered hernias, a frequent injury in plantations in the area that is associated with hard work.

---

41. *Inventaire de la communauté de M. Jean Jacques Haydel fils avec feue Clarisse Becnel sa femme ; 26–28 juin 1826*, SJB-80-1826; Sacramental Records of the Archdiocese of New Orleans, années 1835 et 1839.

42. Sacramental Records of the Archdiocese of New Orleans, 1823–1863; *Inventaire des biens de la succession de la dame Azélie Haydel décédée veuve Marcelin Haydel; 10–12 Novembre, 1860*, SJB-178-1860. The description given here is based on the combination of these two sources.

Lost liberty and homesickness, as well as strenuous labor, were likely at the center of the troubled behavior that affected certain slaves, notably Bernard, a fifty-year-old Kiamba (Tchamba) nation slave, afflicted with "moments of insanity." Manuel, a twenty-five-year-old Creole slave, was described as "a thief and a maroon." One can easily understand that the planters were under legal obligation to record the faults of slaves who were for sale.

Marooning, or the act of fleeing the master's plantation, was very common in Louisiana. The marooned slave exposed himself to graduated punishments, ranging from whip torture, being branded with a *fleur de lis*, amputation of the ears or the hollow of the knee, or the death penalty. In spite of all this, entire colonies of black maroons, especially Creoles, cordoned off the swamps early on, where they developed whole economies around the plantations of their own masters, pillaging the store houses and sometimes killing cattle to feed themselves.[43] The phenomenon lasted until the Civil War and, in 1854, the official parish journal sounded the alarm in these words: "The number of maroon Negroes is considerable on all the Coast. These gentlemen are so sure not to be threatened they build cabins in the woods, very close to the habitations where they live in quietude. Three Negroes have been arrested in the rear of the habitation of Mr. Rousselle. Milk cows and their calves left out at night become prey to the butcheries of the Negroes. . . ."[44] The last inventory of the Haydel habitation, in 1860, indicated two marooned slaves. One of them was the talk of the town for having evaded numerous gunshots and escaping into the swamps after he was discovered on a neighboring plantation.[45]

From January 1820 to February 1839, Haydel Habitation was the joint property of Jean Jacques Haydel Jr. (two-thirds) and Jean François Marcellin Haydel (one-third). This partnership became the subject of a litigation that the younger brother brought before a tribunal. Among his accusations, the plaintiff bemoaned: "The bad treatment inflicted by . . . Jean Jacques Haydel on [him] and his neglect to give proper accounts of his administration of [the] plantation and of the sale of the crops." In a decision

---

43. See Hall, *Africans in Colonial Louisiana*, 202–32.

44. *Le Meschacébé*, December 3, 1854.

45. Ibid., November 23, 1861.

Haydel Habitation (Whitney Plantation)

on June 15, 1839, Judge Buchannan of the first judicial district of the state of Louisiana in New Orleans ordained a legal partition of the estate.[46] In the inventory, which took place the following February, the plantation was described as "established in sugar farming" with "an upper house" and "a lower house" and their outbuildings: "kitchens, infirmaries, store houses, a stable, a grist mill, a rice mill, two pigeon houses, servants' quarter, four chicken houses, twenty slave cabins, a sugar house with two teams of four boilers each, and equipped with all the necessary accessories: a cane mill with an English steam engine, a purgery with a 250-boucaut capacity, a shed, a forge; the crop consists of one-hundred-fifty arpents of planted cane, two hundred arpents of cut cane, and windrowed cane that would plant about sixty arpents, two-hundred-forty-one boucauds of sugar and a quite a bit of molasses."[47]

We will perhaps never know the number of slaves on the plantation at this time because they were not included in the split. According to Richard Follett, the typical size of a sugar working team of the time was about 76 slaves.[48] As the sugar house required two teams, one can easily imagine that the plantation was once again among the region's most important, in terms of its production and the size of its servile population. Marcellin died on November 16, 1839, leaving Marie Azélie Haydel a childless widow. She had bought the plantation at 41,100 piastres.[49] Between 1845 and 1853, or after Norbert Rillieux's invention of the steam boiler, the average production of Louisiana sugar plantations was 250,000 to 310,000 pounds (250-310 hogsheads).[50] The plantation produced 356,000 pounds of sugar in 1844, and a record of 407,000 pounds during the season of 1854-1855. 1856-1857 was

---

46. *Marcellin Haydel vs. Jean Jacques Haydel/Marcellin Haydel petitioner to the Honorable Terence Le Blanc, Parish Judge of the Parish of St. John the Baptist. January 5, 1839.* SJB-42-1840: *First Judicial District Court of the State of Louisiana in New Orleans. Marcellin vs. Jean Jacques / Decision of Justice No. 17.045, June 15, 1839*, ibid., SJB-27-1839.

47. *Procés verbal d'inventaire des biens situés dans cette paroisse possédés indivisément entre les sieurs Francois Marcellin Haydel & Jean Jacques Haydel ; 21 février 1839*, ibid., SJB-27-1839.

48. Follett, *The Sugar Masters*, 24.

49. *Procés verbal de la vente des biens possédés indivisément entre Jean Jacques Haydel & Marcellin Haydel ; 27 février 1840*, SJB-42-1840.

50. Follett, *The Sugar Masters*, 25.

a bad season because of a cold front. In the entire parish, only 3,603,000 pounds were produced, 60,000 of which were on Haydel Habitation. The two seasons of 1858–59 (20,000 pounds) and 1859–60 (75,000 pounds) were also bad due to winter frost, but also because of catastrophic floods.[51]

Epilogue

When Marie Azélie Haydel died in November of 1860, her possessions were appraised at 186,952 piastres, 61,000 of which were immobile goods. Her estate was not auctioned until 1867, after the Civil War, which meant the loss of 101 slaves that were attached to the plantation.[52] After the Civil War, the sugar industry in Louisiana was completely dismantled. The plantations described by Edward King in the 1870s epitomize the depth of this economic stagnation: "The larger ones have been ruined by the war, and have allowed their sugar-houses to decay, and their splendid machinery to rust in ditches. . . . Accumulated losses . . . have made the trade so dubious that dozens of the largest planters in the State cannot secure a cent of advances. Plantations are deserted; owners are completely discouraged."[53] The census of 1860 in St. John the Baptist Parish recorded a population of 3,037 whites, 299 free people of color and 4,594 slaves. In 1870, the black population had diminished to a little over 17 percent. That same decade, the black population of Orleans Parish doubled. New Orleans was probably the most popular destination for former slaves.[54] Around forty slaves who had once been attached to Haydel Habitation became sharecroppers or day workers in the service of Alphonse Becnel, Marie Azélie Haydel's nephew.[55]

---

51. Champomier, Statement on the sugar production of Louisiana, 1844, 1845–46, and 1849–50 to 1858–59, in Menn, *The Large Slaveholders of Louisiana,* 361.

52. *Inventaire des biens de la succession de la dame Azélie Haydel décédée veuve Marcelin Haydel ; 10–12 novembre 1860,* SJB-178-1860; *Partage de la succession de feu Dame Azélie Haydel veuve Marcelin Haydel ; 18 juillet 1867,* ibid., SJB-107-1867.

53. King, *The Great South,* 80.

54. The Free Genealogy site: <http://freepages.genealogy.rootsweb.com/~ajac/lastjohntheb.htm>

55. National Archives, Washington D.C.: M1905, Records of the Field Offices for the State of Louisiana, Bureau of Refugees, Freedmen, and Abandoned Lands 1863–1872, Record Group 105, Subordinate Office Plantation Department, Rolls 27-28-29; Register of Black Persons, undated.

Haydel Habitation (Whitney Plantation)

Sibyl Haydel, wife of Ernest Morial, the first African-American mayor of New Orleans, and mother of Marc Morial, who became the second, had a direct affiliation with Haydel plantation. She was the great-grand daughter of Victor Haydel, who was born of a union between Anna, a black slave, and Antoine Haydel, Marie Azélie Haydel's brother. Victor and his mother appear at the bottom of a list of slaves on the last inventory taken at the plantation. This list also included only one slave who had been born in Africa, Gabriel, of the Congo nation, whom Marcellin Haydel bought from his father in 1820. Being seventy years old at the time, he was respectfully called Vieux [old] Gabriel. He is probably the person who could tell the most complete history of Haydel Habitation, having lived there for nearly fifty years under four different masters. Essentially, the evolution of the slave labor force in this historic place, and in the parish in general, confirms the greater tendencies of the Louisiana slave trade. This trade was at first principally oriented toward Senegambia, before opening up to the Gulf of Benin and to central Africa. This servile population made fortunes for the planters with knowledge they brought with them from Africa or acquired in the colony.

Fleur de lys (emblem of Louisiana), creole

South Louisiana Creoles: Origins and Evolution of a Modern Cultural Identity

Elista Istre

It's Saturday night. Evening shadows lengthen across the prairies of Southwest Louisiana as pickup-driving black Creoles wearing Stetson cowboy hats, pressed Wrangler jeans, and polished cowboy boots make their way to local dancehalls. Set back from the road behind gravel parking lots dotted with potholes, these old buildings reveal the ravages of Louisiana's scorching summers and unrelenting humidity. Generations of paint peel off exterior walls. Foundations that have settled comfortably over the years shift doorframes into slightly tilted positions. To the unsuspecting outsider, these places are relics of times gone by.

But to locals, dimly lit dancehalls like these come alive on the weekend as the accordion-driven rhythm of Zydeco music pulsates throughout the old buildings. Under the low ceilings, cowboy hats bob up and down, boots stomp out beats on hardwood floors, and sweat flies as bodies sway and twirl to the music. The pounding sounds of accordions, drums, bass, and washboards vibrate the buildings and spill out into parking lots, driving away the stress and cares of everyday life for the duration of the four-hour gig.

Dancing Boots

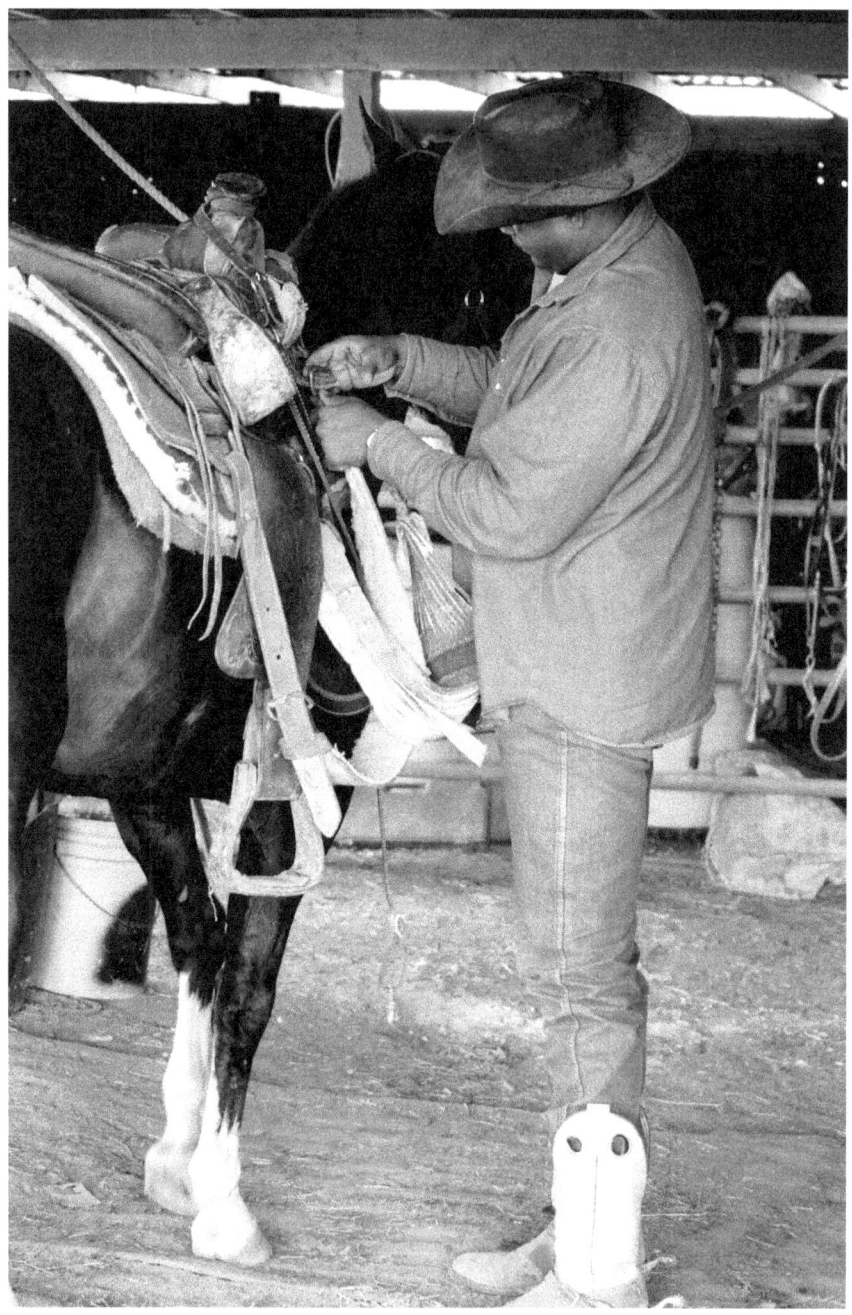

Geno Delafose at home

Tucked into out-of-the-way places in small rural communities, these Creole dancehalls stand as monuments to a way of life that has persisted in South Louisiana for decades. As dancers rub shoulders with others on the crowded floors, conversation flows freely between neighbors and friends who catch up on the local gossip and greet each other with Creole expressions like "*Eh, toi!*" and "*Comment ça va?*" Much more than mere architectural structures, the faded walls of these old dance halls have witnessed Creole efforts to celebrate and preserve their distinct language, music, and culture for generations.

Just as passersby may assume that well-worn dance halls are currently abandoned buildings with historical significance but no modern relevance, many outsiders also view Louisiana's Creole culture to be a flower that has faded over time. Believing that the glory days of the Bayou State's incomparable Creole people disappeared with the influx of American immigrants after Louisiana attained statehood in 1812, many do not realize that Southwest Louisiana still boasts a vibrant Creole culture. What are the origins of black Creoles who live and work in Acadiana today?[1] Why are people surprised to find that Creole heritage still impacts South Louisiana's everyday life and culture?

One thing that may contribute to the misconception that Creoles are a thing of the past is the very nature of the term "Creole" and its many changing definitions over time. The concept of *creolité* is incredibly complex, both within a global context and a local one. Although some may consider the color of one's skin to be the primary factor in determining Creole identity, as scholars Robin Cohen and Paola Toninato point out, "people of all colours can affirm a creole identity through elective processes—speaking a creole language, through friendships or relationships, or simply by identifying with the many expressions of creole popular culture (music, art, dancing, food, syncretic religion and forms of material culture) that are prevalent in their region."[2]

---

1. Acadiana is a triangular-shaped region in South Louisiana comprised of twenty-two parishes that stretch along the Gulf of Mexico from just west of New Orleans to the Texas border and about one hundred miles inland to Marksville in Avoyelles Parish.

2. Robin Cohen and Paola Toninato, "The Creolization Debate: Analysing Mixed Identities and Cultures," in *The Creolization Reader: Studies in Mixed Identities and Cultures*, eds. Robin Cohen and Paola Toninato (New York: Routledge, 2010), 9.

For the past several centuries, groups of people around the world have been labeled Creole or have self-identified as such. For example, people of mixed African and Portuguese descent in the Cape Verdean islands began calling themselves Creoles as early as the fifteenth century.[3] In eighteenth-century Mauritius, the term "Creole" originally referred to whites, primarily of French descent, who lived in Mauritius or on other islands in the Indian Ocean. By the twentieth century, however, Creole had come to mean people of mixed origins there.[4] In Sierra Leone and other parts of West Africa, the Creole (or "Krio") population was comprised initially of blacks who returned to Africa after being awarded their freedom for supporting the British during the American War of Independence. In Trinidad, the fifth largest island in the West Indies, "Creole" typically referred to those of African descent who acquired their freedom and consequently benefited from educational opportunities that allowed them to move up within the colonial system and acquire coveted positions of professional employment and political leadership.[5] Today, perhaps the most easily recognized creole nation in the world is the Caribbean island country of Haiti, whose nearly ten million inhabitants still speak *Kréyol*, one of the country's two official languages.[6]

Just as the definition of Creole varies on a global scale depending on time and location, the same holds true within the state of Louisiana. In order to better understand what it means to be a Creole in South Louisiana within today's modern context, it is necessary to begin with an overview of how this term has been both adopted and rejected throughout the region's history. Doing so should provide some clarity

---

3. Cape Verde is an archipelago located in the Atlantic Ocean some five hundred miles west of Senegal.

4. The use of the Creole label in Mauritius refers to a wide variety of sub-ethnicities as exemplified by the terms "Creole Madras" (those with Tamil heritage), "Creole Sinwa" (Chinese ancestry), "Creole l'Ascar" (Arab descent), and "Creole Morisyen" (of African-Malagasy origin). See Cohen and Toninato, "The Creolization Debate," 8–9. For an additional source on Mauritius's Creole culture, see William F.S. Miles, "The Creole Malaise in Mauritius," *African Affairs* 98 (April 1999): 211–28.

5. Cohen and Toninato, "The Creolization Debate," 8–9.

6. "Haiti," https://www.cia.gov/library/publications/the-world-factbook/geos/ha.html, accessed April 17, 2012.

to the muddied waters of ethnic and cultural identity among Louisiana's diverse Creole populations.

To some, the term "Creole" conjures up images of affluent members of Louisiana's antebellum planter class who descended from French and Spanish aristocracy.[7] To others, "Creole" refers to the descendants of Louisiana-born slaves or free people of color who claim mixed ancestry, including Spanish, French, African, and American Indian blood. Or it might signify a flavorful regional cuisine or the rhythmic sounds of Zydeco music. To still others, it denotes the distinct type of French spoken by the descendants of enslaved Africans and Caribbean islanders. To most, it encompasses several of these aspects. Being a Louisiana Creole today is defined by much more than bloodlines. It is a way of life, a culture, something to be proud of—a heritage worth preserving.

Like their West Indian neighbors, most Louisianans throughout the eighteenth century used the term Creole to refer to anyone who was native-born, regardless of their skin color or ethnic origin. Therefore, during the colonial period, "Creole" distinguished both black and white native children of local origin from African, European, and American immigrants. As sociologists Jacques M. Henry and Carl L. Bankston III explain, the emphasis on birthplace made the idea of creolism "more about displacement than about place; a *creole* [sic] is 'from here' but with roots that are 'from over there.'"[8] Over time, however, the term Creole became more closely associated with racial classifications than geographic origins.

Many white Creoles of French and Spanish descent thought of themselves as members of an emerging colonial aristocracy in the New

---

7. As in other parts of the world, people began calling themselves Creoles throughout the Americas; but a common denominator was having colonists of Spanish, Portuguese, or French extraction settle in the region. As historian Joyce E. Chaplin points out, English-speaking colonists in what became the United States preferred to maintain their British ties. They consciously rejected the term "creole," and, until they rebelled and called themselves "Americans," these British subjects did not favor a New World identity, despite their obviously creolized culture. See Chaplin, "Creoles in British America: From Denial to Acceptance," in *Creolization: History, Ethnography, Theory*, ed. Charles Stewart (Walnut Creek, Calif.: Left Coast Press, 2007), 46–65.

8. Jacques M. Henry and Carl L. Bankston III, "Propositions for a Structuralist Analysis of Creolism," *Current Anthropology* 39 (1998), 561.

World. Even though these early settlers endured desperate conditions in Louisiana's wilderness environment, maintaining the appearance of status remained essential to their identity. Following the European model of feudalism, they desired to own vast amounts of property and engaged in large-scale business ventures they hoped would generate huge profits with minimal personal effort. Naturally, they considered manual labor to be beneath them, and when attempts to enslave Louisiana's native population failed miserably, they began importing Africans to compensate for the severe shortage of skilled and unskilled laborers. The first sanctioned ships transporting slaves arrived in Louisiana in 1719, just a few months after the city of New Orleans was founded.[9]

Although the French slave trade peaked in the 1730s, the port of New Orleans did not directly benefit due to its location some one hundred miles up the Mississippi River. French slavers found it more convenient and cost-effective to drop off their human cargo in the Caribbean sugar islands instead. Due to the lack of imported slaves, New Orleans soon became home to one of the most aged and most creolized slave communities in the New World; by 1741, approximately two-thirds of Louisiana's entire enslaved population was native-born.[10] Creole slaves, unlike those hailing directly from Africa, typically fetched higher prices on the auction block because, as historian Carl A. Brasseaux explains, they were "considered to be more docile, seasoned to the climate, trained for field work or domestic tasks, and, most important, French-speaking."[11]

Although the French introduced slavery to Louisiana, the number of slaves in the colony increased dramatically during the Spanish (1763–1800) and early American periods (1803–1812). Unlike their French predecessors, Spanish and American administrators had witnessed a remarkably

---

9. Daniel H. Usner Jr., "From African Captivity to American Slavery: The Introduction of Black Laborers to Colonial Louisiana," *Louisiana History: The Journal of the Louisiana Historical Association* 20 (1979), 25.

10. Thomas N. Ingersoll, "The Slave Trade and the Ethnic Diversity of Louisiana's Slave Community," *Louisiana History: The Journal of the Louisiana Historical Association* 37 (1996): 137–38.

11. Carl A. Brasseaux, *French, Cajun, Creole, Houma: A Primer on Francophone Louisiana* (Baton Rouge: Louisiana State University Press, 2005), 90.

successful slave revolt in Haiti and realized what creolized slave populations were capable of. As a result, under Spanish rule, nearly all slaves brought to Louisiana came directly from Africa, while roughly three-fourths came from Africa during American rule. The authorities hoped these fresh-off-the-boat slaves would be less likely to stage an insurrection or cause trouble than their Creole counterparts.[12]

This influx of African-born slaves undoubtedly contributed to the Creole slaves' ability to maintain their own identity and somewhat higher status as native-born residents of the region. Many became house slaves and overseers, while the newly arrived Africans took their place working as field hands and common laborers. Some enslaved Creoles felt so strongly about maintaining their status as Creoles, and they eventually tried to separate themselves from the influx of recently imported Africans by forging new biracial and triracial identities—some even passed for white.[13]

Due to a number of factors, including lax manumission laws and the system of *plaçage*, many Creoles of African descent were able to earn their freedom.[14] Some were even born free. Thus, within a relatively short period of time, Louisiana boasted a sizable population of *gens de couleur libre* (free people of color). According to historian Laura Foner, by 1850, about 80 percent of Louisiana's free people of color population was comprised of mulattoes and others of mixed blood, evidence of Louisiana's high tolerance and social acceptance of multiracial relationships. Although most free people of color never could reach the social status of whites due to their darker pigmentation, many became

---

12. Jean-Pierre Leglaunec, "Slave Migrations in Spanish and Early American Louisiana: New Sources and New Estimates," *Louisiana History: The Journal of the Louisiana Historical Association* 46 (2005): 185–209.

13. Ira Berlin, "From Creole to African: Atlantic Creoles and the Origins of African-American Society in Mainland North America," *The William and Mary Quarterly*, 3rd ser., 53 (1996), 284–86.

14. *Plaçage* was a social system that enabled women of color to be "placed" with white men. Oftentimes, mothers arranged for their daughters to meet and establish long-term relationships, also called "left-handed marriages," with white men at public dances known as quadroon balls. Many women of color viewed *plaçage* to be a practical method for securing financial and social stability, as well as freedom in many cases, for themselves and their children.

successful entrepreneurs, plantation owners, and even slaveholders who sometimes enjoyed surprising wealth and prestige prior to the Civil War.[15]

After the Civil War, Louisiana was no longer a tri-caste society with enslaved blacks on the bottom, free people of color in the middle, and whites on top. Instead, Louisiana joined the rest of the United States in becoming a two-tiered society that put all people of African descent on the bottom, regardless of their status before the war. The former "free people of color" segment of Louisiana's population resented being socially classified with the former slaves. To maintain a marked distance between themselves and the newly freed population, they began referring to themselves as "Creoles of Color." As post-war racial tensions escalated, whites became horrified with the attachment of *couleur* to the term *Créole* and desperately began taking extreme measures to prove their racial purity.[16] Whites began insisting that the term Creole applied only to those of "pure" French and/or Spanish ancestry and ignored the fact that people of all skin tones had been calling themselves Creoles for generations.[17] Therefore, at the close of the nineteenth century in Louisiana, the term "Creole" meant purity for whites and miscegenation for blacks.[18]

Throughout the twentieth century, usage of the word Creole continued to be racially polarized in many areas. For example, in and around the metropolitan area of New Orleans, there was a strong divide between white Creoles who claimed untainted European ancestry and black Creoles whose forefathers included enslaved Africans, free people of color, and, in many cases, French and Spanish Creoles. Moving westward into the

---

15. Laura Foner, "The Free People of Color in Louisiana and St. Domingue: A Comparative Portrait of Two Three-Caste Slave Societies," *The Journal of Social History* 3 (1970), 408, 411.

16. Loren Schweninger, "Socioeconomic Dynamics among the Gulf Creole Populations: The Antebellum and Civil War Years," in James H. Dormon, ed., *Creoles of Color of the Gulf South* (Knoxville: University of Tennessee Press, 1996), 63.

17. Anthony G. Barthelemy, "Light, Bright, Damn *Near* White: Race, the Politics of Genealogy, and the Strange Case of Susie Guillory," in Sybil Kein, ed., *Creole: The History and Legacy of Louisiana's Free People of Color* (Baton Rouge: Louisiana State University Press, 2000), 262.

18. Henry and Bankston, "Propositions for a Structuralist Analysis of Creolism," 562.

twenty-two parish region known as Acadiana, however, the term Creole took on a slightly different meaning.[19]

Due to the social stigma attached to people of color, many white Creoles who settled in the prairies and swamps of Acadiana began disassociating themselves from the term "Creole." These white Creoles simply assimilated into French-speaking Acadian/Cajun communities who settled South Louisiana following their expulsion from Nova Scotia during the French and Indian War in the mid-eighteenth century. Cajuns were almost exclusively of French extraction, so to be Cajun meant there was no possibility of racial "tainting" as had been common among the more affluent Creoles in urban areas like New Orleans. In fact, today, many "Cajuns" are actually people of French or Spanish Creole descent who lost or ignored their Creole identity when they became ranchers and farmers in Acadiana. Creoles of Color, on the other hand, continued using the term Creole to refer to themselves. Over time, they eventually dropped the "Creole of Color" phrase and replaced it with "black Creole" or simply "Creole."

So, who are the Creoles in twenty-first century Southwest Louisiana? Deborah J. Clifton, a Creole French language instructor and cultural activist, explains:

> I've heard anthropologists who'll give you ten or twenty definitions of what Creoles are. Maybe they're right, but for me and for the people I know who call themselves Creole, it's a nation, a national identity. It's total, it applies to languages, to fashions, lifestyles, eating habits, houses, everything. Everything from Louisiana and native to Louisiana—that's part of us. Deep down, it's all part of being Creole. . . . People want to come here and study our *blood lines* and everything, who slept with whom, or who married whom in the last two hundred years. But we're a nation, a people, we're not just a minority in the United States. There are people of every color who call themselves Creole, of every race and mixture of race who call themselves Creole. We're the people of Louisiana. The nation of Louisiana, our country.[20]

---

19. The Cane River area around Natchitoches, a town located in Central Louisiana, also boasts a sizable Creole community. As its title indicates, however, this article will focus primarily on the Creoles of South Louisiana.

20. Deborah J. Clifton, interview by André Gladu in *"Zarico,"* National Film Board of Canada Production, 1985.

Yet, despite their history and achievements, as well as their efforts to preserve their heritage, until fairly recently, black Creoles throughout South Louisiana's prairies have been an almost invisible culture subsumed by the dominant Cajun communities with which they coexist. Largely due to the tourism industry that promotes the twenty-two parish region of Acadiana as "Cajun Country," Creoles have often been overlooked or mislabeled "African American" or "black Cajuns." John Broussard, one of the cofounders for C.R.E.O.L.E., Inc., an organization founded "to develop the Creole language and culture in Louisiana," explains, "C.R.E.O.L.E., Inc., is not anti-Cajun. The Cajuns have plenty to be proud of, no question about it. If we were anti-Cajun, we would be denying some of our own identity because we all speak French. We simply want to promote our culture along with that of the Cajuns.... We also feel that the news media needs to recognize all segments of the community and realize that as black people we are not Cajuns, even though we do have a lot in common."[21]

Wilbert Guillory, another Creole advocate and the founder of the Original Southwest Louisiana Zydeco Festival states, "My role is to let people know very strongly that I'm not a Cajun, to let them know, no matter what anyone says, that zydeco is not Cajun music. It is black Afro-American Creole music. Because I am a Creole. That's my best language, Creole French, which is different from Cajun French. So there's no way that I can accept myself as a Cajun, I'm not. I'm Creole and I was born in a small Creole community called Pointe Noire."[22]

Eric Cormier, a native of Lake Charles, Louisiana, describes the difference between being labeled African American and being Creole. He explains, "Well I'm legally, as the federal government says, I'm African American. In Louisiana culturally I fall under the umbrella of—of what they call Creole with a mix of French, Cajun, some Native American, African American, and Spanish. . . . Our family—kind of like all of Louisiana—especially South Louisiana, especially the area south of Interstate 10—is definitely a gumbo. We have a little bit of everything in us."[23]

---

21. Ben Sandmel, *Zydeco!*, (Jackson: University Press of Mississippi, 1999), 129.

22. Ibid., 124.

23. Eric Cormier, interview by Sara Roahen, Lake Charles, La., September 11, 2007, Southern Foodways Alliance, http://www.southerngumbotrail.com/cormier.shtml, accessed February 24,

25th anniversary of C.R.E.O.L.E., Inc.

Throughout South Louisiana, one of the ways Creoles celebrate their identity is through festivals that highlight the distinct aspects of their culture. Perhaps the youngest of these public expressions is the Creole Renaissance Festival that was established in 2012 in order "to celebrate all facets of our culture—the food, the music, the language, and most of all the fellowship." As the festival's website eloquently states,

> Throughout the world the word "Creole" can mean so many different things to so many people. …While many believe Creole is a race identified by a particular skin tone, true Creoles throughout this area know firsthand that Creoles of color can be as pale as a crisp white sheet hanging from your *grand-mère*'s [grandmother's] clothesline, or as dark as a night on a Louisiana bayou; and yet both can be undeniably Creole. That's because being Creole is a lifestyle. From the French we speak, to the gumbo we eat, and the Zydeco we live and die by . . . Creoles are the heart and soul of Louisiana![24]

2010. Cormier is described as a "Creole by ancestry, a Cajun by culture, an African American by complexion, and a Lake Charles native with a newspaper column devoted to the foodways of his peoples—all of them."

24. "Creole Renaissance Festival," http://www.creolerenaissance.com/, accessed February 13, 2013.

What kind of French do South Louisiana Creoles speak? What constitutes "Creole" food today? And where does Zydeco music come from? The answers to these three questions reveal the most distinct cultural elements that set black Creoles apart from their white Cajun counterparts and from mainstream African American culture.

Although many languages have been spoken throughout Louisiana's history, in the early days of colonization, various American Indian groups, enslaved Africans, and a conglomeration of French settlers, soldiers, and administrators turned to French as the region's *lingua franca*. Naturally, the language that emerged from this cultural *mélange* was not limited to one kind of French. Mary Alice Drake, a retired schoolteacher from Lafayette who taught French for thirty-three years, grew up speaking Creole with her family. She stated that even the earliest Creole speakers were far from ignorant; many were tri-lingual. She explains, "In those days, you had different types [of French]. The house woman [enslaved woman of African descent] spoke French with the white mistress and then she spoke another French with the slaves. . . . And the woman of the house [white mistress] told everything to the slave woman so she learned perfect French. In other words . . . she [the enslaved woman] spoke three languages: she had African, she had her [Creole] dialect from that area, and she had Parisian French."[25] Even today, Colonial French, Cajun French, Creole French, and European French are among the types of French still heard in Louisiana.

Enslaved Africans who found themselves in Louisiana hailed from various regions along West Africa's coastline. Naturally, they spoke many different languages before landing on Louisiana's shores. Yet, upon their arrival in Louisiana, many Africans, especially those from the Senegambia region, were already conversant in French as a result of the French trading posts that had been established along Africa's Atlantic coastline long before Louisiana was colonized. Those who were not familiar with the European language had to learn French quickly in order to communicate with their masters. Based on written documentation gleaned from census data, judicial documents, and diaries, Margaret Marshall, a contributing editor to *The Dictionary of Louisiana Creole* (1996), estimated that blacks

---

25. Mary Alice Drake, interview by author, Lafayette, La., June 28, 2011.

in Louisiana were already speaking Louisiana Creole by the middle of the eighteenth century.[26]

Some French scholars and writers such as author Jean Raspail consider Creole French as spoken by Louisiana's black population to be "inferior because of its simplification, its indicative grammar, its lack of gender and number, its shortened form, and its suppression of prepositions and conjugations."[27] Other scholars such as Margaret Marshall argue that Creole is not a substandard language, but rather "a variety of French that the slaves were exposed to, a vernacular French characterized by regionalisms and reduced forms."[28]

Due to the significant number of Africans living in Louisiana, as well as the close contact they had with French-speaking slaveholders, African influences on Louisiana's French Creole language are undeniable. For example, words such as *gris-gris* (a protective place) and *zinzin* (an amulet of support or power) come from the Bambara language. *Congo* (meaning a snake, a dance, or a region in Central Africa), *gumbo* (okra), *zombie*, and *voodoo* also share African origins.[29] Linguist Fehintola Mosadomi paraphrases Haitian linguist Jules Faine's opinion when she explains that "despite the fact that the slaves were forced to learn the language imposed on them by their masters, they nevertheless brought in aspects of their own languages—the harmonious rhythm, the musicality, the tone, the softness, the onomatopoeia, and the system of reduplication such as those found in the Mandingo language, all of which have been observed in Louisiana Creole."[30]

Although some affluent Creole planters were able to send their children to France to pursue an advanced education, the majority of black Creoles remained in Louisiana where opportunities to acquire formal schooling were rare. After the Civil War ended, many sharecropping

26. Fehintola Mosadomi, "The Origin of Louisiana Creole," in Kein, *Creole*, 242.

27. Ibid., 224. Jean Raspail, a native of France born in 1925, has authored several award-winning books and novels in French.

28. For a more in-depth discussion of various scholarly opinions regarding Louisiana's Creole French origins, see Ibid., 223–43.

29. Ibid., 241.

30. Ibid., 237.

families needed their children's help at home, around the farm, or in the fields in order to survive. Even though French was taught in schools and many publications such as newspapers and magazines were printed in French throughout Louisiana, literacy rates remained remarkably low. It comes as no surprise then, that most black Creoles learned French via strictly oral methods well into the twentieth century. When school attendance became compulsory in the early twentieth century, state legislation required Creoles to learn how to read and write in English, not French. As a result, many Creoles born in the early to mid-1900s remember being punished at school for speaking the only language they knew. For example, Alfred Caesar recalls,

> When we started school, we didn't talk American [i.e., speak English]. We learned how to talk American at school—we all spoke Creole. . . . The schoolteacher would stay right beside us to be sure we weren't talking Creole. If they caught us talking Creole, we got a beating. Oh, yes, they didn't want us talking Creole. They knew when the kids from the country got together, we were gonna talk Creole. They would spread us out so we wouldn't talk Creole.[31]

Since so many older Creoles suffered public embarrassment for speaking French and therefore refused to teach the language to their children, many young people have had relatively little exposure to Louisiana's French Creole language. As one woman relates, "My grandmother spoke creole [*sic*] but did not/would not teach it to us because teachers gave Creole speakers a hard time, made fun of them, and thought them less intelligent—so she wanted us to have it 'easier' and to finish school."[32]

Even though most people now realize the benefits of being multilingual, for many middle-aged Creoles, learning a second language as an adult is simply impractical or too challenging a task. Others, however, are fighting to preserve the language. They recognize that Louisiana's Creole French has been spoken for over three centuries throughout

---

31. Gladu, *Marron: La Piste Créole en Amérique*, 2005.

32. This comment was posted by an individual identified as "CoCo" on October 24, 2010, in response to a website created to teach basic Louisiana Creole phrases. See http://learnlouisianacreole.wordpress.com/, accessed October 31, 2012.

the state, and they believe it should not be lost within one generation's time. Although many young Creoles are learning International French in school through immersion programs, some are trying to revive the language of their ancestors by learning Louisiana Creole as well. Since most fluent Creole speakers are not literate in French and therefore cannot teach the language in classrooms, those interested in learning Louisiana Creole today usually learn it via oral transmission as generations before them have done. Most present-day Creole French students improve their linguistic skills by spending time with elderly family members, participating in weekly conversation gatherings, listening to archival recordings, and enjoying Louisiana's French music at dancehalls and festivals. While English is undeniably the predominant language spoken among young Creoles today, consciously or not, Louisiana Creole French is still a part of daily life in one way or another. Even those who do not speak Creole fluently typically recognize and use words such as *gratons* [cracklins] and *fricassée* [smothered chicken] on a daily basis.

Perhaps the most widely known trademark of Creole culture is, in fact, Creole cuisine. Just like the Creole French language, Creole cooking is also a rich amalgamation of European, African, and American influences. Africans introduced staples such as rice, okra, black-eyed peas, collard greens, yams, sesame seeds, watermelons, sugarcane, and coffee. The Americans yielded green beans, butter beans, lima beans, capsicum (peppers), Irish potatoes, sweet potatoes, kidney beans, navy beans, maize (corn), peanuts, and tomatoes.[33] Europeans contributed olives, wheat, barley, citrus fruit, onions, and domesticated meats such as pork, beef, and chicken to the New World.[34]

Historically, South Louisiana has been divided along stereotypical boundaries that divide "Creole" New Orleans from "Cajun" Acadiana. It only follows that many sources celebrate and compare the two excellent cooking traditions. While some chefs typically consider New Orleans's

---

33. James C. McCann, *Stirring the Pot: A History of African Cuisine* (Athens: Ohio University Press, 2009), 26; John Egerton, *Southern Food: At Home, on the Road, in History* (New York: Alfred A. Knopf, 1987), 13; and Reay Tannahill, *Food in History* (New York: Crown Publishers, Inc., 1988), 220.

34. John D. Folse, *The Encyclopedia of Cajun and Creole Cuisine* (Gonzales, La.: Chef John Folse and Company Publishing, 2010), 54.

Cooking Demonstration at Creole Culture Day

Creole food to be "more sophisticated fare" or "*grande cuisine* . . . a kitchen of delicate blends, of subtle combinations and separate sauces," Cajun food is usually thought to be heartier and simpler fare.[35] Perhaps because no definitive work has yet addressed the culinary tradition of Creole people in Acadiana, many outsiders are surprised to learn that Cajuns and Creoles in the prairie regions share more similarities than differences. Josephine Cormier, owner of Josephine's Creole Restaurant in St. Martinville, explains, "My heritage is Creole, but in this area [Acadiana] there's a combination between Cajun-Creole and it's very hard to differentiate it." She adds, "The cooking is basically the same in this area" due to the shared historical experience of the Cajun and Creole people.[36]

Folklorist John Laudun points out that "limiting Creole cooking to a style 'practiced in the areas in and around New Orleans' . . . drives the Creoles of the Louisiana Prairies to no end of distraction." He explains, "Creoles living in Lawtell make a gumbo that has more in common with their Cajun neighbors than Creoles living in Lake Charles, let alone the Creoles of New Orleans or the Creoles of Cane River."[37] Creole accordionist Thomas "Big Hat" Fields clarifies that the Creole food in New Orleans and the Creole food in the "flatlands" or prairies are very different. He says, "We got the regular roux and the old time stuff [in Acadiana]. The sure 'nough gumbo. *You understand?* The *country* type stuff. When you go up to New Orleans, they doctor it up and they put all kind of stuff in it. *We got the real deal here!*"[38]

Much of what the rest of the world has come to associate with South Louisiana cooking is not necessarily what black Creoles ate (or eat) on a daily basis. Despite the popular stereotype that Acadiana residents enjoy gumbo, boiled crawfish, and jambalaya every day, the reality is that many

---

35. Peter S. Feibleman, *American Cooking: Creole and Acadian* (New York: Time-Life Books, 1971), 18.

36. Josephine Phillips Cormier, interview by Sara Roahen, St. Martinville, La., August 20, 2008, Southern Foodways Alliance, www.southernfoodways.org, accessed September 3, 2012.

37. John Laudun, "Gumbo This: The State of a Dish," in Ursula Mathis-Moser and Günter Bischof, eds., *Acadians and Cajuns: The Politics of Culture of French Minorities in North America* (Innsbruck [Austria]: Innsbruck University Press, 2009),159.

38. Thomas "Big Hat" Fields, interview by author, Lafayette, La., June 28, 2011.

of these dishes are reserved for times when families and friends come together to celebrate special occasions. According to Laudun, "In some ways, the *ur*-dish [signature dish] of the region is not gumbo but rice and gravy. Pork steak. Brisket. Meatballs. Even cowboy stew with potatoes: All are served over rice with gravy. What distinguishes one region from another are the stages of browning." He goes on to explain, "This preference for browning may, in part, come from the roasting practices of seventeenth-century French cookery. . . . With the addition of West African foodways to the mix, the browning triumvirate—Native American parching, European roasting, and West African frying—was complete."[39]

Eric Cormier, a Creole from Lake Charles, is a food columnist who observes that having family members from various Creole communities has certainly influenced his own cooking. He states,

> So when it comes to food, that's where my heritage really comes out, because I—we truly identify with smothering food and making gravies, experimenting with smoked meats, boudin, wild game, which is if you have—it's something that historically both blacks and whites in Louisiana have always loved. . . . So culturally I feel connected, and it's something that I like to define in this section of the state, whereas in New Orleans you have Creoles whose heritages [sic] is a little different than on this side of the state because—it hasn't been written down, but there's some folks here in this area who like to call ourselves Prairie Creoles because we come from areas like Lawtell and St. Martinville where folks were farming.

He added that prairie Creoles typically eat food from off the farm that result in dishes like rice and gravy, smothered pork chops, and chicken *fricassée*, along with sides of beans or greens and cornbread.[40] As one cook

---

39. Laudun, "Gumbo This," 164. Laudun explained that the term "*ur*" was popularized by folklorists in the late nineteenth century and early twentieth century to refer to a speculative, idealized, or fictional origin of a term. In this case, Laudun used the word "*ur*-dish" to argue that the most significant dish of the region is not gumbo as many believe, but rather rice and gravy and other foods he lists. Many food writers like to begin a recipe with the phrase "first you make a roux," but Laudun argues that not all regional dishes begin with a roux; therefore, it would be more accurate to state, "first you brown something." John Laudun, phone interview by author, September 26, 2012.

40. Cormier, interview.

states simply, "Creole cooking as we know it today [in Acadiana] is simply glorified 'Soul Food' with a French accent."[41]

Acadiana's Creole cooking, like Cajun cuisine, is not complicated fare. In fact, since their earliest arrival in Louisiana, most Creoles have simply taken basic ingredients that are readily available and cooked them in creative ways to bring out the richest flavors and heartiest tastes. Many women transported from Africa to Louisiana were assigned to be cooks. They often found themselves responsible for providing sustenance for field hands, skilled laborers, and other enslaved workers, as well as for the family and guests of the family to whom they were enslaved. In Africa, women did almost all of the cooking, so it was only natural for women who worked in Louisiana's kitchens to continue cooking as they had been taught. As food historian Patricia B. Mitchell

Creole Lunch House Sign

---

41. Carolyn Shelton, *Zydeco, Blues 'n' Gumbo Cookbook* (n.p.: Chanel Zeno Publishing, 2009), 3.

points out, African women in America "had certain culinary tendencies: the abundant use of leafy green vegetables; the utilization of okra, or nuts and seeds, as thickeners; the addition of peppery/spicy hot sauces; the use of smoked meat for flavoring; the preparation of various kinds of fritters; and the creation of many one-pot dishes composed primarily of rice with 'enhancements.'"[42]

The basis for many present-day Creole dishes varies little from those brought in by African women. For instance, Africans contributed the primary starch still found on Acadiana tables. Long before European colonization began in Africa, rice was already a staple crop. In fact, the captains of the first two slave ships that landed on Louisiana's shore were issued strict orders to "trade for a few [slaves] who knew how to cultivate rice" as well as purchase "three or four hogsheads of rice suitable for planting."[43] The Africans' familiarity with rice cultivation was indispensible since it was the only reliable food crop that could grow in Louisiana's swampy environment. Even when rain and floods destroyed the corn, when Indian wars forced people to flee the region, when maritime shipping was cut off, and when flour from the Illinois Country did not arrive due to ice blockages or war on the Mississippi River, French Louisiana always had rice. Even today, as Merline Herbert, owner of the Creole Lunch House in Lafayette, explains, "It ain't lunch until you have some rice."[44]

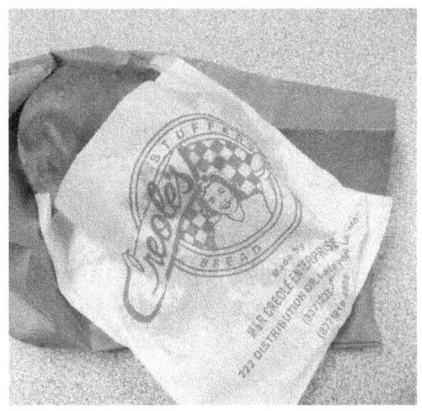

Stuffed Bread from Creole Lunch House

Merline, like many other Acadiana Creoles, recalls meals she grew up with: "Oh, we cooked rice and smothered meat—cooked meat in a pot

---

42. Patricia B. Mitchell, *Soul on Rice: African Influences on American Cooking* (Chatham, Va.: Mitchells Publications, 1993), 18.

43. Henry P. Dart, "The First Cargo of African Slaves for Louisiana, 1718," *The Louisiana Historical Quarterly* 14:2 (April 1931): 173–76.

44. Merline Herbert, interview by Rien T. Fertel, Lafayette, La., March 17, 2011, Southern Foodways Alliance, www.southernfoodways.org, accessed September 3, 2012.

with onions and bell pepper and some beans. You always had meat, rice, and a vegetable, yeah—be it beans or greens or whatever, but you always had meat, rice, and vegetables. And we always had that for lunch." She went on to say, "Now at night we ate sandwiches or we had cornbread with milk or maybe biscuits or cous-cous [couche-couche] and milk. We never ate meat and rice at night when I was coming up. My daddy did not like eating heavy at night, yeah."[45]

For many Creoles, Sunday dinner was the best meal of the week. After attending church, family members gathered together and shared a dinner that usually consisted of chicken, rice, and side dishes. For example, Les Comeaux's grandmother would cook a couple of older hens or surplus roosters from the back yard to feed everyone, normally serving the chicken with gravy over rice.[46] Brenda Placide recalls, "The favorite thing my mother would make that I loved so much back in the days was smothered chicken. Okra and potato salad [and smothered chicken]. That was a Sunday dinner."[47]

Over the years, urban economic opportunities have lured more people off the farms, drawn more women into the workforce, and provided conveniences such as supermarkets and microwaves that have irrevocably influenced the way ingredients are obtained, prepared, and served. Although many Creoles still eat rice and gravy daily, they do not always cook and consume traditional meals at home. Recognizing the desire of locals to continue eating the same dishes without having the time to prepare them, several Creole restaurants throughout Acadiana are filling the void and keeping the Creole cooking tradition alive through their plate lunches. Menus typically include local favorites such as red beans and rice, smothered chicken, smothered pork chops, meatball stew, rice and gravy, and sides of vegetables like black-eyed peas, smothered okra, and smothered cabbage. In keeping with Catholic tradition, Fridays are usually seafood days when crawfish *étouffée*, fried catfish, and other meatless dishes are served. Louisiana specialties like jambalaya, shrimp Creole, and gumbo are

---

45. Ibid.

46. Lesley "Les" Comeaux, interview by author, Lafayette, La., August 8, 2010.

47. Brenda Placide, interview by Sara Roahen, New Iberia, La., February 9, 2011, Southern Foodways Alliance, www.southernfoodways.org, accessed September 3, 2012.

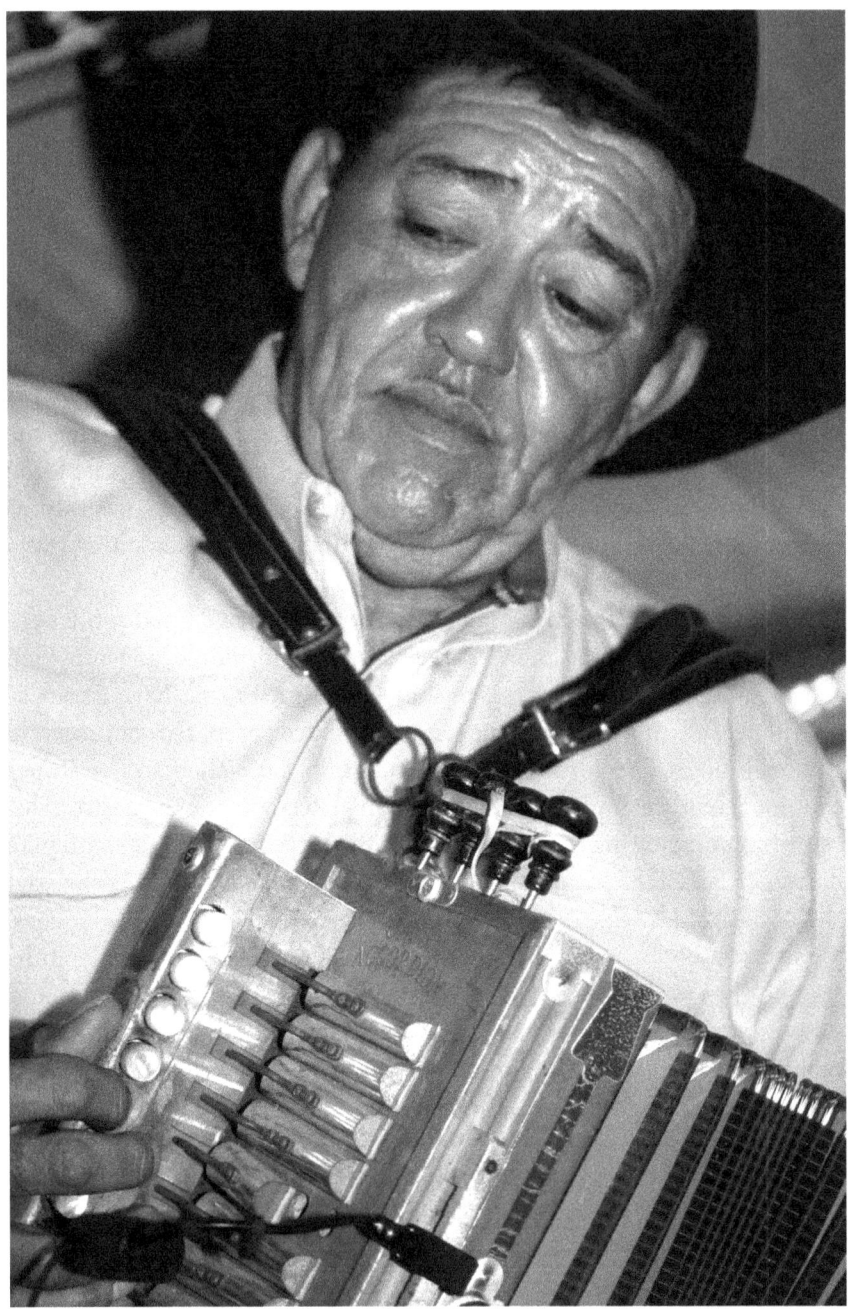
Thomas "Big Hat" Fields

rarely served year-round. As Josephine Cormier explains, "Very seldom will I do a gumbo when it's warm unless it's requested, you know." Like most cooks in the area, she usually makes her gumbo "when the fall comes in or the first cold weather."[48]

While Creoles in New Orleans and Acadiana may share the same ethnic label as a result of their mutual heritage, black Creoles in the prairie regions of South Louisiana are quick to point out that the ingredients they use and the cooking traditions they employ are different from New Orleans cuisine. For instance, much like their Cajun neighbors, Creoles raised in Acadiana typically cook a roux-based gumbo flavored with chicken and sausage, ingredients readily available on the farm. In New Orleans, however, seafood gumbos are more popular because of the port city's easy access to fresh shrimp, oysters, and crabs along Louisiana's coastline. When asked what a true Creole gumbo is, Thomas Fields responds, "It's like a true Creole [person], you understand? You got everything in it. [But] we are plain [here in Acadiana]. We got the roux . . . a little bit of sausage . . . a little bit of Andouille . . . a little bit of chicken. . . . New Orleans—they got gumbo with—shrimp and everything else. But it's not the same gumbo that we have in the flat land, in the prairies of southwest Louisiana."[49]

Just as Creole gumbos are distinct, so are the musical traditions of Louisiana's Creole people. French missionaries and settlers transported European music to the New World, while Africans from different regions introduced their own styles. Within a decade of the founding of New Orleans, dancers and musicians of African descent were gathering on Sunday afternoons in places like Congo Square, an area located on the northern perimeter of New Orleans's French Quarter, in order to celebrate and retain their musical heritage. Travelers and journalists noted that hundreds and even thousands of Africans from various nations formed many clusters, played different kinds of instruments "no doubt imported from Africa," sang songs "in some African language, for it was not French," and

---

48. Josephine Phillips Cormier, interview by Sara Roahen, St. Martinville, La., August 20, 2008, Southern Foodways Alliance, www.southernfoodways.org, accessed September 3, 2012.

49. Fields interview.

Mrs. and Mr. Goldman Thibodeaux

danced according to their own traditions.[50] As one reporter noted, Congo Square was "a place to renew old loves, and to gather new friendships; to talk over affairs of the past week, and lay new plans for enjoyment in the coming ones."[51] Although three centuries have passed since the first dances were held in Congo Square, Louisiana's house dances and dancehalls still serve a similar purpose.

Although no documentation indicates exactly when the style of music known as *juré* emerged, it closely resembles the slave music being played in Congo Square during the antebellum period; it is possible these styles were contemporaneous. In fact, when folklorist Alan Lomax recorded a number of *juré* songs in 1934, he called it "the most African sound I found in America."[52]

50. Gary A. Donaldson, "A Window on Slave Culture: Dances at Congo Square in New Orleans, 1800–1862," *The Journal of Negro History* 69 (1984): 64–65.

51. *Daily* Picayune, December 11, 1864, quoted in ibid., 68.

52. Barry Jean Ancelet, "Zydeco/Zarico: Blues, Beans, and Beyond," *Black Music Research Journal* 8 (1998): 45; and Sandmel, *Zydeco!*, 34.

"Juré," a word derived from the French verb *jurer* meaning "to swear or testify," comes from the traditional expression "*Jurez* (testify), my Lord." As folklorist and Creole music expert Barry Ancelet explains, *juré* is a "localized form of the African American 'ring shout,' consisting of a counterclockwise procession accompanied by antiphonal singing and the shuffling, stamping, and clapping of the dancers, occasionally supplemented by simple percussion such as the ubiquitous metal-on-jawbone scraper or its descendant, the washboard."[53] During Lent or designated mourning times, instrumental music was forbidden, so *juré* singers were called upon to provide dance music. Although *juré* was originally spiritual music, it became progressively secular as time passed and even adapted popular Cajun songs while retaining its African rhythms.[54]

Touted as the origin for the modern-day term for Creole music known as "Zydeco," the phrase "*les haricots sont pas salés*" first appeared in Lomax's collection of *juré* songs. Canray Fontenot, a well-respected Creole fiddler, said, "They never had no such thing as zydeco [sic] music. No such thing as zydeco [sic] music. That's bullcorn... they had a thing they called *juré*. The old people would sing for the young people, and clap their hands and make up a song." Clifton Chenier, known widely as the "King of Zydeco," told Fontenot, "No, I never went to one [*juré* dance], but my daddy used to go. My daddy played the [song] '*zaricots est pas salés*' on his accordion, but he didn't play it in the right speed, he played it like a *juré*. I thought it should go faster."[55] As Fontenot explained, initially the term "Zydeco" referred to the dance itself and the dancehalls where that style of music was played. "But they never had no such thing as Zydeco *music*. Not as far as I know. If you was black, you played Creole." With the passage of time, however, the term "Zydeco" was applied to the revved-up style of Creole music that Chenier helped to popularize and market to the mass media.[56]

---

53. Ancelet, "Zydeco/Zarico: Blues, Beans, and Beyond," 43; and John Minton, "Houston Creoles and Zydeco: The Emergence of an African Urban Popular Style," *American Music* 14, *New Perspectives on the Blues* (1996): 490.

54. Ancelet, "Zydeco/Zarico: Blues, Beans, and Beyond," 45.

55. Sandmel, *Zydeco!* 33–34 (first quote), 38–40 (second quote).

56. Ibid., 40–41.

Jeffery Broussard

In the decades prior to World War II, many Creoles worked hard all week as sharecroppers or day laborers and looked forward to a respite from their toil at weekend house dances known as "French La Las." Hosts shoved furniture aside, prepared food, and hired fiddlers, accordionists, and washboard players to entertain their family members and friends. These house dances rotated from one home to another and served as a means for keeping communities connected. Paydays were especially popular times for hosting house dances, although sharecroppers often found their pay from the landowner to be less than what they expected when the crops came in. Instead of verbalizing complaints outright, however, disappointed workers might tell their neighbors, "*Les haricots sont pas salés*,"

Creole kids on festival stage

a French expression that literally means "the snap beans aren't salty." Since people often served snap beans with salted pork to guests at house dances, when times were lean and pay was short, it meant that the host could not afford to flavor the beans with salted meat. In other words, Creoles used the phrase as a code language to express their frustration without stating their complaints outright.[57]

Although the phrase "*les haricots sont pas salés*" had appeared in songs and conversations for many years before Lomax documented it in 1934, it was not until after World War II that the term "Zydeco" was applied to black Creole music.[58] Due to the frequent repetition of the phrase in many *juré* and Creole songs, the expression gained popularity, and eventually "*les haricots*" [pronounced "layz ah-dee-koh" in English] evolved via numerous spelling variations into "Zydeco," the term by which black Creole music is known today.[59]

Cajun musicians have been recorded prolifically since the 1920s, but unfortunately there are relatively few Creole recordings from those early years. Amédé Ardoin, widely recognized as the father of Creole music, is the notable exception; but even respected ethnomusicologists such as D. K. Wilgus mislabeled his music as "Negro-Cajun music."[60] Over the years, however, Creole music has persisted, becoming more widely known and appreciated in recent decades than ever before.

The style of music that many popular Creole artists such as Jeffery Broussard and Geno Delafose play today fuses Cajun, Creole, and Zydeco tunes, and incorporates their own personal musical and lyrical innovations. Delafose grew up speaking French and played Creole music with

---

57. Linda Langley, Susan G. Lejeune, and Claude Oubre, eds. "Just Exactly What *Is* Zydeco?" in *Le Reveil des Fetes: Revitalized Celebrations and Performance Traditions, Folklife Series*, Vol. 3 (Eunice: Louisiana State University at Eunice, 1995), 73.

58. This information appears in a footnote in Minton's article, "Creole Community and 'Mass' Communication: Houston Zydeco as a Mediated Tradition," *The Journal of Folklore Research* 32 (1995): 13; and in Sara Le Menestrel, "The Color of Music; Social Boundaries and Stereotypes in Southwest Louisiana French Music," *Southern Cultures* (Fall 2007), 90.

59. Norm Cohen, "French-American Music," *The Journal of American Folklore* 102 (1998), 336.

60. D.K. Wilgus, "Cajun and Zydeco Music," *The Journal of American Folklore* 81 (1968), 275.

Elista and Moriah Istre dancing at festival in Lafayette, Louisiana.

his father. Recognizing the fact that so many members of the younger generation do not speak French, Delafose makes a conscious effort to sing in French so the young people can at least hear the language as he heard it. As he explains, "I'm playing what I was brought up listening to. If everybody just goes with the times, the tradition gets lost."[61] Broussard also grew up playing music with his father and speaks French. He concurs with Delafose, stating, "With most of the young bands now, most—basically *everything*—they're singing now is in English." He adds, "My advice to younger musicians is that they need to look back at what's going on and try to get back into the roots because if we don't do this, with the style of music that's being played now, we're gonna lose this culture, this tradition. And I'm gonna fight it as long as I can."[62]

Delafose and Broussard represent a growing number of Creoles who recognize the importance of preserving their culture for future generations. Music, like cooking traditions and linguistic fluency, is not a static entity. In order to survive, it must preserve recognizable elements of the past while forging ahead into the future. As Barry Ancelet, folklorist and founder of Acadiana's largest cultural celebration, *Festivals Acadiens et Créoles*, announced from the main stage in 2013, "Thank God we don't have a heritage hall to preserve our French music! We don't need one because our music scene is alive and well as evidenced by all of the young bands who have shared the stage with legendary artists this weekend."

Since the eighteenth century, Creoles in South Louisiana have celebrated a culture birthed from a fusion of languages, musical traditions, and cooking repertoires that span several continents. As a result, Creoles have contributed significantly to the region's rich cultural heritage for centuries. Unfortunately, because they have sometimes been mislabeled, misunderstood, or simply underappreciated, it may appear to outsiders that Creole culture has, like the paint on old dancehall walls, faded away over time. Once one gets a glimpse into the inside of the culture, however, it becomes apparent that South Louisiana's Creoles are not a relic of the past, but rather make up a vibrant, contagiously energetic

---

61. Geno Delafose, interview by author, Eunice, La., January 31, 2009.

62. Jeffery Broussard, interview by author, Henderson, La., February 22, 2009.

community that is continuing to keep their traditions alive. Time has proven that in spite of outside influences and mainstream pressure to conform, they have successfully adapted to the environments around them while still maintaining cultural traits that characterize them as a distinct group of people.

Artiste invité: Max Diakok. *Association Mamanthé, troupe Massilia Ka.*

Danse Gwoka rythme Woulé

Photographer : Azedine Hsissou

Artiste invité: Max Diakok.   *Association Mamanthé, troupe Massilia Ka.*

Aurélie Bajeux et Mélinée Magen. *Association Mamanthé, troupe Massilia Ka.*

Danse Gwoka, rythme Woulé

Mona Georgelin.
Association Mamanthé, troupe Massilia Ka.

The Gwoka

Mona Georgelin

Creolization

The process of creolization started in the Caribbean islands from the beginning of their colonization by European powers. The Amerindians, the first inhabitants, different African people brought against their will to serve as the slave labor force—the European colonists all contributed to building the creole society that would evolve with the arrival of the "Congos," the Asians, and the Lybio-Syrians after the abolition of slavery. We find this mixture in vegetation, food, religions, languages, and in all artistic forms.

In music, this process gave birth to styles in which we find the African fundamentals mixed with European influences. The slaves immediately adopted many ways of resisting such as marooning, suicide, and revolts. The continuity of their oral and musical traditions, fundamental elements in African societies, also played a role in these acts of resistance. Making drums out of barrels, organizing secret evening gatherings, slaves of different ethnicities knew how to create a common language, experiencing a creolization process. For them music was a creative and liberating force capable of simultaneously preserving their identities, maintaining and preserving the memory of their ancestors, and creating an outlet for communication.

And so musical genres were born that fall within the category of cultural affirmation and legitimation, like "bèlè" in Martinique and "gwoka" in Guadeloupe. After the abolition of slavery, their practice remained vibrant in the countryside and especially in the plantations where many freemen continued to work in sugar farming alongside new workers who came from Africa and Asia.

Gwoka

Gwoka is an integral part of Guadeloupian culture. Although this genre went through a period of decline as people moved into the cities and new musical styles like Biguine arrived, it was back in force by the 1970s, reaffirming a cultural identity modeled according to history. It is not just music or folklore fixed in time. It is a form of artistic expression, a living art, a state of mind taught by the "masters of Gwoka," many of whom are no longer alive (Robert Loyson, Ti Céleste, Esnard Boisdur, Germain "Chaben" Calixte, Kristèn Aigle, Napoléon "Napo" Magloire, Guy Konkèt, Carnot, Marcel "Vélo" Lollia, Henri Délos, Hillaire Geoffroy. . .). Gwoka is a popular art in perpetual evolution, taking inspiration from exterior influences brought by musicians and dancers, all while respecting its fundamental rules.

Gwoka combines music, chants, and dance. The Creole language is generally used to designate the elements that form the Gwoka universe:

Chantè : singer
Répondè : chorus
Tanbouyé : percussionists
Makè : marker (solo drummer)
Boulayen : boula players (rythmic drummers)
Chachayé : chacha player (small percussion instrument made from a calabash)
Dansè : dancer
Rèpriz : reprise (musical phrase that follows a dance cycle that lets the dancers catch their breath before beginning a new cycle).
Swaré léwoz : Léwoz gathering (traditional gathering in which the Gwoka performers form an interactive circle). Léwoz is also the name of a Gwoka rhythm.

There are seven main rhythms. Each expresses a situation, a state of mind, or particular sentiments, and each possesses its own codes that are particularly distinguishable by the drumming, singing, and dancing. The Dansè performs a dance of improvisation solo before the Makè. The Makè must follow the steps of the Dansè, who can play tricks, resulting in a veritable artistic duel. The dance drives the music and not the other way around. Dance appeals to the emotion that the musicians transmit to the dancer and vice versa. All the Gwoka performers are a complementary and inseparable ensemble. The soloist singer starts with a piece and the chorus responds. The ka drums provide the rhythm, accompanied by the cha-cha. The dancers, who can be the public, rotate in the center of the singers and the musicians, who form a circle and play according to the rhythm provided. Like African dance, Gwoka dancing is not choreographed, and there are many ways to execute a single step, with each dancer expressing his own body language and feeling. In Gwoka dancing, we find the same relationship to the ground as in African dancing and steps inspired by European dances like the waltz, the polka, or the mazurka. Although Gwoka dancing is based on very precise movements and codes, it offers great liberty of expression and creation in terms of working the body and the emotions.

The Seven Rhythms of Gwoka

1. "Toumblak" (the most popular) expresses joy, fertility and love. It appeals to agility, vivacity, and the Dansè's sensuality. The postures can be very suggestive. When the rhythm accelerates to a trance-like pace it becomes "toumblak chiré."
2. "Graj" is associated with work, particularly the preparation of cassava. Its name evokes the Creole verb "grajé" which means "to grate." It is a slow, rowing rhythm, and it is danced with graceful, fluid, and restrained movements. It can become feline and sensual when the chanting becomes sentimental.
3. "Mennde" symbolizes celebration and release. Today it is associated with Carnaval. Some attribute its origins to immigrants from the Congo after slavery was abolished. The rhythm is quick and steady, and the dance is strong and energetic.
4. "Woulé" accompanies collective work in the fields. It is reminiscent of a jerky waltz. It is both powerful and aerial with movements that balance range and suspension.
5. "Padjanbèl" is warlike and executed with presence and defiance. It expresses rallying and defending against slavery. It reveals the elegance and pride of the woman who dances it.

6. "Kaladja" is the rhythm of pain and suffering. The dance incorporates many large and aerial movements, but also undulating and contracting movements. When it is played rapidly, Kaladja brings to mind the enthusiasm of the Toumblak.

7. "Léwoz" is the most difficult rhythm to play and dance. It is a trance-inducing dance with a warlike connotation. All parts of the body are used. It is the rhythm par excellence of defiance and theatrical play between the Makè and the Dansè.

According to Max Diakok, a Guadeloupian dancer:

The seven rhythms of Gwoka send us to the edge of various emotions, the goal being not to seek historical truth but to nourish the imagination. A significant example is the Léwoz dance, which makes important use of bigidi (imbalance) and is danced with a stick. The dancer punctuates certain dance styles by pretending to beat the solo drummer. It is a dance charged from the inside that builds up the silence with eyes that do the talking. One can see in it our ancestors' art of diversion, an outlet before the oppression of the masters, a transmutation of weaknesses, of the fragility of the body, a new aesthetic. So, the content of this transmission assumes technical, cultural, and psychological elements.

Bitasyon Gwotanbou

Max Diakok
(Translated by Charles Larroque)

In the ground of Gwoka
I will grow love
Aglaé, Aglaé
The planting moon is right

Go responders
Send the drums
On the wings of Léwòz
Together we will see the moon glow

A collective stirring
Transforms the circle
I heard the hearts
All vibrating in unison

Giving allows receiving
Give rhythm, receive chanted eloquence
Yes, joined around the drum
We are freed from the silence
Here is the root of my strength
Here born was the divine word
Here more beautiful are we all
More than all the frivolities of the greatest king

Aurélie Bajeux. *Association Mamanthé, troupe Massilia Ka.*

Danse Gwoka
rythme Toumblak

Photographer : Azedine Hsissou

Mélinée Magen. *Association Mamanthé, troupe Massilia Ka.*

Mélinée Magen. *Association Mamanthé, troupe Massilia Ka.*

Danse Gwoka, rythme Toumblak

Mona Georgelin.
*Association Mamanthé,
troupe Massilia Ka.*

Interpretation of Aurores Nouvelles I and II. Aurélie Amable.

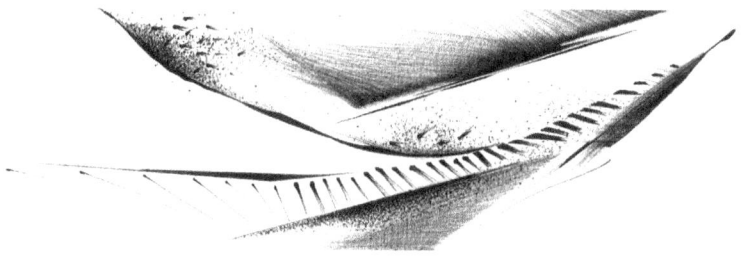

A Linguistic Process: Creole in the Americas

Josette Nonone

Linguists claim that the first descriptions of Creole language appeared little more than a century ago. Many theories have attempted to elaborate on its foundation. Fewer than twenty years ago, Creole studies faced a dilemma: either researchers contented themselves with "European and North American descriptive works, running the risk of accepting the given methods, colored by the observers' occidental viewpoints, or they referrred to the literary works of the Caribbean Negritude movement, knowing that they also have a racial bias and abusive mythical references."[1]

Today, the field has a more scientific orientation. Renowned Creole linguists like L.-F. Prudent, J. Bernabé, and R. Chaudenson, the first two being Martiniquais and the latter being a French resident of La Reunion, have long studied the Creole phenomenon.[2] None of these linguists excludes the colonial centuries from his field of investigation; here they find the essential data on Creole genesis and a model of relations between "language science and ideology, which will enable us to better understand the present stakes."[3]

---

1. Lambert-Félix Prudent, *Des baragouins à la langue antillaise: analyse historique et sociolinguistique du discours sur le créole* (Paris: L'Harmattan, 1999).

2. Dajani Society, *Historial antillais*, vol.1, Lambert-Félix Prudent and Jean Bernabé, *La langue créole, contribution à la sociologie des langues antillaises* (Martinique: Dajani Society, Departmental Archives of Martinique, 1980); Robert Chaudenson, *La Créolisation: théorie, applications, implications* (Paris: L'Harmattan, Intergovernmental Agency of Francophonie, Institute of Francophonie, 2003).

3. Prudent, *op. cit.*, 19.

"Creole appears in a consolidating, developing society"[4] in which there are multiple linguistic tools (that is to say, on a colonial scene in which there are several languages) and where social and economic relations are drawn from violent realtionships. Also, it is appropriate to retrace the conquest of the territories in the Caribbean archipelago. For the Antilles, the process started with Christopher Columbus.

The First Linguistic Exchange Relationship

Having been refused by the king of Portugal, Columbus turned to the Spanish sovereigns to finance his discovery project in the New World. They proclaimed him the "Great Admiral of the Ocean Seas, Viceroy of the Indies, proprietor and governor of all the lands he would discover." During his first voyage, in 1492, Columbus explored the northern coasts of Cuba and Haiti, and during a second voyage in 1493, he continued to reconnoiter the West Indies in search of gold and discovered the Lesser Antilles: Dominique (Dominica), Marie-Galante and Guadeloupe, the Iles des Saintes, Puerto Rico, and Saint Martin. During his third voyage in 1498, he discovered Trinidad Saint Vincent, and it was in 1502, on his fourth voyage, that Columbus came across Martinique (Matinina or Madinina).

In the words of Bernard Pottier (1967), cited by Prudent, "Arriving in the islands, Columbus launched a study of the Amerindian languages, by recording in his *Journal* terms like *canao, cacique* etc. that would soon make their way into the lexicons of European languages."[5] Then, acting upon the powers he had received from his sovereigns, Columbus instigated a linguistic policy of glottophagy, and he gave a new name to all of the islands he discovered.[6] In his "Letter to Santangel," he writes,

---

4. Dajani Society, *Historial antillais*, Lambert-Félix Prudent and Jean Bernabé, "Le Créole apparaît dans une société en oie de constrction et de consolidation" *La langue créole, contribution à la sociologie des langues antillaises* (Martinique, Société Dajani. Achives départementales de Martinique, 1980), 324.

5. Prudent, *op. cit.*, 20.

6. This term was created by Louis-Jean Calvet in *Linguistique et colonialisme, petit traité de glottophagie* (1974). He analysed the relationship between linguistic and colonial discourses on languages and found that the language of the colonized is denigrated, rendered inferior, while that of the colonizer is valorized.

> To the first island I discovered I gave the name of San Salvador, in commemoration of His Divine Majesty, who has wonderfully granted all this. The Indians call it Guanaham. The second I named the Island of Santa Maria de Concepcion; the third, Fernandina; the fourth, Isabella; the fifth, Juana; and thus to each one I gave a new name.[7]

Thus Columbus domesticated the new places, identifying them by names that were known in his country: "They arrive with symbolic markers defining them as human."[8] Using linguistic power, he posits "the foundations of a society in which the Verb takes precedent (an ancient practice anchored in Christian culture) over the appearance of the real. By this fabulous capacity of appropriation, the European's act of naming the Antillean would thereafter be a decisive and magical act."[9] A consequence of this was the suppression of native cultures and languages. According to Bernabé, Columbus discovered his linguistic power by taking possession of the lands and the people who lived there, "colonial speech had just gained a symbolic weight that it would never again lose in this environment, invalidating legitimate aboriginal languages, leaving a small gap so that a few common, colored words feature in the Castilian Authorities' dictionary."[10]

It is therefore in a context of linguistic violence that the first encounter between Castilians and Arawak took place. The entire Arawak civilization disappeared. Only Christianity and the Castilian language survive.

The First Settlements

In the sixteenth century, although the Spanish hardly attached any importance to the Antilles, they attempted to populate Guadeloupe and the neighboring islands, along with Martinique. These attempts did not end well.

---

7. R. H. Major, ed. and trans., *Select Letters of Christopher Columbus, with Other Original Documents, Relating to His Four Voyages to the New World*. 2d ed., (London: The Hakluyt Society, 1870), 2.

8. Jeanne Wiltord, *Les Békés: maîtres et pères*, paper presented at Cenacle of the Cultural Festival organized by Service Municipal d'Action Culturelle, Fort-de-France, Martinique, July 14, 2010.

9. Prudent, *op. cit.*, 20.

10. Bernabé, *op. cit.*, 319.

In 1635, the French took possession of Martinique with the arrival of Pierre Bélain d'Esnambuc and some of the first colonists who were no strangers to the difficulties of colonization: These had been the colonists of Saint Christopher. The reverend Father Du Tertre, quoted by Armand Nicolas, emphasized: "To succeed in this enterprise, he [d'Esnambuc] took around a hundred men, the former inhabitants of Saint Christopher, all manual laborers, accustomed to the outdoors, to work and to the toils of the land, who were all very skilled at clearing land, at cultivating it, and at planting food crops, and very handy with establishing habitations. The population is equally made up of nobles and of indentured servants, or '*alloués*' or (then known as) 'thirty-six months.'"[11] They were voluntary emigrants, but because they could not pay their own passage, they had agreed to work for thirty-six months without pay in order to reimburse the Company of the American Islands. They usually had little education. Convicts, pirates, and ex-convicts made up an equal portion of the islands' population. The Company of the American Islands also organized convoys of white women to the French plantations in America.

In 1640, European corsairs seized Spanish ships that contained Africans and then sold them to the colonies. These Africans came from the Azores, or from the islands off Cap-Vert, the place where they were first transshipped, and would be the first black population in the islands. The first missionaries also arrived in Martinique that year. After 1641, it was through force and violence that men, women and children were transferred, being torn from their psychological, cultural, and social roots in Africa. The colonists thus enlisted the servile African labor force. In effect, "the sold African man became the black slave in Martinique, the possession of a white, French colonist. He entered into a pyramid system, that of the swallowing, dehumanizing, alienating plantations. A system in which his origins had no place: he was on an island . . . with no return."[12]

According to Chaudenson and Bernabé, the Creoles of the Lesser Antilles, notably those in Martinique and Guadeloupe, were formed in the first fifty or sixty years of colonization. Still, according to these authors,

11. Armand Nicolas, *Histoire de la Martinique,* vol. 1, *Des Arawaks à 1848* (Paris and Montréal: L'Harmattan, 1996), 51.

12. Masson-Perrin, Valérie. *Le statut du personnage dans l'œuvre romanesque d'Édouard Glissant.* Ph.D. Dissertation, Université de Cergy-Pontoise, 2006, 73.

Creole appeared at a moment when whites would have been more numerous than blacks. However, according to Alfred Martineau and Louis-Philippe May, Martinique's 1664 census, fewer than thirty years after the beginning of colonization, records a population of 3,515, comprising 1,081 whites, 2,416 blacks, and 18 mulattoes.[13] It would seem that this census is not complete. According to Armand Nicolas, in Martinique in 1654, sugar cane production demanded a labor force that was not to be found on the island.[14] He further states that, "for a sugar habitation that produces fifty to one-hundred thousand pounds of sugar a year, around forty slaves were needed."[15] The reverend Father Du Tertre, quoted by Nicolas, notes that "Our colonies were formed like all the other colonies, that is to say, formed by all sorts of people, gathered from all the world's nations, in every state, of all ages, and all dissimilar in their religions and in their morals."[16]

Population Expansion

The Company of the Americas recommended cotton and sugar industries from the beginning, and it was sugar cane production that proved to have an important place in the European economy. As soon as the colonists disembarked on the islands, they found wild sugar cane growing. Sugar cane, originally from Asia, was imported to the Canary Islands by the Spanish. Columbus then brought it to the West Indies on his second voyage in 1493. Without entering into details, it should be remembered that it was in Portuguese Brazil, beginning in 1533, that the new colonial riches called "white gold" emerged. Thus, "from the beginning of their installation in Martinique, the Company tried to implant cane agriculture and sugar production."[17]

---

13. Alfred Martineau and Louis-Philippe May, *Trois Siècles d'histoire antillaise, Martinique et Guadeloupe, de 1635 à nos jours* (Paris: Society for the History of the French Colonies and Librairie Leroux, 1935), 124.

14. Armand Nicolas, *Histoire de la Martinique*, vol. 1, *Des Arawaks à 1848* (Paris and Montréal: L'Harmattan, 1996), 99.

15. Ibid., 76.

16. Ibid., 61.

17. Ibid., 73.

In 1654, a mainly Jewish Dutch group driven from Brazil by the Portuguese and accompanied by black slaves who were experienced in sugar work, arrived in Martinique carrying the secrets of cultivating and refining sugar. After the Martinique authorities refused them (on grounds of religious obedience), the Dutch turned toward Guadeloupe, where Governor Charles Houël welcomed them. Consequently, Jacques Dyel du Parquet would bring three hundred Dutchmen. He would place them on the Cap de Sac Royal (where the name "Flemish Bay" in Fort-de-France harbor comes from). Although their presence was short-lived, their knowledge of the sugar industry stayed behind.[18] In this way, Du Parquet established the first sugar plantation. In a few years, sugar cane would boom. In fifteen years, there would be 117 sugar farms on Martinique.

Sugar Farms: Crux of the Economic and Social Revolution

The development of cane sugar brought about a social and economic revolution. Indeed, sugar agriculture required important investments, material and human alike. It was necessary, from the standpoint of making a lucrative profit, to have huge stretches of land, which in turn required land redistribution. And so, small land owners would be absorbed by rich planters. During this same period, many indentured servants returned to France. Wealthy landowners, especially sugar planters, had the opportunity to expand their estates. "This process of *concentrating their lands*, somewhat slow at the beginning, accelerated toward the end of the seventeenth century. Thus continued a number of large estates, the future Habitations."[19] Let it be noted that plantations existed only in certain places like Marin, Rivière Pilote, Trou au Chat (Ducos), or in Cul-de-Sac à Vaches (Rivière Salèe).

The population of Martinique experienced new growth. Actually, as Nicolas mentioned, an "abundant" workforce was necessary to cultivate the vast lands. With the rise of sugar, the number of slaves grew: in 1664, the island was populated by 2,904 whites and 3,158 blacks. In the beginning of colonization it was by "means of plunder" that blacks had been introduced to the Islands, and thereafter they officially disembarked in the colonies in this

---

18. Ibid., 74.

19. Ibid., 75.

A Linguistic Process: Creole in the Americas

same way. Indeed, in 1638, with the support of Cardinal Richelieu, the first black trade company was founded: the Senegal Company. It should be noted that the Company of the American Islands was linked to the "Company of Cap-Vert" so as to have the authorization to "send and retrieve Negroes and livestock" in its cargoes.[20] In this way France entered into "ebony" commerce. The colonies in general and Martinique in particular entered into a slaving period. In fact a slaving society was established, and it was composed of three classes: Grand whites (sugar planters, wealthy merchants), little whites, and black slaves. It wasn't until the end of the seventeenth century that the first free mulattoes came on the scene.[21]

In 1664, there were nine militia companies, making nine districts, and there were 684 habitations. This number would more than double in 1671, totaling 1,486. That same year, there were twice as many blacks as in 1664. Each year, seven hundred to a thousand slaves arrived in Martinique.

Formation of the Great Property, Birthplace of Creole

According to Chaudenson, "Creole is a social and human tragedy that represents the rule of threes of classic French tragedy: unity of place, the island; unity of time, a century; unity of action, the colonial slave society." As impossible as it is to determine the "birthdate" of Creole, it is possible to "deal with fixed reference points."[22] Chaudenson says that in these societies, the conditions for the appearances of first generation Creoles were beginning to form, and so he distinguishes the "Habitation societies" from the "Plantation societies." The latter arose with the colonial agro-industrial boom. He situated historic and linguistic creolization in the passage of one to the other.

Habitation Society

Habitation society is the "old, local denomination for the initial unit of production of the colonial societies." "Habitat" and "habitant" were the

---

20. Ibid.

21. Ibid., 180: "They are ordinarily the fruit of a union between a white man and a black woman, of a master with one of his slaves."

22. Chaudenson, *op. cit.*, 37.

terms used in the beginning of colonization to designate "the agricultural unit of production" and "agricultural exploitation." This term "habitation" does not refer to the place in which one lives. Chaudenson explains that the term comes from the fact that the "habitants" did not own the lands that they worked, and that the lands belonged to the Companies. Effectively, they granted lands that had to be cleared and cultivated, and from which they got returns on a portion of the harvests.

Plantation Society

This concept is born of anthropological and economic studies. The lifestyle of these two societies is a social organization. The passage of one to the other corresponds to the growth of the slave population. The genesis of "Creole" languages can only be understood through socio-historic and sociolinguistic studies of the conditions of creolization.[23] According to Chaudenson, "languages are social events." It is important to take into consideration the societies in which they are formed and developed.

Origins and Characteristics of the Populations

All the territories where French Creole is used were peopled by immigrants, who had "exogenous" languages.

<u>The French Colonists</u>
As stated above, it was a heterogeneous population that disembarked on the islands. "The sixteenth century Frenchmen did not have a normalized linguistic tool available to them, as the French language of today would be considered; even the language of Molière and Racine could not reflect even a little of the dialectic and popular distinctions used by the first colonists."[24]

<u>The Slaves</u>
From the Africans' perspective, as soon as they were transshipped they were deprived of words, of language. In effect, they were scattered. Beginning with the first raids, they had been separated out of fear of fomentation of

---

23. Ibid., 90.

24. Bernabé, *op. cit.*, 321.

trouble or revolts. As soon as the captives arrived at their destination, those who had the same ethnicity were separated, and the same procedure was used during sales and on the plantations. The masters feared ethnic gatherings that could lead to groupings that too closely resembled African tribes. According to Prudent, the masters feared the natural element of language, an "ideological and notional bond," above all.

The slaves' languages were totally different. It is of utmost importance to differentiate the peopling of the two great creolization zones: the Caribbean (West Africa) and the Indian Ocean (Madagascar, India, and East Africa). Moreover, one must acknowledge a distinction between "ladino Negroes" who internalized the culture and language of the masters, and "bozales Negroes" who came from Africa. The latter group showed a marked resistance to acculturation.[25]

In Africa as much as in the American-Caribbean zone, the "great linguistic diversity of the servile populations" is evident. Chaudenson asserts that the names of the "nations" by which the slaves were qualified do not signify their origins, "these are not the names of real ethnicities", he adds, "but general designations, and above all, the names of their place of trade or embarkation."[26] He quotes Jean Mettas: "the term can designate multiple peoples and the preeminence of Congolese is certainly a misunderstanding of these peoples on the part of the French slavers."[27]

Construction of Creole

According to Prudent, "the known discourse on the Creole is placed in the general economy of social sciences, under the subjects of colonial or postcolonial societies."[28] He asserts that literature on Creole genesis can be divided into three groups. The first would be polygenist. He dismisses a group of studies that attribute European maternity to each kind of Creole language. Prudent emphasizes the fact that speaking of polygenesis in this case would mean that each colonial situation would have spawned an original pidgin having evolved, or not, into a Creole language. Prudent asserts

---

25. Ibid., 322.

26. Chaudenson, *op. cit.*, 92.

27. *La Traite des noirs par l'Atlantique: nouvelles approaches* (Paris: French Society of History of the Overseas Departments, 1976), 35.

28. Prudent, *op. cit.*, 69.

that according to R. Hall's deduction, "the mechanisms of pidginization and creolization were at work as many times as Europeans found themselves before Africans during the fifteenth, sixteenth, and seventeenth centuries, which justifies the presence of *different* Creoles in the colonial world."[29] The second group of texts would have the epithet of monogenist, meaning the Creole languages all had the same, singular origin of an Afro-Portuguese dialect from the fifteenth century and which would have lexically evolved in different ways, according to different colonial languages. The third vein is characterized by resorting to the population history of the different Creolophone zones in the world.

Like Bernabé, Prudent insists on the fact that it is important to put things in their historical contexts. The first slaves who disembarked on the Antilles were "ladinos," blacks "raised" in Portugal, in the Azores or in Cap-Vert, who had therefore undergone an "intense lusisation."[30] Over the course of the slave trade, the "ebony" that arrived directly from Africa were slaves called "bozales," as opposed to the "Creoles born in the colonies."

Another language also appeared during the trade: the "gibberish of savages." Father Bouton (1640) attests to its existence in Martinique. According to Bernabé, "it is possible that this pidgin had been developing, beginning in the sixteenth century."[31] The multiple disembarkations of Spanish and of French and English pirates in the Lesser Antilles without a doubt permitted language exchanges ("taken language") with the indigenous peoples. According to Bernabé, "the heavy influence of Castilian roots (*manan* = magnane, mater-matté, *mucho* = mouche, *barracho* = bourache) and the fact that all these witnesses date from the beginning of French colonization in Martinique lead us to think that this gibberish was already being used at the end of the sixteenth century."

There were other instances of linguistic creolization, like in Jamaica, Guyana, and Surinam. According to Bernabé, to understand the genesis of Creole languages, it is necessary to return to history, to have an understanding of the present social groups, and to esatablish a linguistic setting, with the goal of identifying eventual kinships.

---

29. Robert A. Hall Jr., "The life cycle of pidgin languages, " *Lingua* 11 (1962): 151–56, cited by Prudent, 71.

30. Prudent, *op. cit.*, 78.

31. Bernabé, *op. cit.*, 322–23.

Creole in the Present

A diglottic situation exists in the former colonies. This diglossia is the presence of two linguistic communications in the Lesser Antilles, for example, with French being the official language although Creole is the mother tongue of a large number of Antilleans. French, the language of the colonizers, is synonymous with social success. A great number of Creole languages are not recognized as such and are referred to as patois, a dialect.

After the slave liberation of 1848, the Creole language was forbidden in schools. In the home, parents forbade their children to use Creole. It was considered the parlance of the "little Negro." Fleischman writes that Creole is "pretty, undoubtedly harmonious, musical, everything you would want . . . but that does not prevent it from being the language of the little Negro, and the quicker it is forgotten, the better for the future of the Antilles."[32]

In Haiti, after the independence of 1804, French became known as the language of instruction at all levels in the education system. It was not until 1979 that Creole entered into the schools, and the Constitution of 1987 granted it legal protection. Once introduced into the education system, Creole became a taught subject and a language of instruction.

In the Lesser Antilles, it is different. The islands are certainly still French dependencies. It is the French language that has been taught there from their educational beginnings. After the abolition of slavery was proclaimed in May 1848, French remained the language of prestige. Using Creole hearkens back to the servile, painful, and punitive colonial period. Speaking Creole also associates one with an inferior social class.

Creole in the French Antilles of America was recognized thanks to the Group for Studies and Research in the Francophone and Creolophone Space (GEREC-F) founded in 1975. It is a group of Creolists working on Creole languages, cultures and populations, with special focus on French-based Creole lexicons and francophone spaces. This group played a role in the creation of Creole CAPES (Certificate of Professional Aptitude in Secondary Instruction) by a decree on February 9th, 2001. The first CAPES for regional Creole language and culture was put in place in 2002, and is still sought today.

32. Ulrich Fleischmann, *Das Französisch-Kreolische in der Karibik: Zur Funktion der Sprache im sozialen und geographischen Raum*, (Tübingen, Germany: Gunther Narr Verlag, 1986), 121; B. Nistl, *Comparaison entre les créoles des Petites Antilles et le francais en ce qui concerne les déterminants*. (Munich: GRIN Verlag, 2003), 2.

The art of tin or "boss-métal" sculpture is very popular in Haiti. This tree can be "read" as a tree of knowledge, or nourishment of all kinds for the birds that knew how to find it.

Defense and Illustration of Haitian Creole in Franketienne's Works

Rafaël Lucas

The production of sophisticated works in Haitian Creole, as is illustrated in Franketienne's numerous books, bears witness to an irreversible mutation in the long under-evaluated rise of this language to a status that is literary in scope. One must start with a literature of *defense and illustration* and then move on to a literature built by poles of reference, in other words, go from the makeshift and marooning to creating a literary heritage. Such a revolution could not be done without a mental rearranging of the language's image, along with forming linguistic capital and developing innovative poetics.

The Creole Bicycle and the French Car

Seventeen years after the first publication of a great novel in a French-based Creole language, Franketienne"s *Dézafi* (1975), Raphael Confiant, one of the authors of *In Praise of Creoleness* (1989), affirmed, in an interview published in *Le Monde* on November 6, 1992, that Creole is a "rural language," whose "conceptual level is very limited," whereas "French is a pre-assembled language with which one can play."[1] He then adds that when given the choice between a Creole bicycle and a French car, it is better to opt for the French car. According to Lambert-Felix Prudent, the conceptual poverty so associated with these languages comes from a "linguistic

---

1. Jean Bernabé, Patrick Chamoiseau and Raphaël Confiant, *In Praise of Creoleness* (Paris: Gallimard, 1989).

Top right: an image of the colonists; slave in ragged pants; master's dog.
Top left: rebellious maroon, torso half-naked, with rudimentary clothing.
Bottom: Toussaint Louverture, represented on horseback, with red and blue hat.

minoration of Creole"[2] that generally applies to words in the vernacular language, as can be seen with the etymologically Latin term *verna*, a slave born on the master's property.

Prioritizing the "French car" to the detriment of the "Creole bicycle" does not necessarily arise from what Edouard Glissant calls a "successful colonization," but rather from a strategy of editorial visibility, through which the limited readership of Creole language works makes the profitability of works in these languages very unpredictable.[3] In the sense that "Creole" literature does not yet have a literary tradition at its disposal, the writer who attempts this adventure often opts for a militant approach, in the spirit of *defense and illustration*, such as what Joachim du Bellay did for the French language in 1549 when he declared that there are no "species

2. Lambert-Félix Prudent, *Du Baragouin à la langue antillaise* (Paris: Caribbean Editions, 1980).

3. Édouard Glissant, *Sun of Consciousness* (Paris: Gallimard, 1997; 1st ed., Paris, Seuil, 1956).

of weak and infirm languages, and others that are healthy and robust."[4] It is incidentally from this same perspective that the Guyanese writer Alfred Parépou published *Atipa* in 1885, the first novel written in Creole.[5] The case for praising Creole is developed in the first chapter, in the form of a defensive conversation between Atipa and Bossobio.

In the preface of the 1980 edition, Lambert-Felix Prudent explained why this work was forgotten for nearly a century. According to him, the assimilationist context of the late nineteenth century in France, very unfavorable for literary recognition of Creole in Guyana, would ascribe numerous deficiencies to the body of work. *Atipa* is composed of twelve chapters that each contains edifying, often simplistic dialogues (which retain nostalgic praise for working class life), ethnographic descriptions, an inventory of Guyana's riches, references to the lives of treasure hunters, some quite contestable remarks about parasitic immigrants, as well as acerbic commentary on local politics.

Translation as a Strategy for Recognition

Prior to the publication of Franketienne's *Défazi*, "Creole" literature consisted mainly of tales, fables, poems, several plays, and translations of European classics. Yet tales, fables, and poems are generally products with weak quantitative scope.[6] As for translations, they served to import foreign works with legitimizing power into the Creole linguistic space with works such as famous tragedies from ancient Greece or from France under Louis XIV.

Let us quickly mention the immense success of La Fontaine's *Fables*, whose diverse translations reveal an already long-standing tradition in the creolophone space: Louis Héry (1828) in Réunion; Paul Baudot (1860) in Guadeloupe; Alfred de Saint-Quentin (1874) in Guyana; Georges Sylvain (1905) in Haiti; Sylviane Telchid (1986, 1989, 2000) in Guadeloupe; and Mont-Rosier Déjean (2000) in Haiti. In the domain of classic tragedies, for

---

4. Joachim du Bellay, *Defense and Illustration of the French Language* [1549] (Paris: Larousse, col. Classiques Larousse), 50.

5. Alfred Parépou, *Atipa* [1885], trans. Michel Lohier [1972] (Paris: Caribbean Editions, 1980).

6. This claim should be qualified with regard to the scope of such works as *Arabian Nights* and *Fables* by La Fontaine, for example. We are not making a negative value judgment here.

Martinique there is Moliere's translation of *Don Juan* and Sophocles' *Antigone* by Georges Mauvois (*Don Jan*, 1996, *Antigòn*, 1997); there are the translations of Sophocles' *Antigone*, titled *Wa Kreyon* (1953) by Felix Morisseau-Leroy, and of Corneille's *Le Cid*, under the title of *Jénéral Rodrig* (1975) by Numa Nono; and Sophocles' *Oedipus Rex* by Frank Fouché (1955). This list must include the Haitian adaptation of John Bunyan's *Pilgrim's Progress* by Carrié Poultre, published under the title of *Ti Jak* (1968).

Concerning poetic works in the Haitian language, outside of the publication of Félix Morisseau-Leroy's *Dyakout* (1953), one must acknowledge the poetic and theatrical works published in the 1970s. In poetry, Georges Castera published *Klou Gagit* (1965), *Boua Mitan* (1970), *Panzou* (1970), *Plon Gayé* (1974), and *Konbèlann* (1976), which is a collection of these and other texts. Haitian language works blossomed in the 1970s, and in addition to poems and the 1975 publication of Frankétienne's and Émile Célestin-Mégie's first novels (*Dézafi* and *Lanmou pa gin baryè*), the Kouidor Theater expanded in this period, bringing together the likes of Georges Castera, Syto Cavé, Jacques Charlier, Hervé Denis, Daniel Huttinot, Josaphat-Robert Large, and Jean-Marie Roumer.

Although the intellectual promotion of Creole is a commendable strategy (thanks to the translation of recognized works), it is confined to the role of redistributing the contents of prestigious, foreign works. The translation of famous works into a pared-down language augments the coefficient of universality, but it is equally important that underrepresented languages gain visibility and also give rise to translations. Translation functions as a label of recognition; it allows us to do away with the enclosure of a vernacular prison. In this sense, it is incontestable that the translation/rewriting of Frankétienne's *Dézafi, The Agonies of Defiance* (1979) has contributed much to the prestige of the original text.

From Literature in Crisis to Reference Literature

With the publication of *Défazi*, Haitian language literature had a work of great scope that made its historical mark thanks to its power of innovation and to Frankétienne's enormous work in producing a written arrangement of Creole.⁷ To use Maximilien Laroche's expression from "*Pwetik lang kreyòl la*" (poetics of the Creole language), it is necessary to move from "collage to montage"; in other words, to go from a literature of immediate comprehension to more complex works.⁸ It was no longer a question of Creole having a place in the "global republic of literature" thanks to legitimizing acculturation abroad, but rather of producing innovative enough texts so that Creole, too, had its reference works. One must no longer adapt to, but seize the field of literary referentiality.

Although *Défazi* (1975) and *Adjanoumelezo* (1987) were written in "the language of the people," that did not gain these publications a wider readership, no more than Rabelais's *Pantagruel* (1532) or *Gargantua* (1534), which, despite their considerable popular impact, were not intended for a broad public. The degree of semantic sophistication of the two aforementioned Haitian works requires an informed reader, capable of appreciating the artistic potential of Creole writing. The following passage from *Adjanoumelezo* would be an example: "*Poutan, kànaval kabal kanibal kanivò kaplata kaskadè chofe pi rèd jouk lan dènye degre rèl eskandal kafe lan ma, kafe fyèlbèf. Latakdelamalpòs/brannbadegrannkonba. Fantomdelopera file sou konpa vantba*".⁹

A first reading of this passage gives the impression of chaotic disorder, so a second approach is needed to appreciate its significance. Immediately noted here is the play on sound and alliteration (*kanaval, kabal, kanibal kaplata, kaskadè*), then the accumulative effect which corresponds to an aesthetic of collage and fragmentary writing, typical of the modernity of the twentieth century. Although Haitian Creole is the national, popular language, the average reader could not immediately decipher Franketienne's Creole text. This reader would not necessarily know cinematic and literary

---

7. We will return later to Georges Castera's pioneering role in this area.

8. Maximilien Laroche, "*Pwetik lang kreyòl la*," in *Teke* (Port-au-Prince: Mémoire, 2000), 12.

9. (*Adjanoumelezo*, 64): "Yet a cascading carnival of cacophonous, cannibalistic cabals whips itself further into frenzy, laughing to the edge of bacchanal hysteria, powdered coffee, coffee bitter like bile soap. Rawhide stage coach robbery/all hands on deck for the big fight. The phantom of the opera slides, belly to the ground, to the rhythm of Haitian *konpa*" (Author's translation).

references like *Rawhide* and *The Phantom of the Opera*.[10] It is clear that this is a sophisticated Creole. Unlike Franketienne's theatrical works, which can be more easily accessed, a work like *Adjanoumelezo* is directed at a highly competent reader. This reader must be, in the words of Umberto Eco, "an insomniac in a state of semantic wakefulness"[11]; in other words, the reader must be permanently vigilant when dealing with text.

It is through concepts drawn from the most popular Haitian Creole, the "*natif-natal*" (local-native), that Franketienne would express the essentially modernizing orientations of his work. This orientation consists of scrambling the readability of the text through a certain opacification, which is reflected in the Haitian terms *andaki*, *alagouj*, and *pale langaj*. The terms *paròl alagouj* and *paròl andaki* are found in the title of the second part of *Dézafi*. To speak in *daki* means to use terms that are known to insiders. *Daki* is also a reference to the language of black maroons, whose Creole was less influenced by French than those who lived in the heart of colonial society. *Pale langaj*, or "speak in the language," has a meaning similar to *pale andaki*, but with a more mystical connotation, as the expression refers to ritual spells spoken by initiates in a language that is pronounced with African consonance (in Benin, often *fon* or *fongbé*). In his 1977 article on Jean-Claude Charles's *Sainte déride des cochons*, Jean Jonassaint expounds on the expressions *pale andaki* and *pale langaj*, showing the respective implications of double meaning in both.[12] As for the term *Alagouj*, it signifies chance, like a throw of the dice (or bones, in Haiti), but, as we know from Mallarmé, "a throw of dice will never abolish chance."

Compared to the works that preceded *Défazi*, Franketienne's "novel" introduced a series of ruptures and innovations. It created a way out of diglossia's heavy constraints. This concept, launched in 1959 by the linguist Charles Ferguson, describes the phenomenon of a splitting of a language into two hierarchical variations: a high form (acrolect) and a low

---

10. We will return later to these two references that appear often in *Ajanoumelezo*.

11. Umberto Eco, *The Limits of Interpretation* (Paris: Grasset & Fasquelle, [1990] 1992), 133.

12. See Jean Jonassaint, "The crossing of American languages in *Sainte dérive des cochons* by Jean-Claude Charles," in *Poétiques et Imaginaires: francopolyphonie littéraire des Amériques*, Directed by Pierre Laurette and Hans-Georges Ruprecht (Paris: L'Harmattan, 1995), 255–65. A reviewed, corrected and augmented version from 2004 is available online at: http://www.lehman.cuny.edu/ile.en.ile/paroles/charles_jonassaint.html.

form (basilect). As Albert Valdman notes, they each have "determined, mutually exclusive functions and areas of use."[13] For us, this concept, also validated by the linguists Lambert-Félix Prudent and Jean Barnabé, presupposes the existence of two variants of the *same* language, as was the case with Greek, the low form (*demotiki*) gradually replaced the high form (*katharevoussa*).[14] This strongly applies to German, where there is a great difference between *Hochdeutsch* and regional dialects, and to Arabic (notably in the Maghreb region) where the modern, high, and classical Arabic (*el arabia el fosha*) coexists with dialectal Arabic (*el arabia ed derija*).

The aforementioned examples are indeed a splitting of one language. In Arabic, German, and Greek, the low form is a simplification of the high form. In these cases of diglossia, intercomprehension between the two forms is still possible but requires sustained attention and effort. Conversely, the case in Haiti is that there are two very different languages (French and Creole). Intercomprehension between a *natif-natal* interlocutor and a French person is almost impossible. To prove this, one would only have to read a page from *Adjanoumelezo* to a French speaker, or even to someone who spoke a different kind of Creole. It is open to debate whether it is appropriate, if one observes the numerous structural differences between the two languages, to categorize Haitian Creole, spoken daily by 95 percent of Haitians, as a variant of low French. Certainly, the intellectual prestige of the French language, its geographic expanse, and its strong literary tradition have rendered it a more elaborate linguistic vehicle than the "creole bicycle," but this should be seen as a transitory state, not an immutable status.

Franketienne's innovation in the field was to create a sort of high Creole, exhibiting enormous lexical capital, in order to put to rest the image of the poverty of "vernacular" vocabulary poverty, deploying an important, stylized device that we will return to later. The author systematically resorts to anthropological heritage (proverbs, nursery rhymes, Vodou characters). He employs narrative outlines and emblematic characters that take an

13. Albert Valdman, *Le Créole: structures, statut et origins* (Paris: Klincksiek, 1978), 314.

14. See Prudent, *Du Baragouin à la langue antillaise*, and Jean Bernabé, *Fondal-natal: grammaire basilectale approchée des créoles guadeloupéens et martiniquais*, 2 vols. (Paris: L'Harmattan, 1983).

active part in a vast symbology, notably when staging power and corruption. In *Dézafi*, for example, the *houngan* (Vodou priest) and the *zombis* serve as the two poles of power: on one side, supreme power, and on the other, absolute alienation. The *houngan*, endowed with an almost comical omnipotence, reappears in Sazarin's character in *Troufoban* (1978). In *Adjanoumelezo*, it is the voice of the Vodou *papagede* that dominates the bulk of the 522-page narrative. *Le papagede*, (Papa Guédé) is a character that has freedom of expression in the setting of Vodou festivals that take place at the time of the Festival of the Dead.

Frankétienne's innovations include a welcome, revolutionary mixture of genres (novel, theater, poetry) that should be placed within a context of disillusionment with academic forms that were being expressed by the Latin American and European avant-garde beginning with Dadaism in the early twentieth century. *Défazi* is not a piece of classical workmanship, as the genre's conventional walls were knocked down in favor of a greater flow of meaning, not to mention subversion of linear devices and page spacing. By tearing down the borders between literary genres, Frankétienne creates diversity in reading codes or multi coding, a characteristic considered by Iouri Lotman to be one of the markers of quality literature.[15] Concerning markers of literary specificity, or "literarity," it is worth noting certain traits that emerge from numerous works on literary theory that are perceptible in Frankétienne's texts.

Of Literarity and Literarization

If Frankétienne's *Dézafi* and *Adjanoumelezo* can be considered events, then they represent a true revolution in the literary use of Haitian Creole. The term "literarity" (*literaturnost* in Russian) represents an important notion in the works of the Russian Formalists (1915–1940), the principal ideas of which are presented in Tzvetan Todorov's *Theory of Literature*.[16] There are numerous approaches to literarity. We wholly share the viewpoint put forth by Gérard Genette in *Fiction and Diction*: "Literarity, being

---

15. Iouri Lotman, *La Structure du texte artistique* (Paris: Gallimard, [1970] 1973). This idea is developed in the chapter "Le texte et les structures extra-textuelles."

16. Tzvetan Todorov, *Theory of Literature* (Paris: Seuil, 1965).

a plural idea, requires a pluralist theory that takes account of the diverse ways language has in escaping and surviving its practical functions, and of producing texts that are susceptible to being received and approached as aesthetic objects."[17]

According to Pierre Macherey, literature is a mythology, a mythification device that equally constitutes a "space of mystification."[18] "Literature is a fiction: that is its first structural definition," wrote Tzvetan Todorov in *The Notion of Literature*.[19] Escaping from practical function, and therefore conserving a "non-pragmatic status," represents one of the main features of literarity, which for Genette is also "the art of language."[20] This implies a double dimension: a technical aspect and an "aesthetic function" (especially for a poetic work) emphasized by Roman Jakobson.[21] Such a literary field therefore constitutes a world apart that has been granted autonomy.[22] It evokes a closed textual universe (Kristeva) that closes in on itself. This degree of autonomy implies a distancing of itself, with the simple function of communicating in everyday language.[23] Such an autonomous universe avails itself of its own internal reference network and therefore of its own "descriptive system" (Riffaterre). However, Henri Meschonnic and Georges Steiner reject the idea of absolutely autonomous literature, based on its inevitable inscription into society and historicity which, for Meschonnic, is inherent "in all language practices."[24] As Steiner said, "No work of art, however abstract, however hermetic and inward it may be, is autonomous. The most private poetry, the most rebellious, abstract painting have their place in a social and historical context."[25]

17. Gérard Genette, *Fiction and Diction* (Paris, Seuil, 1991), 31.
18. Pierre Macherey, *A Theory of Literary Production* (Paris: PUF, 1971), 77.
19. Tzvetan Todorov, *The Notion of Literature* (Paris: Seuil, 1987), 352.
20. Genette, *op. cit.*, 62.
21. Roman Jakobson, *Questions de poétique* (Paris: Seuil, 1973).
22. Roman Jakobson, *Essays on General Linguistics* (Paris: Minuit, 1963).
23. Julia Kristeva, *Semeiotikè, Recherches pour une sémanalyse* (Paris: Seuil, 1969).
24. Henri Meschonnic, *Critique of Rhythm: A Historical Anthropology of Language* (Lagrasse: Éditions Verdier, 1982), 396.
25. Georges Steiner, *Grammars of Creation* (Paris: Gallimard, 2001), 299.

The literary of a work is also characterized by its power to subvert acquired habits and robotic reception of works, hence the destabilizing and "defamiliarizing" (according to Russian Formalists) effects, or a deconstruction that better promotes "the pleasure of the text." Modern literary also distinguishes the dissimilitude between the "prose of the world"[26] and the writer's product. In other words, one must be wary of the "referential illusion" or of what Gérard Genette calls the "mimologic dream" or "realist illusion."[27] Meschonnic refutes an approach to the linguistic sign that is too structuralist and "imperialist," which, according to him, dismisses the scientific in favor of universal pretention. He advocates consideration for the anthropology of words and the historicity of literary forms. Contesting the hegemony of the linguistic sign, in *Critique of Rhythm* (1982) he defends the primordial importance that rhythm has in signification and organizational factors: "Rhythm is an organizer of meaning in discourse."[28] Literary material does not reduce itself to a sign, with its two aspects of signifier and signified, the union of which assures a dynamic meaning, often to the benefit of the signified, except in poetry. Opposed to what he calls "binary ineptitude," Meschonnic pleads for the integration of rhythm, the meaning of which he extends to every manifestation of living. Michaël Riffaterre, like Julia Kristeva, insists on the importance of "*signifiance* as a mark of literarity." Unlike the signification that we deduced from a first reading, the "*signifiance*" results from a deeper understanding of the text. Riffaterre adds over-determination as a "fundamental property of literary text."[29] Over-determination is founded on the different interpretations of meaning that a term can have, as well as on the author's exploitation of a word's link with other contexts of signification. It also has to do with words' potential to draw from all the possibilities of multiple significations (their polysemy) and to listen to the multiplicity of voices (their polyphony) that express themselves in a text (Bakhtine).

26. This expression is the title of the second chapter of Michel Foucault's *The Order of Things* (Paris: Gallimard, 1966), 32–60.

27. Gérard Genette, *Mimologics* (Paris, Seuil, 1976), 376.

28. Henri Meschonnic, *op. cit.*, 70.

29. Michaël Riffaterre, "The Referential Illusion," in *Littérature et Réalité* (Paris: Seuil, 1982), 99.

Equally important are the subversive attempts in the pages' graphic arrangements, with the introduction of calligrams and the use of drawings that are part of the code of icons. A work's literary status furthermore depends on an entire network of institutions (the press, universities, colloquiums, literary prizes, specialized criticism, the media) that function as instances of legitimization. Among the numerous works that have examined this, we will cite those of Pierre Bourdieu and de Pascale Casanova who contest, with evidence to back them, the idea of an autonomous literary work independent of its relationship to the laws of the market.[30] Let it be noted that this criticism had already appeared in 1946 in Roger Caillois' *Babel*, to cite an older example: "All literature makes up civilization. No book comes directly from the beatings of one's heart [...]. A literature exists in a given society: from society it receives its imprint and, in return, imparts to it a direction."[31]

Plurality of voices, polysemy, strategies of confused meaning, by defamiliarization or by deconstruction, often produce an obscuring effect in a text, which brings us back to Frankétienne's words in *daki* and *alagouj*. This is not at all a strategy to transform the literature into an "obstacle course," as Roy Harris says, nor to "punish" the reader by sentencing him to "lexical anguish," as Josette Rey-Debove puts it.[32] The risk would be to sink into "modernery" (Meschonnic) or worse, into "*merde*rnery" as denounced by Michel Leiris. Nevertheless, this complication of the text is one of the marks of contemporary literature. It tests the decoding ability of the reader, or his "inferential comprehension."[33]

With the exception of syntax, which remains relatively classic in Frankétienne's works, the majority of modern literature's trappings can be found in his Creole body of work. In a "relatively classic syntax" the

---

30. See Pierre Bourdieu, *Les Règles de l'art: genèse et structures du champ littéraire* (Paris: Seuil, 1992); Pascale Casanova, *La République mondiale des lettres* (Paris: Seuil, 1999).

31. Roger Caillois, *Babel* (Paris, Gallimard, [1946] 1996), 157.

32. See Roy Harris, *La Sémiologie de l'écriture* (Paris: Éditions CNRS, 1993) ; Josette Rey-Debove who writes in *La Linguistique du signe*: "Lexical anguish is a component of discomfort, a sentiment of inferiority, of suspicion and punitive urges in the absence of the given objective of the unknown word." (Paris: Armand Colin, 1998), 141.

33. These ideas are developed by Dan Sperber and Deirdre Wilson in *Relevance: Communication and Cognition* (Paris, Minuit, [1986] 1989).

classic order of subject, verb, and compliment is maintained. Franketienne does not use subversive forms such as are found in the poem "To Moccasin the Verb" by Robert Desnos, in *Langage cuit* (1923): "You suicide me docilely /I'll die of you, though, one day. / You and me and I'll meet this ideal woman [. . .] You, we love our eyes so little/ and this tear will fall down / without reason why and without sadness."[34] Franketienne's audacity involves typography, page management, the creation of neologisms and an important investment in styling and referential systems. As for punctuation, in *Défazi* the forward slash is used abundantly. In his *Treatise on French Punctuation*, Jacques Drillon recommends limited usage: "The forward slash has a restrained usage. It is used to closely link two terms, opposites or not."[35] Roland Barthes uses it relatively frequently. In *Défazi* the frequent use of the forward slash brings out a modern tick that is associated with writing on a keyboard, but it also serves to punctuate enumerations and to give the text a choppy rhythm. Such is the style in the passage where Clodonis, in a zombified state, sees the scenes from his childhood unwinding before his eyes like a video clip: "*Latou, li kòmansé vizionnin. An miyèt-moso tchaké, vi-li débobinin pòtré lan youn rèv: kalbas sou tèt / l-ap binyin lan sous / jouèt marèl maré / mayi boukannin / tonbé-levé / lago-caché lan jadin bannann / chout grinn zaboka / boul toual roulé devan kalvè / bo latranblad nan rinyin kay.*"[36]

Franketienne's Haitian Creole Corpus

We will mention here fourteen works by Franketienne: apart from *Défazi*, nine plays (*Troufoban*, 1978; *Pèlin-Tèt*, 1978; *Bobomasouri*, 1984; *Kaselezo*, 1985; *Totolanmanwèl*, 1987; *Melovivi*, 1987; *Minwi mwen senk*, 1988; *Kalibofobo*, 1988; *Foukifoura*, [1999] 2000) and four "spirals" (*Zagoloray*, 1983; *Adjanoumelezo*, 1987; *Voix marassas*, 1998; *Rappjazz*, 1999). *Voix marassas*

---

34. This poem is published in *Corps et Biens* (Paris, Gallimard, [1930] 1968), 79.

35. Jacques Drillon, *Treatise on French Punctuation* (Paris, Gallimard, 1991), 430.

36. "In that same moment he started to watch. In finely chopped pieces, his life unwinds like in a dream: a calabash on his head / he bathes in a stream / fierce hopscotch matches / grilled corn / he falls and gets back up/ hide-and-seek under the banana trees / he kicks the avocado stone / a dust cloth rolls down Cavalry's slope / trembling kisses hidden from the houses." (Author's translation) This excerpt is from *Dezafi* (Port-au-Prince: Éditions Fardin, 1975), 290–91.

(Twin Voices), which has a bilingual title, exemplifies the author's tendency to write in Haitian and French (*Rappjazz*, 1999, *Foukifoura*, 2000), which permits a creative exit from diglossia's prison and from the colonial pact that makes Creole a low, rudimentary version of French. In the preface of *Voix marassas*, Frankétienne puts an end to the stereotype of postcolonial relations between French and Haitian, recalling that French is already territorialized in Haiti and that instead of "conflicting" liaisons with Creole, it is possible to envision a fruitful marriage and an anti-totalitarian hybridity: "Fertile androgyny. A mind-blowing, hallucinatory marriage of two languages that, to varying degrees, are part of our cultural heritage. [. . .] A wager on the future of transphonic/franco-creolophonic/schizophonic/ transgressive, hybrid writing . . . A bizarre literary adventure with a fabulously playful dimension" (*Voix marassas* 8–9).

As for the titles' meanings, they are often a mixture of symbolic dimensions and playful aspects. *Défazi* refers to the mortal combat of a cockfight, but also to existential combat. *Troufoban* simultaneously invokes a lost locality and a place where all kinds of pirates meet (a pirate's haunt). *Pèlentèt* is a deadly trap, a "head trap," really a mental trap, where romantic lies and theatrical truths combine. *Bobomasouri* (kiss me, I will smile) and *Kalibo fobo* (There is beauty there, but it is artificial), are examples of playful titles, along with *Foukifoura*. *Totolanmawèl*, like *Foukifoura*, tells the story of a rebellious actor, Bolo Bèlòm, who lives under a dictatorship and is forced into hiding. He gives a solo performance every night so he will not disappear entirely.[37] *Zagoloray* can literally be translated as "rain boots." *Adjanoumelezo* invokes a moment in the popular carnival *raras*, when participants enter an all-permitting psychological state. The way Frankétienne uses it, this state reflects the generalized chaos of a drifting society. This chaos is expressed through an untamed language, that of the *guédés*, Vodou figures who use a vitriolic and satiric language (*pawòl pimanbouk*) during the Festival of the Dead. *Kaselezo* alludes to "the breaking of the water pouch" during childbirth. This play's plot concerns a two-hundred-year-old pregnant woman who refuses to give birth in a deadly environment.

---

37. For a comparison of the two texts, see *supra* Alvina Ruprecht, "*Totolomannwèl*: Frankétienne et le one-man-show," and *infra* Jean Jonassaint, "Matériaux pour une édition critique: condordances des premières et dernières éditions des oeuvres françaises de Frankétienne."

If we exclude the eight "metamorphoses" of *L'Oiseau Schizophone*, it becomes clear that the number of works published in the Haitian language is about equal to the number of French language publications. This quantitative aspect, together with the originality of the writing and a coherent editorial approach, confers on Frankétienne an important role in the emergence of a sophisticated "Creole" literature. In this literature, defense and illustration accompany the writer's enormous creative effort that reconciles numerous avant-garde conquests with the stylistic exploitation of the entire Haitian anthropological heritage, in terms of referential materials and resources of expression. Even so, one of the preoccupations of a writer who expresses himself in a minor language is to demonstrate the language's rich lexical and expressive potential.

A Reading of Haitian Reality through Haitian Language

Frankétienne's choice to literarize Haitian through stylistic processes is inseparable from his use of Creole terms as concepts that illustrate Haitian reality: *pawòl pimanbouk* (radical language); *zenglen* (shard, a metonymy for the suffering of the poor); *jamèdodo* (the insomnia of vigilance); *aganman* (combativeness); *bòwonm* (the brutality of power); *lwijanboje* (brawling, macho behavior); *makonnen, trip, deplòtonnen* (twisting imagery, spirals of suffering); *lavalas* (debacle); *malouk, makawon, mangonmen* (perilous incertitude); *deblozay, adjanoumelezo, tchaka, lòbèy* (the entire semantic field of carnavalesque chaos); and *défazi* (fighting to the death).

This survey of Frankétienne's work allows us to return to a decisive phase of establishing Haitian Creole literature and to producing a collection of texts that will thereafter fuel a corpus of classic works in the Haitian language. The attempt to develop a literary realm in Creole represents a well-established preoccupation in Haitian literature. It should be stated here that it is not only inaccurate, but unjust to attribute a founding role in the literation of Haitian Creole to Frankétienne alone. Important authors such as Félix Morisseau-Leroy (*Dyakout* - 1953) or Georges Castera (*Konbèlann* - 1976) should not be forgotten. Castera elaborates on his contribution in an interview with Rodney Saint-Éloi: "From the beginning I gave myself the task of putting Creole into writing. My collection *Konbèlann* marked the end of my first stage in writing

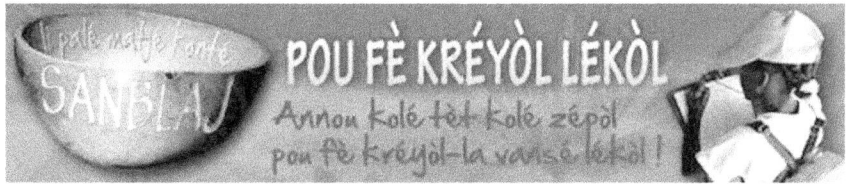

The calabash:
Sanglaj: union, collaboration.
POU FÉ KRÉYÒL LÉKÒL: FOR EDUCATION IN CREOLE.
Annou kole tè kolé zépòl: all united in head and shoulders.
Pou fè kréyòl-la vansé lékòl!: to develop Creole in school!

poetry, and is a regrouping of several collections, the last of which contains pictorial poems. This silent reading with the eyes, which I recommended to my readers, was a way of exiting orality."[38]

The Kouidor Theater and the *Sèl* Review contributed to promoting a Creole that is conceptually and aesthetically dense. As for historical studies, the imposing work of Rolph Trouillot, *Ti difé boulé sou istoua Ayiti* (1977), and the efforts of Maximilien Laroche in his literary and anthropological essays *Teke* (2000) and *Prinsip marassa* (2004) should be noted.[39] Franketienne's strides are not isolated; they are a part of a movement to promote Creole that gradually became more visible over the course of the 1970s.

Franketienne's work in the literarization of Creole, outside of diversifying the genres, benefits the movement quantitatively, not only with the number of his published works, but with the volume of certain works, like the 522-page *Adjanoumelezo*. Following the example of Georges Castera, Franketienne learned to anticipate profound mutations in the literary adventure of Haitian language literature. In addition to the task of augmenting the aesthetic visibility of the language, the form must also be innovated. New, literary Creole would integrate the audacity of modernity while conserving the heritage of the original culture, all while exploring the sonority of the spoken language in all of its social richness.

---

38. See Rodney Saint-Éloi, "Écrire en créole," *Notre Librairie*, 133 (1998), 97.

39. Maximilien Laroche, *Teke* (Port-au-Prince: Éditions Mémoire, 2000); *Prinsip Marassa*, (Sillery, Québec: GRELCA, 2004).

Mona Georgelin. *Association Mamanthé, troupe Massilia Ka.*

Danse Gwoka rythme Pajanbèl

Photographer : Azedine Hsissou

Mona Georgelin. *Association Mamanthé, troupe Massilia Ka.*

Mona Georgelin. *Association Mamanthé, troupe Massilia Ka.*

Danse Gwoka, rythme Pajanbèl

Artiste invité : Max Diakok. *Association Mamanthé, troupe Massilia Ka.*

Mélinée Magen. *Association Mamanthé, troupe Massilia Ka.*

Danse Gwoka, rythme Pajanbèl

Artiste invité : Max Diakok.   *Association Mamanthé, troupe Massilia Ka.*

Creole/Creolism/Creolization/Créolité

Jacques de Cauna

The term "creole" (and its derivations "creolism," "creolization," and "créolité"), pervasive as it is in the American lexicon, must be examined from a continental perspective due to the diversity of meaning it has had in different geographic areas. This is the purpose of the corresponding article of the same title in a forthcoming dictionary of the Americas, of which we present here as a preview, and as a point of departure for deliberation, a short excerpt centered on the Caribbean, and in particular the former French colonies.[1]

Here the term has recently and progressively endured important alterations and reductions in meaning that today tend to limit it, not only in the general usage but also in the majority of dictionaries, to meaning "white people born in the American islands," and only in the continental colonies of Guyana and Louisiana, but not in *Nouvelle-France*. This usage is also limited, in a paradoxical manner, to a language that we often esteem to be uniquely "created and spoken by black populations" of African descent, born of trans-Atlantic slavery.

The etymology of the term "creole" dates from the earliest colonization of the Americas and is found in the Portuguese *crioulo* and the Spanish *criollo*, based on the Latin *criare*: "to raise and feed a servant in the home." Originally, it was applied in the accounts of chroniclers in the French islands, principally in the seventeenth and eighteenth centuries, as a noun or an adjective, referring to all persons white, black or of color, born or raised there. One would qualify, for example, a "creole" slave as one "made

---

[1]. Michel Bertrand, Jean-Michel Blanquer, Antoine Coppolani, Isabelle Vagnoux, Dictionnaire des Amériques, Laffront, collection Bouquins, 2016.

in the colony" rather than a *Bossale*, an African who had experienced the journey of the slave trade or made the middle passage. It could also be said that Josephine de Beauharnais, born in the Trois Ilôts, was a Creole. The Mulattoes, a (nearly always) pejorative term applied to those of black and white ancestry, were without a doubt "Creoles," and considered themselves as the "only true Americans." More numerous in the former colonies of Martinique and Guadeloupe, in Santo Domingo the Creoles represented the principal colonists of the region (the "inhabitants"), in contrast with the widespread absenteeism of the great proprietors (the "*Grands-Blancs*"). In Martinique the term "*Békés*" took hold, even though elsewhere, "white country" was more readily used.

Finally, by extension we apply the term as an adjective to each creature, object, product, and material or immaterial good of the same origin: a creole pig, creole cuisine, a creole song, creole jewelry, or even, more simply, just "creoles" for ring shaped earrings. The most remarkable usage in this sense, and the one that has endured, is applied to "creole language," which came to be called just "Creole" (Haitian, Martiniquan, Guadeloupian, French Guianan, Louisianan), a communication tool born of colonial contact among groups that did not all speak French (two-thirds of the French people at this time spoke a regional language as their first one) and of slaves reflecting a huge African linguistic diversity.

Creole dialects are associated with languages of maritime contact, or pidgins. Their originality stems from the fact that they are the product of a shared slave history and that they exist theoretically in all the islands which belonged to Europeans in the Antilles: dialects of French, English (broken English or Jamaican patois), Dutch (*Papiamento*)…, but at different developmental degrees, and less distinctly in the Swedish, Danish, and Spanish islands. The quintessential example of this would be the small Franco-Dutch island of Saint-Martin, where over a half dozen languages, dialects, creoles, or patois remain, one of which is a Norman regional variation. French creole dialects are relatively inter-comprehensible, including those of the Indian Ocean.

Creole languages, close to their vehicular languages, are characterized by a lexicon based on the dominant language of the colonizer and a morphological or syntaxical simplification resulting as much from their original usage for the transmission of simple orders as from the borrowing from the local vernaculars of slaves, indigenous Native Americans and neighboring Europeans. One of their principal characteristics is their faculty for rapid evolution and innovation. One sometimes hears them qualified as the "successful Pidgins." Their resemblances are attributable to an analogy of the conditions of use more than to the common characteristics of the original languages, of superstrate or of substrate. The French Caribbean Creole (*kreyole*), spoken especially in Haiti, Martinique, Guadeloupe, Dominque, and Saint Lucia, is the second most common language of the Antilles after Spanish. The derivation "creolism" is employed to identify an idiomatic expression, a linguistic form, a term or construction belonging to the creole language and without equivalent elsewhere, principally in a situation of standard French elocution (the official language), which explains why the term had been long considered pejorative in a diglossic context constrained by the norm.

One may also speak of the "creolization" of a person, or of a civilization or culture, in the sense of naturalization, or of becoming autochthonous. This process consists of demonstrating the complete adaptation to the ongoing norms in the country. It is on this basis that certain researchers and thinkers have advanced the concept of "créolité," together with the constantly evolving values specific to the unification of identity in a vast American region revolving around the islands of the Caribbean basin, Louisiana, Brazil, and the Guyanas, and certain communities on the shores of Central America.

Bibliography:

Jacques de Cauna, *Haiti, The Eternal Revolution* (Monein, France: Éditions PyréMonde PRNG, 2009), Revised and updated edition of H. Deschamps, Port-au-Prince, 1997.

Robert Chaudenson, *Les Créoles* (Que Sais-je? 2970) (Paris: Presses Universitaires de France, 1995).

Moreau de Saint-Méry, Louis-Médéric-Elie, *Description of the French Part of the Isle of Saint-Domingue*, 2 vols. (Philadelphia, n.p., 1796–1797), re-edition Maurel, Blanche, et Taillemite, Étienne, *French Society of Overseas History*, 3 vols., 1958.

Images of Being, Places of the Imagination

Article by Edouard Glissant
with Comment by Olivier Douville

The following is the text from a presentation at a conference held at the Espace Analytique association in Paris in 2008. The conference was organized in collaboration with the psychoanalytic association Le Cercle Freudien by Olivier Douville and Patrick Bellamich, and the proceedings were published in Psychologie Clinique, 2008, No. 2.

Edouard Glissant:
I will begin with what I call and what is naïve thinking; naïve thinking, as opposed to what can be called scientific thinking. I will start with a sort of timid but resolute praise of naïve thinking. Of course, naïve thinking can lead to forms of what one would call anthropomorphism, that is to say that it ingenuously attempts, tries to bring what is real into the very model, the very structure of man. There is another form of naïve thinking that interests me; it is what I will call geomorphism, which aspires, through a contrary movement, to transport man's components to a poetic geography that exceeds man's structures while at the same time integrating them. The two movements—anthropomorphism or geomorphism—are contrary in their direction, but perhaps they deeply correspond to something more imperceptible, which is that man has a tendency to posit equivalence and solidarity between the movements of his being and the movements of the world.

This has always been the poet's ambition. We know that beginning from the moment when Plato defined the Laws of the city and banished its poets, it was in the name of pure reason, what we would later call scientific thinking, and at that moment he felt fear of the poets' dreadful ability to let themselves fall into the obscurity of myth and origin legends. By consequence, naïve thinking, which does not have a good reputation, is in fact a public form of this essential movement of poetic vindication, since Plato's banning, of the possibility of poetic consciousness.

Plato confined my poets to the expression of feelings, what we will later call "limited poetry (?)," limited to the expression of the sentiments of joy, suffering, love, hate, etc., to better forbid them the possibility of entering the realm of consciousness with a voice not initiated by Aristotle, but a voice of scientific consciousness—a voice that would be that of a poetic consciousness and that would in some way revisit Plato's fears, a consciousness of depth. He who says consciousness of depth also says that which becomes more and more obvious, particularly in the history of Western culture; that is to say that there is something there that is to be desired and that the ways of logic, and therefore science, do not allow us to really attain.

There is therefore, at the beginning of this movement—I remind you of what Claudel says in one of his great works, *The Muse . . . Grace*, he says: "And the poet responds: 'I am not a poet.'" "I am not a poet," that means "I am not a poet as Plato defines it. I am not a poet who is there to make you laugh or cry, or to amuse you; I am a poet who aspires to go into the depths of the abyss and develop the principles and seeds of another consciousness." All that belongs in theory to naïve thinking, and if I begin there, I think there are two phenomena there that interest me, namely that this thinking, which is not yet poetic thinking, which is not yet deep seeking, but which is already the refusal of certain thought frameworks, this thinking does not conceive, firstly, of absolute truth and that, secondly, this thinking does not conceive of a system of thought.

From the viewpoint of this naïve thinking, I would like to begin by trying to approach what these Western philosophies have called "Being and being."[1] Being appears as an absolute, as the unattainable and as a transcendence, the sublime. One must examine these characteristics if

---

1. From the German *Sein/Seiendes* and translated in French as *l'être/l'étant*.

one wants to speak of the possibility of characterizing Being. The absolute cannot be characterized and neither can transcendence. However one can designate these so-called characteristics as attributes of Being.

The second form of being (lower case) appears to be relative, or contrary to that which is true of Being: one can explore being. This being has territory; it has extension and area. More than Being, being has qualities. In effect, it is difficult to speak of the qualities of Being, but is it possible to speak of the qualities of being. So there I would like to—still from the viewpoint of naïve thought, consisting of both these dimensions conquered particularly but not only by Western thought—for Muslim mystics and for Buddhist mystics, there is this dimension of Being. There is an Islamic mystic who once considered Being as a scandal, and that is very interesting in relation to Heidegger's ideas on Being, which are concepts that are fixed and a bit limited. There is . . . in this relationship of Being and being, which was developed mainly by Western cultures. I would now like to introduce—and this is what interests me—the notion of borders.

It seems obvious that if, through a principle of geomorphism, we geographize being—we'll say it like that—it appears all of a sudden that we can easily introduce the notion of the border. Borders separate two states of being, like a real border separates two regions of the world or two communities in the world, etc. This notion of borders, in a completely insidious and surreptitious way, has inclined intellectual forms of the humanities toward the notion of system. A system is that which has two borders. In other words a system moves in one direction and does not consider the left or right border, does not consider that which is on either side of it; a system goes between two borders and by consequence defines an ambition that is, let us say, linear. This is a radical notion of borders because it defines at once what is the same and what is other; it defines, in an indivisible manner, that which separates choice and other. And in these conditions, Western thought has evolved in a linear manner that I believe is toward an idea that defines goals as sufficient in and of themselves, that is to say as placed on this line between two borders which moves the mind and makes it advance. What I propose is that this notion of borders is absolutely obsolete, and one can consider that after all these movements to advance thought, particularly in the West, the moment comes when borders are no longer air-tight and no longer even have a reason to exist, and that being is not a geographic territory delineated by borders, but that being is an inexplicable structure in perpetual revolution around itself that bypasses the notion of borders. Consequently, what were considered borders, as being—in this geomorphism that I practice—the very condition of being, we learn in the contemporary world—and we can say why and how—that it is no longer true and that borders, in this sense, have become a series of passages, a series of interspaces that are, comfortable or not, nevertheless surmountable.

On the other hand, the idea of borders does not at all apply to Being. Being has no borders; Being, in traditional conditions, is an absolute; Being is sublimity. Consequently, there is no border to Being. My claim is that if we continue to consider the notion of Being, there are borders in Being, that is to say that the absolute of Being is not one of them. Being, such as we have conceived it, implicates borders that we must define. All efforts of contemporary thought, across all kinds of manifestations for which we could establish a list—tarot, psychoanalysis, etc.—all these activities of the mind show that in its depths Being has borders. The difficulty of these activities is, firstly, to know how to find the borders and, secondly, to know how to cross them; and that the function of a border as an instrument of reflection and of work is to be able to cloak itself within the geo-poetics of being, while at the same time outlining the geopolitics of Being. I realize that this is a series of absolutely heretical affirmations, but I think that the situation of the humanities in the present day at least permits the formulation of a hypothesis in this area.

In other words, being, which today tends to perpetually expand—I saw yesterday that the expansion of the universe will stop and that we will arrive at a stasis in which the universe will stop expanding; these are the newest discoveries of physics. And so we will maintain equilibrium in that way, and perhaps we will begin to retract—one never knows—until we become the first molecule that the Big Bang gave to the universe. It is a formidable perspective, of course, but I think that we have billions of years ahead of us, surely. But it does not relax the mind to know that in ten billion years we will be reduced to the first molecule. But it does not

Images of Being, Places of the Imagination 181

prevent us from saying, in my geomorphism, that being tends to expand, and we can also say—from a perspective just as formidable, gloomy, and ghastly—that Being tends to narrow, because perhaps we will discover or experience, or in any case be conscious, even if it is not true, be conscious of experiencing that Being has internal borders, that borders of Being are internal while borders of being are external. The borders of Being are internal and consequently Being tends to narrow as being tends to expand. And here also is a formidable perspective. Will Being not reduce us again to a primordial molecule, and render hopeless our conditions for the exercise of thought?

All that, from the viewpoint of naïve thought. Do not take me to mean that I aspire to formulations—these formulations are hazardous, hypothetical, unsure of themselves, but they appear to me to be formulable from the standpoint of work, whatever the realm of that work may be. What does this mean? This means that, from the standpoint of Being, today we must undertake the passage from Being to the self, that is to say to the identical, and from the identical to identity itself. And we realize today that one of the fundamental principles of this exercise in the humanities rests on the question of identity, because it is through identity that we conceive of the identical, and that we can conceive of the self, and that we can conceive of Being. Being, in its formulation, has always been, not homeomorphic but anthropomorphic, and if we reflect carefully on the question of identity, we arrive perhaps at a plan for the famous rapport between Being and being that reformed an entire branch of thought.

Reflecting on the question of identity, I belong to a community which, contrary perhaps to Western communities and cultures, let us say in the majority of Europe, to a community whose identity has always been historically refuted. That is to say that the very principle of identity, from the beginning, was refuted as a principle, which poses a problem for the "shrink" who wants to try to analyze a Martiniquais or an Antillean. Reflecting upon this question of identity, I find that one of the calamities of colonial societies has always been to adopt, without critical reflection, the principles of identity driven by the colonizer, especially in countries which I call composite, that is, countries born from history itself.

Composite Society

These countries I characterize as composite societies because they have not procreated, invented, sparked, developed a genesis. These are the societies whose origins do not go back to a mythical time—we come back to Plato and his reproach of poets who concern themselves with myths and original depths. In composite societies—I belong to a composite society, a Caribbean creole society—origins do not go back to myth. I would say that we think of our composite societies as against atavistic societies, and I call them atavistic if they have created their own myth, or a genesis. It is well understood that composite societies can adopt the geneses of others, in the same way that they are colonized. For example, if I am Caribbean and Catholic, I will believe in Adam and Eve, etc.; I will adopt this genesis. But composite societies do not produce, do not create geneses because their origin is historical. I repeat all the time that the genesis of my culture is the belly of the slave ship; it is not an original paradise, etc.; it is the historical belly of the slave ships.

Consequently, what I rebuke in our societies is adopting without a critical view the very notion of the identity that the colonizers prescribed for us. Furthermore, the majority of anticolonial struggles were carried out in the name of these ideas. That is to say, why are anticolonial struggles most often catastrophic in their outcomes? It is because they are carried out in the name of the colonizers' ideas, and particularly the idea that identity, like Being, is an absolute, an aim in itself that belongs on that line I talked about, with borders on each side. We understand that very easily in Western societies—perhaps I will not delve into this illustration, this demonstration—that which constitutes identity is descendence by filiation and the total legitimacy of a genesis given by presence in a territory. I am absolutely authorized to possess a territory because I am absolutely linked through direct descendence to the very creation of this territory, or the very creation of this world. There are many variants because there are varied geneses in atavistic African societies, but we see the difference right away: lineage in African societies is completely permeable, meaning a foreigner can enter the ancestors' lineage; if he serves the community he can enter the line. This is not the same principle as in Western societies.

Also as an example, in Latin America, the Amerindians do not have an absolute genesis. The Aztec gods get it wrong three or four times before they successfully create man, and consequently the creation of the world is relative, which is not the case, for example, in the Bible or in the Old Testament in Genesis. This conception of identity, which is a conception that I call the "sole root"—I took it, of course you know, those who have read me know, that I adopted the image of Deleuze and Guattari who applied it not to identity but, largely (to enter into philosophical language), to categories of understanding, and who then applied this image to modes of thinking, while I applied it to modes of identity. And the "sole root" identity, which proceeds from an absolutely legitimate line of affiliation beginning at the genesis and ending in the present.

So, I juxtaposed this image of the "sole root" identity with the image of the "rhizome identity" or the relation-identity. This rhizome identity or relation-identity corresponds to the real situation in so-called composite cultures in relation to atavistic cultures, and it secondly leads to a new conception of both Being as being, and of being as it strives to become Being. Otherwise said, the great difference, the separation, the great hiatus between Being and being and between the absolute and the relative in Western cultures, seems to me not to work when applied to composite cultures.

On the other hand, it seems to me that in the current situation, if we want to analyze, or penetrate or attempt to understand human beings, which is of course never possible, as much for individuals but also for cultural participants and communities, it seems to me that ancient atavistic cultures tend to become composites. That is to say that belief in the extraordinary force, the imperative and absolute affiliation with the original myth diminishes, to the extent that in the present world, what I call the present chaos-world, the geneses mix. For example, it is an irrefutable observation that there are thousands of religious sects in the world and that the principle of these religious sects is that they mix their geneses and we arrive at absolutely incredible situations. There are—I saw them every day in New York on the way to university—a sect of black people who say that they are the only Jews in the world, that the others are imposters, that Jesus Christ was a black Jew. What is that?

They took a part of the Christian Genesis, a part of the Jewish Genesis and then they mixed it. And that we cannot prevent because all the conditions were united so that they mixed together. Consequently, that poses undoubtable problems for the analyst. Sorry for telling you that.

So, there is this fundamental problem that the question of identity is not only one question—it is both a political question and a poetic question. It is a poetic question insofar as poetics attempt a consciousness of depth, and we see today that we can approach nearer to this consciousness of depth, by abandoning the systems of ideas and/or ideas of systems. And I summarized this new way by saying that Being is closer to intuition and creates images, and that being is closer to the imaginary and creates place. What I have left to say to you is to try to see what are this image and this place.

The image that creates the approach to Being is the very sign of the intelligibility of the relation. I call relation that which I relay, reconnect, and relate all the elements of the world, not leaving out one. In other words, the relation that is the realized quantity of all the differends in the world, thus absolutely opposes the universal, the realized quality of an absolute in the world. It seems to me that today, relation is what serves as our bridge, our passage, our ford between all the differends in the world, whereas the universal, yesterday still, tried to abstract all the differends of the world in an absolute truth that joins truth and Being.

Relation

I call place that which in this relation and in the relation of all the differends of the world cannot be circumvented, meaning that through place we understand that relation is never a dilution, it is never a soup in which everything melts together and dissolves, it is never a kind of hodgepodge where only God can find his own. The relation conceived by the imagination is founded on all possible places in the world. Place is inescapable. That means that one cannot ignore or pass through it, but neither can one go around it, because if one goes around it, one encloses it and this enclosed place does not enter into relation. That may seem to you a bit systematic as a system, although I maintain that we must beware of thinking about systems and systems of thought.

Images of Being, Places of the Imagination 185

However, it is not systematic because what unifies and differentiates all these differends in their relation is what I call the inextricable, the poetics of relation that gives us knowledge of relation, not scientific thinking. So it would behoove us to renounce the idea that we could, by intuition of Being or by the imagination of being, by the foundation of image or the foundation of place, arrive at an absolute and definitive truth that would hold us to a beacon, a line, a viewpoint and a focal point, etc. Places are founded in the inextricable of the world; the world is inextricable.

The qualities of Being as being, and the qualities of being as Being in this inextricable can be described in three words: opacity, trembling, and trace. Opacity is not the obscure; opacity is that which a place affixes to another place through the freedom of its relation to that place. In this sense, I reclaim for one and all the right to opacity—a dubious perspective for a psychoanalyst. I demand for all the right to opacity, and I say that this attempted transparency of truth, that we have strived for since the time of Plato, is precisely what prevents us from seeing that links to the inextricable are fruitful and not paralyzing. It is not because there is an inextricable that we are tied and paralyzed. We can return to this question of opacity later on in the discussion if you find it necessary.

The thought of trembling, that is what seems to me to characterize the process of approaching the inextricable in the world; trembling is not fear; trembling is not hesitation; trembling is not incertitude erected in phantasm. Trembling is the deliberate vocation of renouncing the systematic view and the consecutive view and the equational development on a line, on a linear principle such as physicists and chaos sciences would say. Well, trembling is the intuition of depth, that is to say the intuition that there is something in both anthropomorphism and geomorphism that is not to be rejected, not to be criticized systematically, and that makes possible all sorts of intuitions, connections, and contacts that allow us to move around in the inextricable of the world and in this composite of the world. It consists of moving around in the composite of the world and no longer in the atavism of the world.

And finally, trace: this allows trembling to advance. I developed the idea of trace thinking. Why? Because of our cultures in the composite countries, I use them as an example, but I do not give them as a model. No one in the world today has the right to propose models to others. The model no longer exists as such. But trace is what allows us to advance. For example, the creole cultures of the Americas have advanced through trace. Why? Because they are the countries where the essential is the population—whether it came from Africa or the Indies, but especially Africa—the population arrived naked, meaning having lost the use of their language, their gods, their usual objects, their customs, etc., and it was necessary, for the Antilleans, for example, to recompose the desolate savannas of memory with traces of what remained of the old culture, and atavistic culture. Black, sub-Saharan African cultures are atavistic cultures. But I showed you the difference that there was between this atavism and the Western atavisms. They had to reconstruct it by traces. American jazz is a trace, meaning it took black Americans in the southern United States recomposing the traces of the very founding of African rhythm. They did not arrive with African songs, like the Irish arrived in the United States with Irish songs, the Italians with their Italian songs, the Scottish with theirs that they sing at marriages, burials, baptisms, etc. The Africans arrived naked. They were skinned of everything in the belly of the slave ship. Consequently, they had to recompose the traces of the bases of African culture and associate that with a phenomenon of colonization by using Western musical instruments—piano, saxophone, trumpet, trombone, etc. They created a valid music for everyone, a music that was no longer valid just for them but for everyone because it was a creolized music. The creole languages of Martinique, Guadeloupe, Haiti, and Guyana were made with traces. When the slaves fled the plantations, in the forest or in the mountains, they had traces, but the traces were sufficiently light, firstly so as to not harm the forest, and secondly so as to not be found by their pursuers and so that only they could find each other. Consequently, the habit of proceeding by traces is an extremely fruitful habit, and I would say that Western cultures are also starting to proceed by traces. We can prove, with examples of music and in other areas as well, like literary structures, we can prove that there is this phenomenon of traces that opposes systematic thinking and ideas of systems, and it better corresponds to the present situation of the humanities in the world.

Images of Being, Places of the Imagination

Olivier Douville:

Thank you so much for agreeing to this meeting, which has had aspects that I do not hesitate to qualify as impressive in terms of our thinking habits.... Edouard Glissant, I was very touched by all that you expressed; I would like to articulate two or three points.

Firstly, I believe that you are decisively renewing enunciation as a form of political thought. I will explain it in this way: I go to Africa frequently, I sometimes go to the Antilles and effectively I have always been surprised, perhaps a bit troubled with each visit by the emphasis on the theme of dignity that accompanies the theme of identity. So much that, at the same time, I see men, women, many young people of these societies, who all while claiming an identity—which, after all, cope with a difficult situation when they feel mistreated—contribute to what you call rhizomes, and what I myself would call "forms of digression," forms and processes that often permit the emergence of a new way of representing one's affiliation, body, voice, and presence—ways of representing themselves and also presenting the other.

I find it, for my part, extremely important that you have at the end of your presentation emphasized music. It seems to me that for the history of these musical styles, the least of which we can say have had a decisive effect on the sonorous aesthetic of our age, the relationship to memory is something completely surprising for someone who would content themselves with musicographical reconnaissance. The memory of the body in this music is umbilical, surrounding an immemorial of voice, of rhythm, just as jazz is always spiraling around blues and gospel. It seems to me that beyond what we can call *jazz*, this insolent term that is now a buzzword for selling albums or arrangements and collections, rustles and affirms the effective participation of imagination and aesthetic creation. If it results in the creation of traces or indicates another relationship to sensibility, memory, the body and the very structures of exchange, it is preferable to that which prescribes a credo of identity that is too rigid. Jazz is like a ferry that produces and propels events, that carries out the internal laws of the history of the people who make it while at the same time creating new possibilities. By internal law I mean not only the constraints of an aesthetic code, but a regime of bodily resistance, a regime that produces bodies of truth that do not allow themselves to be reduced to historical conditions of servitude or exclusion. I will close this jazz parenthesis here, which I am a bit enamored of, and I will return to you and your texts.

I would like to now say that certain works of yours—not all, of course—but *Le discours antillais*, *Le quatrième siècle*, and your last book, *La Cohée du Lamentin*—are books that have frequently accompanied me while listening to these subjects, without deliberately wanting them to. I currently receive patients from these composite societies, as you call them, and I will try to say and explain something about it, because after all, it is here where there would perhaps be, according to you—and I think it is right—something decisive and unavoidable. For example, take the question: "What is negation"? Negation is something that is obviously foundational for identity, because if there is a border, there is division. I am A, and I am not Not-A. It appears to psychoanalysts who are aided by the ferrymen of memory in an open present, that negation is not simply a logical operation; it is equally a historical operation. That is to say, colonial systems are—and we all know it—built upon a drastic form of negating the other, and they have operated a universal negation, in the very name of universality.

For example, the universality of rights should concern everyone beyond their particular situation. The colonial situation is such that rights are not for everyone. This is the judicial discourse founded on universal reason that excludes some humans who are involved in universal ambition, in universality—the same for any "apartheid." But I would also say that for the plan of resistance, negation is very important. It is no longer a denial of the human condition of the other, but a strategy of refusal or of returning meaning to the colonial other, an opening in monolingualism. For the most part, both in doing historical research—for which I am far from an expert—and in hearing these analysts, it seems to me that societies marked by colonial violence are also marked by eminent gestures of refusing colonial violence. We know you to be one of the first, if not the first, persons to have made an archetype of the "black maroon" figure, an insurgent fleeing slavery. I'm referring to the *Mawon* review from the Center for Cooperative Research and Caribbean-Guyana-Reunion Studies launched a few years ago by Jean Galap, Lyne Lyrus, Hughes Liborel-Pochot, and myself. Today, another strategy of negation could be the evasion of indirection, a play on codes that is very intense in its relationship to "foreigners." It is a disconcerting means that places little on assignation, but much on ways of subverting codes, the conventional means of presenting and representing oneself. These are the societies that have capitalized on hybrid input, marked by violence, trauma, dread, but also enchantments; the variation of the self and the motif of the other become tangled in undecipherable modalities in which space and time return. If this rhizome identity is no more than an exotic, transitory stasis, a decorative mixing possesses in itself a formidable power to transmit the past, to displace sleeping ancestors, stripped from our present and returned to a memory which, far from resembling eternal renewal, must be constantly realized anew.

Anthenor Firmin (1850-1911).
Archives of Cidihca, Montréal, Québec

Is Creolization a Philosophy of History? The Colonial History of the Antilles, Globalization and "Globality"

Edelyn Dorismond

There are many reasons that gleaning a unitary conception of history from the work of Édouard Glissant is a great challenge. Firstly, Glissant adopts a very critical stance toward what he designates "History," meaning Occidental history in particular, whose full form is characterized by the Hegelian philosophy of history in which reason unfolds linearly toward an absolute finality and its own completion: absolute Reason. Thinking of history according to the logic of a philosophy of history sheds light on the reasons why non-western or non-European societies are considered as peripheral, and in all likelihood, as non-history.

Secondly, Glissant considers that Antillean—and particularly Martiniquais—societies do not have a history since theirs is nothing more than the "development of a neurosis."[1] Yet, from a psychoanalytic point of view, neurosis brings about history's impossible culmination from an obstructed narration in the realm of the "unexplored, on whose shores we wander, wide-awake."[2] A paradox is already imposed at this stage, where the non-history of Antillean societies is clarified in relation to European History. Non-history is thus understood as being the act of developing a historicity in History's margins, or even as being an objectified effect of this History. However, it is this same objectified history that could be

---

1. Édouard Glissant, *Antillean Discourse* (Paris, Gallimard, 1997), 229.

2. Ibid.

considered as the advent of a form of historicity that thwarts the cavalier European version. We are faced with histories that, provoked by History, have come to proclaim new forms of historicity that put together a historical framework of the current world, a creolized world. So, instead of living in a world carried by History that enlists all societies on the periphery of the western world, we observe constant attempts to evade this linear historicity that is indifferent to difference, benefitting from a heterogenization of histories whose proliferations are profusely intertwined. Seen from this angle, we can characterize creolization by the diversification and establishment of world histories, giving rise to a dense history in which geography is grasped by diverse historical logics.

Arriving at this stage in world history, we should say that universal history, the one whose philosophy inherited fundamental structure, no longer has the attributes of unity, linearity, or foreseen, precise finality. Henceforth, it is distinguished by other attributes, none of which remove its global vision of world operations. However, we must admit that a vision of the world proposed by creolization appeals to other attributes: diversity, the curved line that coordinates the heterogeneous interlacings of histories, and the unpredictability that underscores the impossibility of knowing what will come at the end of time.

According to this last consideration, the plurality of these histories hinders the goal of unification, domination, and exploitation of colonial societies and leads toward a philosophy of history, or a unitary vision of world history. This process risks provoking a number of reactions in favor of creole-oriented thought, which appear as a contemporary effort against universalism, or oneness-oriented thought. Contrary to this exalted notion of creolization, we maintain the position that creolization remains a notion of globalized history, even if it shares the diversifying effects of European or western History, which, by its centralist dynamic, paradoxically gave birth to the societies that are considered "without history" because of their social and political organizations that differ from Europeans' and because of the real consequences of domination, slavery, colonialism, etc. The irony of history: these societies are gradually given the freedom to invent their own history, which, according to Glissant, is opposed to "History." Colonial histories seem to take their revenge in provoking a new theory and a new "region" of the world, made up of diverse histories that, in their ascent, force History to shed its murderous arrogance. The name of this new region is creolization, where "memories" and "histories" are connected; the world then has a new historical logic: examining relationships between different and diverse histories. It would be a poor judgment not to see a reinterpretation of the philosophy of history in this dynamic of "multiplicity" and "opacity."

We must refer to creolization as a philosophy of history. To accomplish this, we must take into account the internal coherence of Glissant's works that claim to be a critique of universalism for the benefit of the notion of "diversality." Furthermore, if thinking of history as heterogenic dynamic seems to break with the progression of "reason in history," it is important to question the philosophical status of this logic of differentiation with which histories constantly stamp out the possibility of bringing about the anticipated finality. Additionally, it is not impertinent to ask whether these interlacing histories follow a logic that is itself unifying. Admitting that it is impossible to know the future, Glissant's masterstroke banishes failure from his line of reasoning. Finally, we should adopt the position that creolization leads to the unknown, as a teleological principle that conceals the eschatology that Glissant either did not know or did not want to assume: a cosmic maelstrom that recovers blurred origins as recounted in *The Philosophy of Relation*.[3]

Glissant's Notions of "History" and "histories"

"*Where histories converge, History ends.*"[4] This sentence contains a theoretical position that will be taken up in *Caribbean Discourse*.[5] Glissant traces the red line that guides his theory of history, understood with a sense of the tension between "History" and "histories"; but this philosophical and epistemological premise also feeds his critique of Occidental History, to the benefit of the histories that are scattered in the periphery. Thus we insistently return to this tension that seems to drive away at the necessity to dismiss History, taking into account the actual existence of histories,

---

3. Édouard Glissant, *La Philosophie de la relation* (Paris, Gallimard, 2009), 11–15.

4. Édouard Glissant, *L'Intention poétique* (Paris, Éditions du Seuil, 1969), 215.

5. Ibid., 227.

even when they run the risk of not being fully developed histories. In any case, Glissant considers Antillean societies to be on the side of non-history, particularly Martiniquais society. However, this non-history, this absence of historical consciousness can be reabsorbed into the critique of History, whose objective consists of appropriating conscious control of "dispossession" that hinders its "return"—"the first urge of a transplanted society, which is not sure of maintaining in its place of transfer the old order of its values. Return is the obsession of the one."[6] The historical reason is that Antillean societies were taken by Europe's, or the West's civilizing dynamic, which are based on the notion of being. If we return to the classical equation of being and one, as it is proposed by Parmenides and taken up by Plato in *Sophist*, his treatise on being, we can clarify Glissant's proposition, considering that European History maintains an ontological equation that is not without consequences for the future of Antillean societies.

Politics will not be hampered any less in the traps of such an ontology. History, driven by the politics that it in turn feeds, is informed by ontology, the notion of oneness, the politics of being, and allows itself to be apprehended by the phenomena of slavery and colonization.

Truthfully, without invalidating the idea of ontology as a condition of history, it would be preferable to hypothesize that Christian theology, corresponding to Greek ontologies—Aristotelian, Platonist, or Stoic—nourishes a theology of history carried by the coming of the kingdom of God that the Christian must carry out. In effect, this theology contains a notion of a hierarchy of being that places the European Christian at the top. This onto-theology, as Heidegger would say, represents the wellspring of what would become slavery, colonization, in short, the European international relations that instituted this hierarchy of cultures and cultural practices. Orality, myths, and societal ways of life that are not "Euro-Christian" are qualified as inferior under this onto-theology, this confusion of God and being, this view of history as God's way of coming to Earth in his fullness.[7] In some way, this is what Glissant wants to identify. For him, western

---

6. Édouard Glissant, *Le Discours antillais, op. cit.,* 44.

7. We are borrowing this expression to demonstrate the cultural and religious complex of the European Christian in Dominique Deslandres's work on "seventeenth century French missions in France and in the colonies." Dominique Deslandres, *Croire et faire croire. Les missions françaises au XVIIe (1600–1605)* (Paris: Fayard, 2003).

Is Creolization a Philosophy of History? 195

societies are fed by the "ambition of being, that defines transparent models of humanity, and that organizes the scales of rising to humanity." This ambition, "tied to the appearance of the sign, particularly the written sign,"[8] leads to the rejection of oral forms of expression.

The philosophy of history inspired by Christian theology produces other effects than the disregard of orality: it creates a duality, giving being to Christians and non-being to non-Euro-Christians.[9] Such a dualist discourse penetrates societies according to criteria of "civilization" and "barbarism," and justifies uprooting, colonization (appropriation of others' lands), and slavery (appropriation of others' bodies) as a "natural" ascent of these cultures toward civilization, Christianity, and being.[10]

Western history presents several attributes by which it becomes easy to ascribe a more or less satisfying intelligibility. We will consider three of them: the characteristic of the philosophy of one and being that gives it its metaphysical foundation that Nietzsche, Heidegger, and Derrida sought to "deconstruct," and of which postmodernism insists on showing the inoperability, seeing as it hinders—as much as it is itself hindered by—a taking charge of particularities and produces murderous effects carried out in the name of essences and absolutes that are today becoming obsolete. In this sense, Glissant is a figure who cannot be left out of this critique of the great accounts that characterize theologies and philosophies of "Euro-Christian" history. His critique of History (capital H) proceeds from this deconstruction.

Next, it becomes necessary to identify politics of expropriation and of exploitation supported by the philosophical legitimization of the domination of other attributes of this history that imposed itself on the world in the name of a teleological vision of salvation. Dominating other cultures makes sense in this generalized ecology and expands in the process of wrenching these societies from the reign of nature. This is what all the fields of western knowledge are yoked to, from literature to history and

---

8. Édouard Glissant, *Écrire la "parole de nuit." La nouvelle littérature antillaise* (Paris: Gallimard, 1994), 112.

9. Let us clarify that the Haitian Creole retains this confusion of "Christian" as man differentiated from animal. A "Christian" in the deepest sense of Haitian Creole is a man.

10. In a poetic and arresting manner, Glissant exposes the "chasm" experienced by "transshipped" Africans. Édouard Glissant, *Poétique de la relation* (Paris, Gallimard, 1990), 17–21.

philosophy: "the ambiguity is that Literature and History are at the same time proposed, in the West, to act as Totality (wrapping primitive linearity in globality), but in this supposed Totality is inserted the unheard-of ambition of animating man with a western image, with degrees of elevation, from Caliban to Prospero."[11]

Finally, exteriorization and identification represent European policies' anticipated effects. Placing societies at a distance, thinking of them as foreign and outside of Europe favors everything that was forbidden within Europe: warring among Christians, making war for rights of commerce or asylum, etc. Also, this concept of just war (Francisco de Vitoria), was upheld in the name of Christian, European being that must be spread to the four corners of the earth: conversion and evangelizing are procedures of identification and alienation by which, scorning native cultures, identification is made on European cultural terms.[12] This is the tension between action and ideal. Action, always finding itself in a different phase than the norm or the ideal, persists in realizing the evil exploit that we, with Glissant, name "dispossession." Because in fact colonization and assimilation have resulted in West Indians who have no consciousness of their history, and who conceive of themselves as outside of history.

Such is the general apparatus of western civilization that Glissant proposes we put to the test, firstly by recognizing that it itself creates an exteriority that embodies other logics. It starts with orality, which from the "kingdom of existing, the extant," to the contact between the written and being, leads to "our eruption of modernity."[13] Here modernity must be understood in a new sense, if we admit that western modernity quarantines non-European cultures' orality in favor of writing.

Indeed, the eruption in modernity can be understood as a way of overthrowing European dominance, or the preeminence of writing as it happens to be in this case. The "chaos-world" will be a new configuration of the world in the context of returning "histories" to "History," a per-version of the unitary logic of modern rationality by an opaque and diversified

---

11. Édouard Glissant, *Le Discours antillais*, op. cit., 242–43.

12. See Dominique Deslandres's work cited above (note 7) in which he exposes missionaries' methods of tenaciously evangelizing "pagans."

13. Édouard Glissant, *Écrire la "parole de nuit,"* op. cit, 113, 117.

rationality. In reality, the principal approach to undertaking the invention of a "new region of the world" consists of dismissing a "general idea of science"—even the "general idea" itself—so as to break down the interstices of the great "Euro-Christian" accounts and give free reign to oral practices and diverse histories. Thus, "our diversified histories in the Caribbean today produce another unveiling: that of their underground convergence. In doing so, they inform us of a dimension that is unsuspected because it is too evident in human actions: transversality. The eruption of Antillean history (the converging history of our people) clears us of the linear and hierarchical vision of a History that has run its course."[14] The history of Caribbean peoples, or of other regions in the world, permits the invention of a new temporality, like orality permits us to create another relationship to writing, by which writing can be made to tremble: "we have a conception of spiraling time that does not correspond to the linear time of Westerners, nor the circular time of pre-Columbian peoples or Asian philosophies, but which is in a sense a result of both, that is to say, a circular movement, but always with a means of escaping this circularity toward something else—this is what constitutes the spiral."[15] In place of History's linearity and transparency, histories spark "transversality," "spiral," and "opacity."

To better understand this new configuration of world history made by "histories" constantly defeating "History," it is necessary to come back to one of Glissant's formulas, especially concerning colonial, assimilationist, and Caribbean histories, but also the histories of all world societies that are being shifted by their citizens. The "world is becoming creolized." In other words, the logic of transversality, made up of spiraling and opacity, is winning the world by becoming its own historic structure. We are moving from a specific historicity of Caribbean societies to a "universal" historicity, as in the "universal" history explored by medieval chroniclers or by Bossuet, Kant, Schiller, and Hegel: it acted as a universal history from a cosmo-political (global politics) standpoint, as a global vision of Providence's or Reason's march, giving sense and meaning to isolated incidents, which politics were supposed to relay.[16]

14. Édouard Glissant, *Le Discours antillais, op. cit.*, 230.
15. Édouard Glissant, *Écrire la "parole de nuit," op. cit.*, 123.
16. Emmanuel Kant, *Idée d'une histoire universelle au point de vue cosmopolitique* (Paris:

And that's right, yes, because you have to put everything together at the same time. The splintered, heaped, swarmed aesthetics designate totality. There, arranging everything on the same scale, the offensive histories whose veils need to be lifted, and the unknown countries that we suddenly revere and whose genres we patronize, particularly the presque-isles and the rocks that are introductions to islands and archipelagoes, but equally to continents, and the continents themselves which continue in quitting the straight and triumphant path of their old dominations to enter into the muddled pleasures of multiplicity and sharing, and this very disorder is not the announcement of diluting or partitioning the self, yet the not guaranteed assurance that the definitive and systematic truths of yesterday are gangrenous to the humanities, and this or that problem of diversity or praise of countries does not remove religion or dissipating beliefs, and the muscular efforts and great organisms of the All-World, like a great, stiffening body moves to delude justice and equity between peoples.[17]

Such is the new plan of the All-World that represents the "new region of the world," the new configuration of the world in which "multiplicity" serves as unity, "murkiness" to "transparency," with an eye to "progress" that must be understood in the sense of augmenting "justice and equity between peoples."[18] That being said, we are obviously in the presence of a global vision of history whose characteristics consist of replacing the generalized economy of unity, transparence, linear history, and surface geography with a historical transversality marked by opacity, multiplicity, and geographic interlacings in the direction of an energetic organicism.

Ellipse, 2011); Friedrich Schiller, *Qu'est-ce que l'histoire universelle et pourquoi l'étudie-t-on ?* Available online at http://www.larecherchedubonheur.com/article-3724848.html; Friedrich Hegel, *La Philosophie de l'histoire* (Paris: Livre de Poche [La Pochothèque], 2009), *La raison dans l'Histoire*, Éditions 10/18, 1965.

17. Édouard Glissant, *Une Nouvelle Région du monde* (Paris: Gallimard, 2006), 158.

18. "And I am sure that one day, in the crashing of cultures, the humanities' sensibility will be such that we will learn to appreciate cultures, or literary and artistic works not as a function of the comprehension we would have gained, but as a function of the effect on their own sensibility, and the opacity of these cultures or artworks. In other words, I am sure that the humanities will reach a point where we can better appreciate opacities just as much as we understand transparencies. And that would be an immense *progress*." (Emphasis added) Édouard Glissant, "Le chaos-monde, l'oral et l'écrit," in *Écrire la "parole de nuit," La nouvelle littérature antillaise* (Paris: Gallimard, 1994), 127.

We recognize that our position would need further argument to justify it in regards to the joyous reception given to notions of creolization. However, the space we were given in this article permits us only to outline this question that we will inevitably undertake in the development of other studies. Here it was a question of sketching aspects of a philosophy of history that contains notions of creolization.

If we cannot avoid recognizing the strength of certain positions put forward by Glissant, who attempted to decentralize European History by pointing out its reifying power, and, paradoxically, the fact of giving birth to objectified histories that learned to reverse the heterogenizing relations to a chaos-world, a chaos history, as it is deplored by some and exalted by others, we have shown the necessity of resisting the charm of notions of creolization that would hinder the process of emancipation in the straight line of notions of "globalization." So it is more to a contradiction of Glissants works, which proceed from a critique of History, western rationale, linearity, transparence of the self, unity, etc. to the benefit of an aesthetic and a poetic of opacity and multiplicity, that we call attention. This aspect will receive ample attention in later works.[19]

If we can present creolization as an attempt to read the history of Europe or the West from a viewpoint that emphasizes aspects of exploitation, objectification, and seeing non-European cultures as exterior, this project must not be seen simply as corrective and critical posturing toward a civilization that denied humanity to exotic cultures; it must also be shown—what we have attempted here—that creolization can elicit a conception of history that redirects the denial of differences as a condition of globality. For this, it is necessary to create a distinction between globality and globalization, considering that the two go together, and that globality is a modality of globalization. At this stage, it is less a question of thinking that globality will resist globalization, and more a question of showing the ways in which creolization represents a philosophical frame for understanding the historical and cultural dynamic of globalization, understood as fluxes in encounters and relationships.

Another question presents itself concerning the pertinence of a historical Caribbean scheme that becomes the measure of explaining the order

---

19. See Edelyn Dorismond, "*Comment Deleuze et Derrida voyagent dans la pensée glissantienne de la créolisation*," Rue Descartes, 2013:2n78, 34–47.

of the world, the chaos-world. How can the history of Caribbean societies include the history of the world? It is inevitably necessary to explain how colonial experiences of slavery contribute to the explanation of the development of so-called advanced capitalism. The fusion of Caribbean history and world history is not obvious. It should once more be shown how the Caribbean integrates the order of the world from which it was excluded, as an exterior colonial space of slave exploitation and mercantilism. As for this exclusion of the Caribbean from European history, we cannot only postulate the possibility of the perversion of the history of the world, it is further necessary to justify going from a creolization of the Caribbean to a creolization of the world. From the very start, this would entail explaining the phrase "the world is becoming creolized."

If this theoretical assumption leads us toward a universal conception of history, one in which post-slavery Caribbean societies become the setting for interpreting the general dynamic of world history, we are, consequently, in the presence of a universal vision marked by opacity, wandering, multiplicity, and of the imaginary in place of politics, transparency, and unity. We have considered that such a vision of history updates the old philosophies of history in bringing to them the rectifications tied to the structures of so-called diversified societies: a systematic view of history that begins with a historical experience toward a finality, which determines the meaning, orientation, and significance of the world's course. Therefore, it is not without pertinence to consider notions of creolization, as much as they proceed toward the poetic theming of relations as a modality of being in the time and space of the contemporary world, characterized by meetings and sharing, as a systematic vision of human actions and things of the world.

Finally, our particular preoccupation was to suggest that a certain criticism of occidental universalism is not spared the renewal of universalism, even diversal. The notion of creolization that claims to be above all a criticism of universalism and the forms of domination that it instituted is caught in the trap of all criticism, in that it is processed in the very terms of the object it critiques. In this sense, the lesson that this work invites meditation upon is a strategy of putting in place the deconstruction of universalism, all while refusing to reinvent a predatory universalism. How will post-slavery Caribbean societies advance without drowning in the great river of the History of the world? How can we conceptualize Caribbean societies as "not on the side of" the enslaving universalism of western capitalism? This will be the question with which all rereading of universal History must begin.

Louis-Joseph Janvier (1855-1911)
Archives of Cidihca, Montréal, Québec

Creolization: Some Observations

Carlo A. Celius

As widespread as the idea of creolization is, it still provokes numerous enquiries. Some questions persist on its scope and its limits,[1] as can be witnessed by the most recent publications, that evaluate the extent of these debates.[2] Here I would like to make a few brief observations in the margin of these discussions.

The Shadow of Glissant

Edouard Glissant is certainly one of the principal theorists of creolization. Certain authors refer only to him or discuss only his propositions when approaching the question. His reflections undeniably constitute a decisive moment, but the issue of creolization has been studied over the course of a long development in disciplines as far-ranging as anthropology,

---

1. This was the subject of a previous personal reflection. See Carlo A. Célius, "La créolisation: Portée et limites d'un concept," in Sélim Abou and Katia Haddad, eds., *Universalisation et différenciation des modèles culturels* (Montréal/Beyrouth: AUPELF,UREF/Université Saint-Joseph, "Universités Francophones: Actualité scientifique," 1999), 49–95. The text is available online on the AUF's site. For this same perspective, I organized an international colloquium in 2004 at the University of Quebec in Montreal. See Carlo A. Célius, ed., *Situations créoles: Pratiques et représentations* (Québec: Éditions Nota Bene, collection "Société," 2006). For a more recent contribution see Carlo A. Célius, "Créolité et bossalité en Haïti selon Gérard Barthélemy," *L'Homme*, 207–8 (2013): 313–32.

2. Among the most recent French language publications are Alain Ménil, *Les voies de la créolisation: Essai sur Édouard Glissant*, De l'incidence éditeur, 2011; *Archipélies*, 3–4 (2012): "De la créolisation culturelle"; *Revue des sciences humaines*, 309:1 (2013): "Entours d'Édouard Glissant"; *L'Homme*, 207–8 (2013): "Un miracle créole ?"; Edelyn Dorismond, *L'ère du métisssage. Variations sur la créolisation politique, éthique et philosophie de la diversité* (Paris: Anibwé, 2013); ibid., "Comment Deleuze et Derrida voyagent dans la pensée glissantienne de la créolisation," *Rue Descartes*, Collège international de philosophie, 78:2 (2013): 34–47.

linguistics (creolization is a central notion of creolistics), sociology and history. A definition, still considered current, was proposed in 1884 at a meeting of the Anthropological Society of Paris, during which the Haitian intellectual Louis Joseph Janvier offered his contribution.[3] We make note of an English language reference in a 1928 letter addressed to the American anthropologist Melville J. Herskovits, sent by Joonker L. C. Van Panhuys, a researcher from the Netherlands, where the word may have become fashionable.[4] During the 1950s and 60s the idea became the focus of anthropologists' and linguists' reflections, most particularly during two international conferences on creole languages in Mona, Jamaica, in 1959 and 1968.[5] Glissant, who rarely cites works on the subject that predate him, began to really take an interest in the early 1990s, after having thematized antillanité.[6] Even the idea, so dear to Glissant, according to which the world has become creolized, was advanced by Ulf Hannerz in a 1987 publication.[7]

When we look closely, it is clear that Glissant began to think of creolization in reaction to *créolité*. Jean Barnabé, Patrick Chamoiseau, and Raphaël Confiant published *In Praise of Creoleness* in 1988.[8] If they recognize in this work their debt to Glissant, if they apply themselves to his analyses, they nonetheless intend to move beyond his notion of *antillanité*, which seems too restrained, confined to a geographic horizon, having above all a geopolitical scope. It is undoubtedly to this that Glissant reacted, and rightly so, so that the new literary movement would not bypass him. He in turn

---

3. Armand de Quatrefages, "Observations relatives à l'action exercée par le milieu américain sur les races de l'ancien continent," *Bulletins de la Société d'anthropologie de Paris*, series 3, vol. 7, fasc. 1–4, 579–85. The *Society*'s discussions of the idea are reported and commented upon by Jean Benoist in "La créolisation: locale ou mondiale ?" *Archipélies*, 3–4 (2012), 19–30, and by Jean-Luc Bonniol in "Au prisme de la créolisation. Tentative d'épuisement d'un concept," *L'Homme*, 207–8 (2013), 237–88.

4. Richard Price, "Créolisation et historicité," *L'Homme*, 207–8, 2013, 289.

5. Carlo A. Célius, "La créolisation: Portée et limites d'un concept," *op cit.*

6. Cf. Édouard Glissant, *Le Discours antillais* (Paris, Gallimard, "Folio/essais," [1981], 1997); *Poétique de la relation* Poétique III (Paris, Gallimard, 1990).

7. Ulf Hannerz, "World in creolization," *Africa*, 57, 4, 1987, 546–59.

8. Jean Bernabé, Patrick Chamoiseau, and Raphaël Confiant, *Éloge de la créolité* [1988]/ *In Praise of Creoleness* (Paris: Gallimard, 1993). This work is a continuation of a previous publication: GEREC, *Charte culturelle créole: Se pwan douvan avan douvan pwan non!* (Fort-de-France, 1982).

critiques the notion of *créolité*, pointing out the fixed nature of the flexional ending "ity" (this would be a "regression" toward identity, a search for essence), with which he contrasts a procedural approach that is meant to render the notion of creolization, one that he certainly supports with force, but not without tension, contradictions, often inextricable "entanglements," "opacity," to its maximum extent. Often commentators on his work in the moment when he addresses the notion, tend to reduce the entirety of his approach to the perspective of creolization. However, it should be noted that this treatment is linked to an inflection in his thought. This is far from insignificant because, according to Peter Hallward and Chris Bongie, it is equivalent to a veritable depoliticization of this thinking.[9] From Dominique Chancé's perspective, this is a passage from anthropology to aesthetics. She explains:

> The latest essays certainly do not fail to remind us of 'suffering, massacres, famines, epidemics, the exhaustion and the binding of so many peoples and so many individuals,' enumerated, but we are called upon to 'enter into a new region of the world' and to conceive of another relation. ... From this point of view, writing continues to spare a sort of diagnostic space, a sort of overwhelming reality of the world (one of globalization, conquest and oppression), all while breaking through a threshold. Here the writer executes a veritable epistemological leap, ceasing to describe, analyze, or detail the process of creolization. Glissantian creolization therefore ceases to be an anthropology.[10]

---

9. Peter Hallward, *Absolutely Postcolonial: Writing Between the Singular and the Specific* (Manchester, U.K.: Manchester University Press, 2001); Chris Bongie, *Friends and Enemies: The Scribal Politics of Post/Colonial* (Liverpool: Liverpool University Press, 2008). See Celia Britton's contrary viewpoint, "Globalization and Political Action in the Work of Edouard Glissant," *Small Axe* 20 (November 2009) 1-11. See articles by Nick Nesbitt, Celia Britton, H. Adlai Murdoch, and Cilas Kemedjio in *Revue des sciences humaines* 309:1 (2013). "Entours d'Édouard Glissant," addresses the political dimensions of Edouard Glissant's ideas. Christine Chivallon envisions creolization as "the invention of a new relationship to power." This necessitates "a distancing from Edouard Glissant's perspective," which, she says, "brings nothing to the enrichment that it continues to dispense." Christine Chivallon, "Créolisation universelle ou singulière ? Perspectives depuis le Nouveau Monde," *L'Homme* 207-8 (2013), 64.

10. Dominique Chancé, "Edouard Glissant, de l'anthropologie à l'esthétique," *Revue des sciences humaines*, 309:1 (2013), 51.

Alain Ménil emphasizes that Glissantian creolization should be understood in an anthropological and not a linguistic sense. But understood as a process, Glissantian creolization ceases, according to Chancé, to be an anthropology. It *ceases* to be, and therefore we know that it was. In other words, the entirety of the work falls under creolization thought. It is true that Glissant himself explained that the notion has been present in his writings for a long time.[11] Furthermore, when he started putting this forward, he articulated it according to his previous reflections. However, although he effectively evoked the idea in *Le discours antillais*, it was done without analyzing its problems and also with a meaning as restrictive as it is negative.[12] It is difficult to affirm that he was thinking of creolization as such. It would then be without knowing it or even without wanting it, given his understanding of the word and its disqualification. But it is always possible to name *a posteriori* or to rename. The arrival and the adoption of a new idea always leads to requalification, makes new interpretations possible, opens new avenues of intelligibility. This is still not without problems, such as eventual inadequate projections, or possible uncontrollable effects of linearization or of enclosure in circularities.

Characterizing a Process

If were are particularly attached to the moment when he formulates it, Glissantian creolization will be, according to these evaluations, nothing more than an aesthetic, a depoliticized form of thought, a contemplative posture of the world, an imaginary future. . . . In this thinking, the "Relation" is the "muscle" to exercise, according to Michel Giraud, who recommends doing away with "all the smothering fat surrounding the essence."[13] Without a doubt it is because there is something to preserve that Edelyn Dorismond, interviewing Glissant, conceives creolization "as the

---

11. Fred Reno, "Lecture critique des notions de domination et d'identité chez les écrivains-militants de la créolité," *Pouvoirs dans la Caraïbe,* special edition, Série Université de Juillet, "Sciences Sociales et Caraïbe. Session 1997" (1998), 203–22.

12. See Carlo A. Célius, "La créolisation: Portée et limites d'un concept," *op cit.*

13. Michel Giraud, "La créolisation. Le muscle ou la graisse," *L'Homme,* 207–8 (2013), 346.

new face of political philosophy."[14] He brings up "the political, ethical and judicial impasse toward which we drive Glissantian thought on creolization with regard to harmony, to forms of domination requiring recognition or reestablishment of human dignity."[15] Michel Beniamino remarked that "The effectiveness of Glissantian poetics undoubtedly finds its limits in the pertinence of the social sciences, which his analysis dismisses with surprising . . . and infrequently analyzed levity. . . ."[16]

It is difficult, following these critiques, to maintain that Glissant devised a "ready to use" concept of creolization. One of the principal difficulties identified is the result of the effort exerted to give it its maximal extension. This criticism has been and still is addressed by many authors, especially those whom Mimi Sheller calls "the unattached guardians of 'global' culture."[17] However, an attempt at extension was and is perhaps still inevitable. In linguistics, the legitimacy of creolistics rested on the demonstration that its objective does not constitute a "special case" but is rather exemplary and of high heuristic value. In other words, understanding that creole languages are not special languages, that the possibility of documenting their geneses constitutes a considerable advantage in understanding the way other languages form, that the value of their studies extends to the mechanisms for language learning… all considerations that justify the distinction between process (creolization) and product (creole language), the first not necessarily resulting in the second. We develop in this way an analytic instrument to offer to the general scope of a discipline of creolization. First, its discipline: hence the distinction, established by certain creolists, between *internal usage* (linguistic) and *external usage* (other disciplines) of the idea. The authentication of this "right of property," by demarcating boundaries, attempts in a way to subordinate uses of the idea to *internal* theories. Actually, "internal uses" have been tried, meaning we have tried to apply linguistic theories to other dimensions of social life.

14. Edelyn Dorismond, *L'ère du métisssage...*, op cit., 424.

15. Ibid., 406.

16. Michel Beniamino, "Glissant, la créolisation et les sciences humaines," Les Caraïbes: convergences et affinités, *Publifarum*, 10, pubblicato il 15/02/2009, consultato il 13/07/2013, url: http://publifarum.farum.it/ezine_articles.php?id=87.

17. Mimi Sheller, *Consuming the Caribbean: From Arawaks to Zombies* (London: Routledge, 2003), 196, cited by Richard Price, "Créolisation et historicité," *L'Homme*, 207–8 (2013), 304.

Many researchers did not need to resort to thinking of creolization as an historical and anthropological phenomenon. At this level too we wondered about the possibilities, the conditions, and the interest of learning the use of an idea beyond the defined spatio-temporal horizon. Today we willingly insist on the necessity of recentering, recommending *historicization* and *contextualization*. Much is left to describe and analyze in order to arrive at a better understanding of what truly is (or would be?) creolization in the "restrained" ("first" or "initial") sense of the word.

In 2002, Christian Ghasarian explained in an article how he perceives the phenomenon on Reunion Island. He notes:

> Three great, conjoined forces, in constant relation and tension, which have always been at work on the island: acculturation, creolization and cultural reinvention. If acculturation presupposes the existence of two systems and cultural models, one of which imposes itself upon the other, creolization contrarily suggests a mixture of cultural models ending in a compromise of these models, in a new, more or less syncretic form. Cultural reinvention manipulates imposed models, and models made by forced contact, in order to produce, often explicitly, new social meanings. None of these dynamics can in and of themselves pertinently realize social processes at stake on the Island. In effect, these three processes, constituting the current complexity of Reunion society, collectively catalyze social, cultural, political, economic and religious stakes, as well as existential representations of the self and of place in local, metropolitan and global society. The angle of French models of integration, and of assimilation pure and simple, like the total creative mixture of novelty and innovation, are in and of themselves insufficient for Reunion anthropology, and their exclusive evocation reveals ideological positioning above all.[18]

First, creolization is both historical and present—it is still not a global phenomenon, but a dynamic among other phenomena. It distinguishes itself from *acculturation* and is not conceived as *cultural reinvention*. The effort to demarcate, the search for precision, the will of specification, must

---

18. Christian Ghasarian, "La Réunion: Acculturation, créolisation et réinventions culturelles," *Ethnologie française*, 32:4 (2002), 663.

be emphasized, given the synonymy frequently established with other ideas, rendering imperceptible that which neatly characterizes creolization.[19] However the proposition is far from being satisfying. Richard Price remembers that creolization is a "tool of analysis applied to infrequent processes of cultural change born in the colonies of the New World," adding in a note that these are: "Processes that, beforehand, had been conceptualized according to theories of 'acculturation' (Herskovits 1938), 'transculturation' (Ortiz 1940; Malinowski 1940) or 'cultural interpenetration' (Bastide 1960) that are outmoded today."[20] It should be noted, however, that several authors based their theories of creolization on Herskovitz and/or Bastide when considering creolization.[21] The elements of the Bastidian conceptual apparatus (assimilation, interaction, reappropriation, diversion, syncretism, derivation, adaptation…) are still considered useful, if not necessary, to the understanding of the creolization phenomenon.[22] They would designate processes that would be internal to it, that it would envelop. Of course, Bastide himself did not conceive of them as such; creolization was not a global phenomenon for him.[23]

Understood as a genetic global process, creolization implicates various mechanisms. These would be at work during a limited period, if we refer to Jean Benoist, who speaks of a "particular yet temporary process of opening and incorporation that permits growth, evolution, the construction of a society. But it will not be disassociated with what follows and what necessarily inverts the process." In fact, this observation, which allows us to

19. Carlo A. Célius, "La créolisation: Portée et limites d'un concept," *op cit.*

20. Richard Price, *op cit.*, 289. Complete references to authors cited: Melville J. Herskovits, *Acculturation: The Study of Culture Contact* (New York: J. J. Augustin, 1938); Fernando Ortiz, *Contrapunteo cubano del Tabaco y el azúcar* (La Habana: Jesús Montero, 1940); Bronislaw Malinowski, "Introducción," in Ortiz, *Contrapunteo cubano del Tabaco…*, xv–xxiii; Roger Bastide, *Les religions afro-brésiliennes: Contribution à une sociologie des interpénétrations des civilisations* (Paris: Presses universitaires de France, 1960).

21. See Carlo A. Célius, "La créolisation: Portée et limites d'un concept," *op cit.*

22. Marie-José Jolivet, "Acculturation, création, créolisation . . . Étude de cas en Guyane," *Bastidiana*, "Les Amériques noires et la recherche afro-américaniste," 13–14 (January-June 1996), 143–61; Marie-José Jolivet, "Modèle occidental et créolisation: L'exemple de la Guyane," *L'Homme*, 207–8, 113–34 , esp. 116–17. See also Jean-Luc Bonniol, "Au prisme de la créolisation . . . ," *op cit.*

23. See Carlo A. Célius, "La créolisation: Portée et limites d'un concept," *op cit.*

take on the question of creolization, concerns the entire history of human societies and cultures. He emphasizes that

> ...creolization is neither an exception to nor a result of this history. It is a phase that takes on, depending on the time and place, dissimilar faces, but that maintains the same functions: clearing the horizon of the barrage of old values and allowing the entrance of the conditions for building a new society. In the same way that biological mixing is one of the major forces of the biological evolution of species, creolization is a force that is capable of reuniting disparate inputs, of engendering new configurations. But these forces have no future if they become crystalized. For this reason, the societies that seem the most open build their identities by withdrawing into themselves. The movement of history also shows us the alternation between homogeneity and mixture, and teaches us that they are a united couple.[24]

We must acknowledge that these affirmations do not refer to a creolization of the world. Benoist had already stated his reservations on the pertinence of the idea of presenting the "creole worlds" as a "paradigm of globalization."[25] He wrote that creolization, which stimulates the creation of new cultures, extensively postpones the erosion of older cultures through the fragmentation of subjects, and the permeability of borders. In the previously cited article, he observes that his endeavor "as it applies to the contemporary world . . . stems above all from a representation of the world, of a project for the world that poses to our societies the ideal of being 'creolized.'"[26] In other words, his general considerations (previously mentioned) concern a past moment in history. He confirms it by indicating the entrance of "creole societies" into a "closing" phase. "What this mixture built only has a chance at lasting if the mixture slows one day, and on that day, the doors will close. Is creolization itself not beginning to define an orthodoxy?"[27]

Creolization, precisely! Let us examine what one of those who have

---

24. Jean Benoist, "La créolisation: locale ou mondiale ?" *Archipélies*, 3–4 (2012), 28.

25. Jean Benoist, "Les mondes créoles comme paradigme de la mondialisation ?" in Sélim Abou, Katia Haddad, eds., *Universalisation et différenciation des modèles culturels* (Montréal/Beyrouth: AUPELF,UREF/Université Saint-Joseph, "Universités Francophones: Actualité scientifique," 1999), 96–104.

26. Jean Benoist, "La créolisation: locale ou mondiale ?" *op cit.*, 25.

27. Ibid., 28.

pronounced *créolité*'s eulogy, Jean Barnabe, the well known linguistic specialist in creolistics, said on the subject in the same issue of the journal *Archipélies* as the above passages by Benoist. The article is best summarized in this excerpt:

> Language and culture constitute the 'places' that are commonly assigned the qualification of 'creole.' But these are also epistemological objects as much as they are ideological, which admittedly must be evaluated when our interest is the issue of creolization. The distinction between language and words is like the distinction between civilization and culture. From this point of view, this article is attempting to differentiate the primary order of reality from a secondary representation, the abstract from the concrete, and the factual from the structural. The different modes and types of creolization are linked to the diversity of conditions under which populations come into contact; they are contradictory due to the unequivocal character of the process of creolization, just as much as the modes of globalization are. If it is possible to establish the existence of so-called creole languages, without suggesting that they are special languages, it is daring to attribute the structural quality of creole to culture and society. On the other hand, there is nothing unreasonable in validating the concept of *créolité*, not as the expression of an essence, but as a constructivist notion, as the thing that carries out the project of 'ancestral sharing,' and doing so against all atavistic ideologies of 'sole root' and ethnocentric withdrawal.[28]

Bernabé then returns to the line of demarcation traced by Glissant. He reaffirms the validity of the notion of creolization and repeatedly rejects the idea that it is the expression of an essence.[29] The linguist takes on the

---

28. Jean Bernabé, "Créolisation des langues et des cultures: approche épistémologique et analytique d'un mécanisme asymétrique," *Archipélies*, 3-4 (2012), 84-85.

29. In *Prolégomènes à une charte des créoles* (Fort-de-France: K. Éditions, collection "Créole Fondamental," 2013), Jean Bernabé proposes definitions for several terms derived from the word "creole" as well as for the characterization and the processes of creolization. He recognizes the essentialist dimension of the notion of *créolité*, or rather accepts this notion and says that he is engaged in rereading *Éloge de la créolité*. From this perspective he writes: "I would not know how to go along with the preliminary, emblematic sentence of this essay: 'Whether Europeans, Africans or Asians, we all proclaim ourselves to be Creoles.'" (p. 61, note 29) He goes on to say, "A creole identity does not exist." (p. 62) He had previously categorized *créolité* among derivatives of the word creole, "the meaning of which

Glissantian qualifier *atavistic*[30] to explain what creolization is not: neither the search for the sole root, nor an ethnocentric withdrawal. It is more a notion of "carrying out a project of 'ancestral sharing'" and should be understood as a constructivist process. The author assumes what numerous studies have attempted to establish: ideological and political dimensions are inherent in the *créolité* movement. In reality, this dimension has always been linked to *the creole question*. We find it in the founding principles of the arguments that developed creolistics.[31] The sociologist Jean Casimir refuted the idea of creolization put forth by Anglophone Caribbean intellectuals because of its ideological positioning, which did not correspond to his.[32] Mimi Sheller said the same thing in the 1970s when she noted that creolization was a politically charged term, used by Caribbean thinkers to

---

is subject to controversy." He explains, "créolité: according to *Éloge de la créolité* (1988), this term is criticized by Glissant (1990), because of its essentialist character, for which he blames himself. More interested in the procedural character of creole realities, he prefers the concept of **creolization**. He goes so far as to relate creolization and globalization, a viewpoint I disagree with, as these phenomena are completely different in regard to their nature and implications. In a paradoxical way, Glissant (1997), for the second time, somewhat separates his first approach from the concept of globalization and puts forth the concept of **globality**, which in both its morphology and its semantics in the lexical medium, does not seem any less essentialist than *créolité*. From the way that Glissant is perfectly willing to denounce a certain conception of *créolité*, we should be surprised that he does not treat globality in the same way. We find ourselves before the illogicality of the chiasmus *créolité*-creolization/globalization-globality, which will surely bring about the ideological dimension of the debate." (pp. 24–25; creolization and globality are in bold type in the book). References cited: Jean Bernabé, Patrick Chamoiseau, Raphaël Confiant, *Éloge de la créolité* (Paris: Gallimard, 1988); Édouard Glissant, *Poétique de la relation*. Poétique III (Paris: Gallimard, 1990); Édouard Glissant, *Traité du Tout-Monde*. Poétique IV (Paris, Gallimard, 1997).

30. Glissant distinguishes "atavistic cultures" and "composite cultures." The first are armed with a body of mythical tales of legitimation, most often taking the form of the creation of the world, a Genesis. The second do not elaborate the founding myth of a Genesis; there is therefore "digenesis." In atavistic cultures, "creolization took place a long time ago, when the culture was made," whereas creolization happens before our eyes in composite cultures. But we witness the creolization of the world, and therefore of atavistic cultures, which are the result of an original creolization. This circularity makes the history of creolization unattainable and reveals that it is not behind the distinction between genesis and digenesis. See Edouard Glissant, *Traité du Tout-Monde*. Poétique IV (Paris: Gallimard, 1997), 194–95.

31. Cf. Carlo A. Célius, " La créolisation. Portée et limites d'un concept," *op cit*.

32. Jean Casimir, *La Caraïbe une et divisible*, coédition, CEPALC-Nations-Unies (Port-au-Prince: Éditions Henri Deschamps, 1991).

conceive of Caribbean societies.³³ Bernabé reaffirms this theory by rearticulating *créolité* and creolization. When several researchers address the removal of ideological envelopes, the links in the subject matter between ideology and epistemology become inseparable (and thus they rejoin those who demand engaged, political thought). All this is in perfect coherence with constructivism, which asserts the will to de-essentialize and assumes the political stakes of naming and producing knowledge in the field. The term "creole" can therefore be understood as a quality that is "assigned" to "places" (languages, cultures). From this point of view requalifications are possible, as are interrogations on the balance between qualifications and "places." The author believes it is appropriate to use the word "creole" to designate languages but does not concede the existence of structurally creole societies.

Reflexivity and Space-time

One of the particularities of *the creole question* that underpins the political dimension is that it has always been strongly tied to the discourse of the self. Jean-luc Bonniol emphasizes this indirectly when he mentions Louis Joseph Janvier's talk at the July 17, 1884, meeting of the Anthropological Society of Paris: "Also as evidence is the identity of the speaker Louis Joseph Janvier, a Haitian, and therefore from a society that produces individuals who are apt to foster analyses of self-reflection; strongly characteristic of, and still central to these studies in which 'organic' intellectuals and exterior observers confront each other."³⁴

We should examine this *1884 moment*, which became an important milestone in the genealogy of the idea of creolization. Louis Armand de Quatrefages read to the Society from a letter from Mr. Paul Lévy, who proposed using the term *creolization* to explain the transformation the races undergo in the American environment, resulting from their adapting to their environment and making them more like indigenous races. De Quatrefages gives his approval by saying that he had long observed that in the colonies, "ethnic characteristics" of European whites and

---

33. Cited by Richard Price, *op. cit.*, 303.
34. Jean-Luc Bonniol, "Au prisme de la créolisation…," *op cit.*, 240.

African blacks had undergone modifications, which led him to talk about "derived races." Then Janvier spoke. After addressing his propositions, Bonniol observes:

> This exchange undoubtedly marks one of the first appearances of the term 'creolization' in the intellectual sphere (but it is certainly used frequently, as Louis Joseph Janvier has taken the opportunity to show us), and we can learn much from the meaning that we can ascribe to this new word at the end of the nineteenth century, at the end of a long lexical trajectory of which this terminological innovation is the culmination.[35]

And later:

> We thus see that the principal parameters associated with creolization, that is to say the processes in response to a new environment and long-term mixing of original populations, are already in place. Inventing the notion of creolization seems accomplished, even before it was introduced as such to the field of linguistics: there is no need to affirm that its adoption by the social sciences is tantamount to a linguistic metaphor. The discourse on creolization had already been in place for half a millennium, expressing elements of popular thought that emerged at the beginning of colonial relationships, taking after both the identification of people and the recognition of cultures, and permitting the realization of the old opposition between metropolitans and colonials.

Janvier seems not to have continued to use the idea. There still needs to be an attentive rereading of his writings for verification, but if he used it frequently, we would have likely already noticed it. In any case, he certainly did not make it a central idea in this later writing. However he did take "the opportunity" with such ease that it seemed he was on familiar territory, and he was. What did he say? He said that the black race in Haiti transformed itself through climate and infinite ethnic mixing. For beneath black skin, even when we don't perceive it, Amerindian, Spanish, English, or French blood sometimes courses. This adds to political influence and to power struggles. "We see creolization of the black race especially in Haiti. From a physical point of view, creolization constantly forms a particular human group, an original group in the intellectual and moral sense, it

---

35. Ibid.

rapidly approaches the nations that belong to what the philosopher Pierre Laffitte calls the western group."[36]

Here Janvier is not proposing a new idea in terms of his own thoughts or the ideas formed in Haiti throughout the nineteenth century. Under pressure to defend the new Haitian state (which officially gained independence on January 1, 1804), the intellectuals conduct a reading of their past situations and record it in "the history of humankind."[37] Logically, they reject fixism and focus on "the instability of human things."[38] That goes for the building and the disintegration of empires, the shifting of civilization, the migration of peoples, and the transformations that result from them. Haiti's existence is understood through such a dynamic, with the peculiarity that it came from "the barbarity of the slave trade". These ideas stated by deVastey in the 1810s were developed by other authors. For example Thomas Madiou, in the introduction of his monumental 1847 *History of Haiti*, remarks that the first inhabitants of the island were exterminated and replaced by black Africans.[39] "This race from Africa" would form "a new nation." "It would be a new proof that different areas of the earth are not the domain of different species of the human race. The whole world belongs to the human race: one people succeeds another, one race succeeds another. Men form paths that cross in all directions. In the areas occupied by today's nations, we encounter few aboriginal populations; reviewing history we see nothing but immigration

---

36. Cited by Bonniol, ibid. See Benoist's considerations (*op cit.*) on the idea of biological mixing in response to the Lévy letter and the interventions by de Quatrefages and Janvier.

37. Baron de Vastey, *Réflexions sur une Lettre de Mazères, ex-Colon français, adressé à M. J. C. L. Sismonde de Sismondi, sur les Noirs et les Blancs, la Civilisation de l'Afrique, le Royaume d'Hayti, etc.* (Cap-Henry: Chez P. Roux, imprimeur du Roi, mars 1816), 77.

38. Ibid., 33.

39. From Baron Pompée Valentin de Vastey, see, among others, *Le système colonial dévoilé* (Cap-Henry: P. Roux, Imprimerie du Roi, 1814). This work was re-edited by Société haïtienne d'histoire, de géographie et de géologie, (Port-au-Prince, 2013), with a preface by Michel Hector and presented by Jean Casimir. On de Vastey, see Marlène L. Daut, "Un-Silencing the Past: Boisrond-Tonnerre, Vastey, and the Re-Writing of the Haitian Revolution," *South Atlantic Review* 74:1 (Winter 2009), 35–64; "The Alpha and Omega of Haitian Literature: Baron de Vastey and the U.S. Audience of Haitian Political Writing," *Comparative Literature* 64:1 (Spring 2012): 49–72; "From Classical French Poet to Militant Haitian Statesman: The Early Years and Poetry of the Baron de Vastey," *Research in African Literatures* 43:1 (Spring 2012), 35–57.

and transplanting. The human race only progresses through this friction, this fusion of races."[40]

From this same perspective, Anténor Firmin, a member of the Anthropological Society of Paris present at the July 17, 1884, meeting, deconstructs the scientific elaborations that validate racial inequality in his book *On the Equality of Human Races*, published the following year.[41] Firmin argues the non-fixity of humans by citing the example of Haiti, among others. In his consideration on "the beauty in human races" he disqualifies the validity of the aesthetic criteria used to classify races and arrange them in a hierarchy, and he does not hesitate to celebrate the beauty of the mulatto woman. This point, which magnifies Janvier's position as noted above, should be emphasized because it highlights the fact that the deconstruction of racial hierarchy should be completed. Haiti confirmed, in the eyes of several authors, the state of degeneration that would affect groups of mixed heritage. The proof would be the mulatto elite who were incapable of moving the nation forward. The fight against racial inequality thus implied rejecting the fear of miscegenation. Firmin arrives at the conclusion that analyses must consider the social state of human groups and he recommends leaving the notion of race out of it. "This word," he says, "implies a certain natural and biological fatality that has no analogy, has no correlation to the degree of aptitudes offered up by the different agglomerations of humans spread across the globe."[42]

We are, let us repeat, engaging in a thought process concerning civilizational dynamics, and Janvier placed himself within this process. His considerations should be understood as they appeared in an 1883 writing on imitation, a practice for which Haitians were reproached. The interest generated by this question is evident in the postcolonial studies inspired by Homi Bhabha.[43] Janvier affirms that "it is man's nature to imitate." He asks himself, "What is civilization, then? It is a pastiche or a copy, everywhere.

---

40. Thomas Madiou, *Histoire d'Haïti, I, 1492–1799* (Port-au-Prince: Éditions Henri Deschamps, 1989 [1847]), viii–ix.

41. Anténor Firmin, *De l'égalité des races humaines (Anthropologie positive)* (Paris: Librairie Cotillon, 1885, new edition by Ghislaine Géloin, Paris: L'Harmattan, 2003).

42. Ibid (édition 2003), 403.

43. Homi K. Bhabha, *Les lieux de la culture: Une théorie postcoloniale* (Paris, Payot, [1994], 2007).

Creolization: Some Observations 217

All civilization consists of an exchange of more or less appropriated, intelligent, and opportune imitations."[44] He uses the French as an example, in the area of arts:

> France, very artistic at this point in time, was not at all before Charles VIII's wars with Italy. We indeed saw a new art developing on the green banks of the Loire and the laughing shores of the Sequana after Francois I returned from Italy, covered in the laurels of Marignano.
>
> Modern French art, as cosmopolitan as it is subtle, was formed through association with and refinement of Indian, Assyrian, Egyptian, Greek, Roman, Gallo-Roman, Arab or Moorish, Spanish, Italian, German, Flemish, Dutch, English and even primitive, Oceanic arts from Africa, Asia Major and the Americas, from which the masterpieces are gathered and piled one atop the other in the halls of the Louvre, the Cluny museum, Saint-Germain and the Hotel Carnavalet. Still today, France sends her brightest young erudites to study in Italy at the Villa Medici (the Roman school), in Greece (the Greek school) and in Egypt (the Alexandria school). . . . Are these not the former prizes of Rome, the Carpeaus, the Bonnats, the Carolus Durans, the Gounods, the Lefeuls, the Chapus, the Falguières, the Merciés, who for the past twenty years, and even still, are the leaders of contemporary French painting, sculpture, architecture and music?[45]

The primary preoccupation of nineteenth-century Haitian thinkers was to prove the humanity of all men in a world where colonialism and slavery still existed. They began with their awareness of belonging to a new society, showing that this, the result of particular historical conditions, is inscribed in the horizon of humankind's history. They affirm that the displacement of human groups, their adaptation in times of extreme exploitation and their exchanges are the basis for the formation and the transformation of societies. In this frame of mind, Louis Joseph Janvier participated in a debate over whether the results of colonization in the American context were familiar territory. He could take the opportunity

---

44. Louis-Joseph Janvier, *La République d'Haïti et ses visiteurs (1840–1882)* (Paris: Marpon et Flammarion, 1883), 511.

45. Ibid., 512–13.

to show that this phenomenon qualifies as creolization and bring examples from his own country. It should be noted that de Quatrefages accepts this notion, judging that it corresponds to his previous reflections. The same is true of Janvier. For all that, were they really operating in a framework of creolization? From this perspective, perhaps yes. We should not forget that Janvier's thinking developed in the absence of such a conceptualization and *would certainly not adopt it*. It is understood that this thinking, however well-known, does not provoke *the creole question*, which is attested by what Janvier said to Moreau de Saint-Méry (an essential writer for the Haitians of the nineteenth century because of the knowledge they gained about the colonial period).[46] In other words, the nineteenth-century Haitians' self-reflection expresses their consciousness of belonging to a new world, but without taking a ready-made theory on the subject, *creole thought* developed during the colonial period.

Such a reprise should have facilitated adopting the idea of creolization. It was not so, though, because it was in a frame of redistribution, of re-elaborating and reorganizing categories beginning with the political establishment of a new society. The new state is proclaimed, the new territory is rechristened, individuals are renamed, and all are integrated into the same nationality. A discourse of renewal is established, one that absorbs the creole thinking of Saint-Domingue and attaches the qualifier "creole" to precise facts, particular and specific qualities.

Considered from the perspective of a discourse on the self, the creole question has been the object of disappropriation. This has also been observed in the American hispanophone world,[47] for which many of the general reflections on creolization do not apply. We must therefore inquire about the permanence, the survival, the disappearance, and the resurgence of the creole question, here and there, yesterday and today. We must be sensitive to its temporality and its spatial distribution, which, *a priori*, draw

46. See Elie Moreau de Saint-Méry, *Description topographique, physique, civile, politique et historique de la partie française de l'isle de Saint-Domingue* [1797] (Paris: Société Française d'Histoire d'Outre-Mer, édition établie par Blanche Maurel et Etienne Taillemite, 1984), 3 vols..

47. See, among others, the example of Colombia as analyzed by Anne-Marie Losonczy, "Le criollo et le mestizo: Du substantif à l'adjectif: catégorie d'apparence et d'appartenance en Colombie hier et aujourd'hui," in Carlo A. Célius, ed., *Situations créoles. Pratiques et représentations* (Québec: Éditions Nota Bene, collection "Société," 2006), 187–207.

Creolization: Some Observations

out a cartography that is differentiated by the period in question. From there, diverse situations offer themselves up for analysis and comparison, according to the demands of contextualization and history, without necessarily seeking to eliminate all political dimensions. We will perhaps see that a *process called creolization*, a *situation that qualifies as creole* is not intrinsically emancipating, just as *creole, creolitary or creolizing thought* is not liberating in itself. According to the case and/or the viewpoint, this can be colonial and enslaving, autonomist or separatist, anti-establishment or conservative, integrating or exclusive.

Theorizing About Caribbean Society: From Plantation Society to the Post-Colony and Creolité

Anthony Bogues

Introduction

A recent issue of the journal *Sargasso* edited at the University of Puerto Rico was devoted to the subject of alternative identities and included among its articles and interviews a conversation with writer Patrick Chamoiseau. In the conversation/interview, Chamoiseau responded at length to questions about *creolité* as cultural project and "imaginary [which] opens up a path towards the Caribbeanization of culture in the Antilles."[1] For Chamoiseau, the notion of *creolité* and the process of creolization "allows us to apprehend a unity concealed . . . within the generalized process of creolization that constituted the Americas." In his perspective the creolization process produced various *creolités*, thus making a distinction between process and consequences. Reading the interview made me pause and reflect on the ways in which the notion of creole/*creolité* has been deployed in the intellectual history of the theorization about Caribbean society.

The high point of efforts to theorize Anglophone Caribbean society in the twentieth century was bound up with nationalist claims and desires to find both language and categories in which Caribbean society could reveal

---

1. "Warrior of the Imaginary: A Conversation with Patrick Chamoiseau, Interview with Juan Carlos Canals," in *Sargasso*, "Alternative Identities: Belonging and Resistance" (2007 –2008) No. 1, 9–23.

itself. This nationalist project, in part a federal project, has floundered and the Anglophone Caribbean post-colonies are today island nation –states with each defining its Caribbeanness in insular island terms or in geological, geographical terms. This means that complex historical experiences which turned fragmented colonies into a unitary region with a singular historical experience of colonialism and racial slavery layered with forms of indentured labor and servitude does not have any weight in much of the Anglophone Caribbean as a set of relevant ideas. It is important to note that the theorization that emerged at this time in the Anglophone segment of the region paid great attention to institutions—on the ways structures work.

Theories of Caribbean society

From the 1950s to the 1970s there were two distinct waves of theorization about Anglophone Caribbean society.[2] Beginning in the 1950s with research at the Institute of Social and Economic Research at the University of the West Indies at Mona and the Institute of Caribbean Studies at the University of Puerto Rico, there emerged a wave of theorization about the Anglophone Caribbean in which the work of historians, sociologists, and anthropologists laid down theoretical markers about the nature and character of Caribbean society. The event that brought together these disciplinary fields and some of the key individuals working through these notions at that time was the December 1956 symposium on Caribbean Research held in the United States. In 1957, the symposium papers were published by the Institute of Social and Economic Research in collaboration with the Research and Training Program for the Study of Man in the Tropics at Columbia University.[3] The publication, entitled *Caribbean*

---

2. I am limiting myself here because I am not going to discuss the emergence of the theoretical framework of Marxism that emerged in the 1970s and posited a theory of Caribbean society. The Marxist theory of Caribbean society did not propose any unique features of Caribbean society but in the main attempted to fit Caribbean society within the framework of conventional Marxist categories. There was little or no effort to Caribbeanize Marxism and the main currents often neglected a genealogy of Caribbean Marxist thinkers like C. L. R. James. There is a story here waiting to be told about the reasons for this neglect.

3. Note the title of the institute and the use and placement of the word tropics. There is a long genealogy of the word tropics and its meanings with reference to uncivilized areas, particularly in reference to the Caribbean. In colonial texts about the region it begins with

Studies: A Symposium, included papers on the plantation model, the place of African heritage in Caribbean society, the racial and family structures in the region, and "The Present Status of the Social Sciences in the British Caribbean," the latter an intriguing paper by Lloyd Braithwaite.

In his paper, Braithwaite noted that the impetus for social science research in the region came from a report of the Irvine Commission. This report not only recommended the establishment of the University of the West Indies but argued that, "We have already stated our belief that the West Indies provide abundant opportunity for economic, historical and sociological research in the widest sense."[4] Funding for social research was provided by the Colonial Development and Welfare Acts enacted in Britain at the time. Of course the external push to engage in major research on the Caribbean was shaped as well by the regional nationalist sentiments of the period, as any review of some of the participants who attended the symposium would indicate. The paper on race was delivered by Eric Williams and the one on African heritage in the region by M. G. Smith.

Braithwaite's paper presents us with a useful overview of social science research in the Anglophone part of the region at that time. Dividing Caribbean Studies into disciplinary fields, he noted that developments in the field of anthropology "followed the British tradition . . . rather than the American one of cultural anthropology." In this regard he pointed to the various studies of kinship and peasant life and studies on family. For Braithwaite what was important about these studies was the fact that they identified the process "of cultural amalgamation . . . long at work" in the region and therefore created the conditions for the merger of "sociological and anthropological analysis . . . and comparative work."[5] In particular Braithwaite identified the theory of plural society as one that has a "deceptive analytic flavor," but he notes its pervasiveness as a framework not only in the work of M.G. Smith but also of Edith Clarke and Andrew Pearse.

---

the 1590 publication of Jose De Acosta's book, *Natural and Moral History of the Indies*. This book has recently been republished by Duke University Press in 2002.

4. Cited in Lloyd Braithwaite "The Present Status of the Social Sciences in the British Caribbean," IN *Caribbean Studies: A Symposium*, ed. Vera Rubin (Kingston: ISER, 1957).

5. Ibid.

Braithwaite advocates a structural—functional approach to the study of the region. In the remainder of the paper he pays attention to what he calls the "search for Africanisms within folk culture . . . stemming from a nascent nationalism of the West Indies."

There are major difficulties with Braithwaite's analysis of these research trends on the Caribbean. In the first instance he situates social science research paradigms in a field where the nuances of American and British social science research play out. Thus the Anglophone Caribbean becomes a research laboratory where various Western scholarly battles are played out. There is no discussion from Braithwaite and others of what precisely constituted the Caribbean on its own terms. Secondly, he ignores the significance of culture. And here I am not speaking of culture as a "body of intellectual and imaginative work" but rather, in the language of Raymond Williams, I am referring to culture as a "structure of feeling,"[6] of a society and a period, one which is contingent because it operates through the passages of time. Here culture is, in part, *ways of life*—a set of practices that we invent and rework, mediated through power and therefore both entangled and sometimes resistant to power's capacities.

It is safe to say that the first wave of Anglo-Caribbean theorization in the mid-1950s was externally driven and focused on structures, kinship, family and these were also the preoccupations of anthropology and sociology at the time. These social and structural categories where used to mark difference and the "other." However the second wave, while focusing on social structure and political economy, was preoccupied with asking and answering the question: What is the Caribbean?[7]

---

6. Raymond Williams, *The Long Revolution* (Ontario: Broadview Press, reprint, 2001), 64.

7. One should of course also note that Caribbean literature during this period had already begun to develop thematic approaches to Caribbean society. For a discussion of some of these approaches see, Alison Donnell, *Twentieth-Century Caribbean Literature* (New York: Routledge, 2006). What is interesting in Caribbean literature at the time were its preoccupations with colonial power and the sense that the nationalist political process would not lead to fundamental decolonization. Included in this preoccupation were discussions about modernism and the Caribbean nation and the development of a perspective on modernism from the "margins." For a discussion of this see Simon Gikandi, *Writing in Limbo: Modernism and Caribbean Literature* (Ithaca, N.Y.: Cornell University Press, 1992). What should be noted is how social science research at the time ignored Caribbean literature as a form of knowledge.

In this second wave, two theoretical paradigms stand out: The plantation model and the theory of creolization.

The Caribbean as Plantation Society

It is with the New World group, that remarkable collection of regional Anglo-Caribbean intellectuals, that the conception and theorization of Caribbean society as a plantation society emerged as one of the most important frameworks for thinking and describing Caribbean society. The impetus for the formation and the desires that drove the group's collective and research agendas were distinctly different from that of the first wave. Formed towards the end of 1962, the purpose of the group was "to give a correct description of the problems and an indication of what can be done."[8] Research and scholarship for members of the New World Group focused on engagement and social change. Importantly, the categories in which change was going to be thought about and advocated were "appropriate to the native Caribbean imagination," in the words of the first editorial in the group's journal, *New World Quarterly*. This marked a decisive shift in Anglo-Caribbean thought, particularly in the domain of the formal social sciences.[9] The writings of George Beckford and Lloyd Best with their different concerns represent the major statements on the plantation as a theoretical model of Caribbean society. In 1966, Best's formulation of a "model of pure plantation" argued that there was an exploited hinterland linked structurally in unequal ways to the former colonial power. One of Best's objectives was to push Caribbean economic thinking beyond traditional political economy, so he posited a

---

8. Cited in Denis Benn, *The Caribbean: An Intellectual History, 1774–2003* (Kingston: Ian Randle Publishers, 2004), 123.

9. The key members of the group were Lloyd Best, George Beckford, Norman Girvan, C.Y. Thomas and Havelock Brewster, Miles Fitzpatrick, David De Caires, Kari Levitt, and Owen Jefferson. Of course Lloyd Best's seminal essay, "Independent Thought and Caribbean Freedom" remains a key moment in post-colonial Caribbean thought. For a rich discussion of this essay and the thought of Lloyd Best in general see, Selwyn Ryan, ed. *Independent Thought and Caribbean Freedom: Essays in Honor of Lloyd Best* (St. Augustine, Trinidad: Sir Arthur Lewis Institute of Social and Economic Studies, 2003.) For a review of the thinking and activity of the New World group as a whole see, Brian Meeks and Norman Girvan, eds., *The Thought of New World* (Kingston: Ian Randle Publications, 2010).

new school of political economy that would collapse the divide between the social sciences and the humanities. Beckford, however, in his work *Persistent Poverty*, presented us with a theory of Caribbean "underdevelopment," thus formulating a description of Caribbean economy and of society as a totality. For Beckford the concept of a plantation economy was one in which a country's economic, social and political structures were dominated by the plantation system. In social institutional terms a plantation society had its own laws of motion that governed social change. One distinguishing feature of plantation theory of Caribbean society was that it begins with the historical formation of the Caribbean: slave plantations dominated by sugar production. It recognized the unequal power arrangements of colonial and imperial power in relation to the colony and then post-colony. The plantation created the conditions for the historical emergence of Caribbean society, one in which different races and labor regimes of servitude were consolidated. Thus in an effort to answer the question "What is the Caribbean?," the plantation school of thought began with the historical encounters and formation of the region in the period of colonial modernity.

Clearly any theory of Caribbean society cannot ignore the historical formation of the region. Thus one perennial issue would be: "What were the defining features of this history and what kind of society had been produced?" From the perspective of the plantation school of thought, Caribbean society was a modern society created by colonial conquest and plantation slavery. And it was not only this school that operated from this perspective. For example, in the appendix to his 1962 classic *The Black Jacobins*, C. L. R. James announces that "Wherever the sugar plantation and slavery existed, they imposed a pattern. It is an original pattern, not European, not African, not a part of the American main, not native in any conceivable sense of that word, but West Indian, *sui generis* with no parallel anywhere else."[10] If the plantation school of thought attempted to discern and describe the structural patterns, then the other important theory of the period—creolization—attempted to describe what kind of society these patterns produced.

---

10. C.L.R. James, *The Black Jacobins* (Essex: Allison and Busby, 1980), 391–92.

Creole Theory

By the time the concept of creole enters into Anglo-Caribbean discourse it inhabits a slippery history.[11] Debate surrounds the etymology of the word itself, which may have African origins, designating someone born outside of Africa.[12] Within the Anglo-Caribbean, the word and the theory of creolization emerged as cultural explanations about the nature of Caribbean society. The historian and poet Kamau Brathwaite, in his seminal 1974 piece *Contradictionary Omens*, makes the point that "creolization . . . is a specialized version of the two widely accepted terms acculturation and interculturation."[13] For Brathwaite, a human population group—no matter the conditions they faced upon their arrival in the Caribbean—had to adapt and adjust themselves to the new landscape. The late Rex Nettleford puts the matter well when he notes, "But more properly it refers to the agonizing process of renewal and growth that marks the new order of men and women who came originally from different Old World cultures . . . and met in conflict or otherwise on foreign soil."[14] Brathwaite notes that this adjustment created mimic men, but he argues that in the circumstances this was the only kind of imitation that was possible.[15] This has always been a problematic point in the formulation of the theory in the Anglo-Caribbean. Here the question is not so much what culture/s have been produced but on *what basis* has this production occurred and how has it been sustained? How has power, and in this case colonial and racial power, shaped cultural production, and how can creolization theory give an account of resistance? In this regard

---

11. For a discussion about the theory of creolization in the Caribbean see O. Nigel Bolland, "Creolization and Creole Societies: a cultural nationalist view of Caribbean social history," in Alistair Hennessy, *Intellectuals in the Twentieth-Century Caribbean* (London: Macmillian, 1992), 50–79. For a very good etymological reading of the word see Carolyn Allen, "Creole then and Now: The problem of definition," *Caribbean Quarterly* 44:1&2 (March-June 1998), 33–49.

12. For a discussion of this see Maureen Warner Lewis's paper "KiKongo Origins of some Portuguese and Spanish words of the slave period," August 1994.

13. Kamau Brathwaite, *Contradictionary Omens* (Kingston: The Times Printery, 1974), 11.

14. Rex Nettleford, *Caribbean Cultural Identity* (Kingston: Institute of Jamaica, 1978), 2.

15. Brathwaite, *Contradictionary* Omens, 15.

it would be useful to note that Sylvia Wynter has argued that there was a distinction between creolization and what she then calls "indigenization." Following closely (while reworking) the writings of Aime Cesaire on Negritude, as well paying attention to the Jean Price-Mars's *So Spoke The Uncle,* Wynter notes that "While the 'creolization' process represents . . . a more or less 'false assimilation' in which the dominated people adopt elements from the dominant . . . in order to obtain prestige or status, 'the indigenization' process represents the more secretive process by which the dominated culture survives; and resists."[16] Despite Wynter's caveat, creolization became the accepted social/cultural and theoretical description of Caribbean society. Wynter's concern, however, points us to something about theorization and Caribbean society that should make us pause, and that is: How does one develop a theory of Caribbean society without thinking about power? How does one think and theorize within a framework of both domination *and* the ways in which that domination has been contested to give shape to new cultural and social forms in the region?

All this takes me back to the interview with Patrick Chamoiseau.

If in the "Anglophone" Caribbean the theory of creolization was a theory of the cultural, social, and historical process of Caribbean society, in the Francophone Caribbean the theory of creolization and its accompanying concept of *creolité* has been primarily deployed by poets and novelists with an important investment in language. Furthermore, as was made clear in the manifesto, *In Praise of Creoleness*, "to be creole . . . will be for us an interior attitude—better a vigilance, or even better, a sort of mental envelope in the middle of which our world will be built in full consciousness of the outer world."[17] It is therefore not a formal theory but rather a way of seeing and of speaking. So, if in the Anglophone Caribbean creolization was about forms of a cultural encounter and the processes of adaptation, then in the Francophone region creolité is about constructing a cultural practice through which buried cultural forms dominated

---

16. Sylvia Wynter, "Jonkonnu in Jamaica" *Jamaica Journal* (June 1970), 39. In this formulation, Wynter is of course influenced by the Haitian scholar and thinker, Jean Price-Mars.

17. Jean Bernabe, Patrick Chamoiseau, and Raphael Confiant, *In Praise of Creoleness* (Baltimore: Johns Hopkins University Press, 1990), 75.

by French colonial power are made visible. Patrick Chamoiseau makes the point when describing Martinique:

> There is a general regard of French Culture, which responds mostly to French–Occidental values, and everything which comes from the deepest recesses of our country is buried, just as the memory of slavery is buried . . . You see, there is a part of us which is generally underestimated, and so it is not appreciated or celebrated . . . we must begin by exhuming those cultural values; not in order to find refuge there, or to find solace in a bleated traditionalism, but exhuming them in order to better position ourselves vis-à-vis the whole world.

In this process matters of history become important, not as facts of the past but rather as historical knowledge. In other words, how is the past recounted? In what language will we tell the stories of the past? And here I would draw attention to Chamoiseau's novel, *Texaco*, in which the language of history does not move through plantation to the present but rather from the perspective of the ex-slave's journey through different landscapes and habitations.

In the novel, Chamoiseau gives the reader a different take on the history of the Caribbean. He begins with the *The Age of Longhouses and Ajoupas* and ends his historical sequence with the *"Age of Concrete."*[18] What is being done here is an attempt the retell the history of the Caribbean from the perspective of the slave. The theorization which is being gestured towards integrates slave voices.

---

18. When one reads *Texaco* one cannot help but think about the remarkable poem of Lorna Goodison, "Never Expect," in particular the following lines:

> Burchell the Baptist
> Handed you the landpapers
> You were not in a position
> To read them, so you call
> The name of your place
> Into the responding wind
> By so doing recreating
> Your ancestral ceremony
> Of naming. "Never Expect"

Hence the structure of the novel is one in which the real source of this history is Marie-Sophie Laborieux. It is she who would tell a history in which "old men of the Doum reveal stories beneath History most essential for understanding us, stories no books speak of."[19]

I think this is where were we are in any present theorization of the Caribbean. It is not about cultural values or geographical spaces but rather about how to integrate the human experiences of the ordinary person into any theory. How can we get to the stories that "no books speak of"? And when we do so what will they tell us about Caribbean society? This move of opening buried histories and memories creates another possibility—changing the terms of the battles we currently engage. Chamoiseau makes the point that "even those who free themselves from colonial subjection fail to emancipate . . . their imaginary."[20] It is a point common enough in post-colonial Caribbean spaces. However what we often do in reciting this as a mantra is to forget to ask ourselves what is the relationship between imperial power and forms of domination? So the imaginary that we may need to create is one that may be buried in an archive of memory, but is also one about a future which ruptures a past. One part, therefore, of a theory about Caribbean society from below is grappling with events that have posed the significant questions of our modernity. In this regard the Long Haitian Revolution remains an extraordinary marker.

George Lamming in *Season of Adventure* begins the end of the novel when the narrator observes that the real problem that led to the collapse of the first independent republic was one of language. He writes: "But the main problem was language. It was language which caused the First Republic to fall. And the Second would suffer the same fate; the Second and the Third, unless they tried to find a language which was no less immediate than the language of the drum."[21] Here the point to note is not about language in our conventional understanding, but rather it is about the capacity to name and from there to conduct an

---

19. Patrick Chamoiseau, *Texaco* (New York: Vintage, 1998), 35.

20. Interview with Patrick Chamoiseau, 18.

21. George Lamming, *Season of Adventure* (Ann Arbor: University of Michigan Press, 1999), 363.

inventory of ourselves. In the end, my argument is a simple one. Patrick Chamoiseau's interview triggered the question . . . what would a theory of Caribbean society look like? What would be its main features if we took into account the ideas and human experiences of the ordinary person? Perhaps the next stage of theorizing about the region may begin from this frame and in that process the issues posed by the stance of *creolité* become central to that intellectual labor, marking another opening not an end.

Mona Georgelin. *Association Mamanthé, troupe Massilia Ka.*

Danse Gwoka
rythme Kaladja

Photographer : Azedine Hsissou

Mélinée Magen et Mona Georgelin. *Association Mamanthé, troupe Massilia Ka.*

Mélinée Magen. *Association Mamanthé, troupe Massilia Ka.*

Mélinée Magen.
Association Mamanthé,
troupe Massilia Ka.

Mélinée Magen. *Association Mamanthé, troupe Massilia Ka.*

Mélinée Magen.
*Association Mamanthé,
troupe Massilia Ka.*

Aurélie Bajeux. *Association Mamanthé, troupe Massilia Ka.*

Danse Gwoka, rythme Kaladja

Aurélie Bajeux. *Association Mamanthé, troupe Massilia Ka.*

Creolization Metaphors in the Southeast Asian Context

Bryce Beemer

In an article on the Burmese classical music tradition, scholar Khin Zaw puckishly described the 1767 Burmese sack of Ayutthaya, the capital city of Thailand, its neighbor and principal political rival, as the "time that our cultural store-house was filled with Siamese [Thai] loot."[1] Interstate slave gathering warfare was an endemic feature of statecraft in the lightly populated Southeast Asia region. Kingdoms rose and fell based on their ability to accumulate some portion of a rival's population and protect the people in their own territory from capture and relocation. Siege warfare and slave gathering play prominently in mainland Southeast Asian history. While there are many features that distinguish the systems of slavery found in Southeast Asia from those in the Atlantic World, one difference bears heavily on our discussion in this brief essay. War captives in Southeast Asia were frequently sorted according to their useful skills and then incorporated into the royal service system in their captors' state. Thus, farmers were resettled in sparsely populated farming zones or charged with clearing and settling new farmland. Captives with military experience were incorporated into the military. More pertinent to the discussion at hand, artisans and performers were settled in the capital or surrounding suburbs, some into ethnically distinct quarters and villages, while others were incorporated into pre-existing work groups. In the period after the 1767 destruction of the Thai capital, captured Thai dancers

---

1. Khin Zaw, "Burmese Music (A Preliminary Enquiry)," *Bulletin of the School of Oriental and African Studies, University of London*, 10:3 (1940), 724

and musicians assumed positions alongside other elite performers within the Burmese palace, leading to what I would argue were multiple creolizing transformations of Burma's royal dance and music.

Within Burmese art historical studies, the most well known piece of "cultural loot" appropriated from Thai captives is *Yodaya thakyin* (Ayutthaya music), a genre of Burmese classical music named for the conquered Thai capital.[2] Even today in modern Burma (or Myanmar), *Yodaya thakyin* continues to have cultural relevance. It is one of a handful of musical genres that college-level music students must master in order to graduate with a degree in classical music and performance. However, as much as this music is alive in the present, there is a mystery to its origins that has long confused historians. *Yodaya thakyin* does not sound Burmese to Burmese ears, it sounds foreign and exotic. Yet, when it is played for Thai audiences they find nothing in the music that they recognize as their own. The question is intriguing: what is the *Yodaya* musical genre in Burma?[3]

The metaphorical framework at the core of creolization theory provides a convincing and, to-date, underutilized tool for understanding cultural exchange within the Southeast Asian system of slavery. Creolization theory posits that, in the context of slavery, when two or more cultural groups come into contact there is a potential for processes of convergence and reformulation that can produce new third cultural variants. Or, said in another way, the cultural rupture of capture and enslavement can set in motion processes of cultural reinvention and transformation that produce novel artistic practices, systems of belief, food culture, dress, and behavior. This model has allowed scholars of American slavery to escape linear models of assimilation and/or cultural survival that viewed slave culture as existing on a sliding scale of acculturation, and

2. *Yodaya* was also the Burmese word for people originating from the city of Ayutthaya. The term has a range of meanings including the political (non-ethnic) conception that a *Yodaya* person was a subject of the king of Ayutthaya. It was also used as an ethnonym for Tai-speaking people originating from Central Thailand. In modern Burmese, *Yodaya* and *Thai* are sometimes used interchangeably as ethnonyms for people from Thailand, but *Yodaya* is considered an out-of-date term.

3. This quandary is discussed in Myint Kyi, "Three Yodaya Songs Representing the Thai Element in Myanmar Classical Music," presented at the 6th International Conference on Thai Studies, Chiang Mai, Thailand, 1996, n.p.

to better appreciate the agency of enslaved peoples in the reinvention of their social world.[4]

By using the creolization metaphor we can unwind the mystery of *Yodaya thakyin* music by understanding it as a novel art form born from the cross-fertilizing interactions between Upper Burma's palace elite and captive performers and musicians from Ayutthaya. Ethno-musicological research by Daphne Wolf has shown *Yodaya thakyin* retains some elements of the Burmese and Thai classical music traditions, while simultaneously containing elements that are found in neither of them.[5] Considered in this way, *Yodaya thakyin* is similar to other more commonly acknowledged creolized musical traditions in the Americas such as calypso, the songs that accompany capoeira, and the still emerging "chutney soca" genre.[6] The creolization framework provides a breakthrough framework for re-understanding processes of cultural exchange within Southeast Asian slavery. Yet this theory was developed to describe cultural processes within the Atlantic slave system with its very different systems of racial hierarchy, violence, and labor organization. In the Southeast Asian setting the skills and talents of captured people were not necessarily diminished or degraded because they had origins among a defeated people. In fact, the opposite was frequently true. The artistic practices of captured people—performance and the plastic arts—were often incorporated into the state's public spectacles and architectural projects. In this way Southeast Asian royals could project an image of themselves as universal monarchs ruling over foreign kings, and as unifying leaders of vibrant multi-ethnic polities.[7] A brief descrip-

---

4. I draw here from the discussion in Robin Cohen and Paola Toninato, "Creolization Debate: Analysing Mixed Identities and Cultures," in *The Creolization Reader: Studies in Mixed Identities and Cultures*, ed. Robin Cohen and Paola Toninato (New York: Routledge, 2010).

5. Daphne Wolf, "*Bamarische Musik: Yodaya-Lieder im historisch-kulturellen Kontext Myanmars*" (Berlin: Regiospectra, 2010), 49–53, 71–72, 90. I thank the author for providing me with a draft translation of key passages from her German language thesis and for pointing me to important Burmese language texts on this subject.

6. "Chutney soca" describes the blending of South Asian and Caribbean musical traditions that has become common since the 1980s on Caribbean islands with South Indian populations.

7. For a broader discussion see Bryce Beemer, "Southeast Asian Slavery and Slave Gathering Warfare as a Vector for Cultural Transmission: The Case of Burma and Thailand," *The Historian* 71:3 (March 2008).

tion of the development of *Yodaya thakyin* in Burma elucidates the pitfalls and challenges of adapting the creolization concept to the Southeast Asian system of slavery.

It is difficult to determine how Thai musical traditions were performed in the court or for the public, between the years 1767 and 1789, the years immediately after the capture and transfer of Thai performers to Burma. The scholarly assumption is that Thai performance traditions were carried out in ways roughly similar to how they were performed in Ayutthaya. By December 1789, the popularity of Thai performance traditions resulted in a royal order establishing an eight person committee of elite poets and musicians (several of them royal) charged with collaborating with representatives from the Yodaya community to translate Thai plays and songs into Burmese poetic verse "appropriate" for presentation in the king's inner palace.[8] One of the plays translated at this time was the Ramayana dance-drama. Early editions of this theatrical work show that it was orchestrated for music from both Thai and Burmese ensembles that participated simultaneously.[9] Music from this period no longer exists, but the highly regarded music historian, Myint Kyi, argues that the post-1789 translations of Thai song would have had a transformative effect on the music due to the profound differences between the Thai and Burmese languages. Numerous melodic adaptations would have to have been made to join the translated Burmese lyrics to the song's original Thai melody.[10]

According to Myint Kyi's scholarship, 1804 marks the birth of *Yodaya thakyin*. In that year the Burmese crown prince sponsored a pagoda consecration ceremony for a Buddhist temple in Mingun, a town a few miles upriver from present day Mandalay. The prince wanted to enliven the event with a competition between an orchestra comprised of captured Ayutthaya people (and their descendants) and a Burmese orchestra. He asked the

---

8. Pe Maung Tin, "*Yodaya hma yashi thaw yinkyehmu mya* [The Culture received from Thailand (Ayutthaya)]," in *Nawarat Ko-Thwe* (Yangon: Sabei Oo Sarpay, 1974), 29–32.

9. Thein Han (U) and Khin Zaw (U), "Ramayana in Myanmar Literature and Art," in *Yama Saung Ba Baung Khyo [Collected Articles on the Ramayana]* (Rangoon: Pagan Book Printers, 2005), 297–98.

10. Myint Kyi, *Myanma tegita anusape thamein: pukam khe hmu kounbaun khe aso [A Literary History of Myanmar Music]* (Rangoon: National Center for Human Resource Development, Ministry of Education, 2001), 229–30.

court minister U Sa, a member of the 1789 translation committee and artistic polymath, to create a composition that both orchestras could play on relatively equal footing, making the competition more fair and perhaps more thrilling. U Sa produced two songs (*Kha nwei san* and *Iwan pou aung*) that mark the first experiment in what would become a decades-long project of merging Thai and Burmese musical traditions. The songs composed in this burgeoning style came to be called "*Yodaya thakyin.*"[11] This experiment quickly developed into a popular royal musical genre with roughly one hundred surviving examples. Years later, U Sa headed a project to create a formal canon of Burmese court music in which roughly five hundred songs were collected into a single volume called the *Maha Gita* [The Great Songs]. The first anthology was completed in 1849. The cannon continued to develop so that by 1870 a more thoroughly organized *Maha Gita* emerged in which every song was classified according to six official genres, one of which was *Yodaya thakyin*.[12] In this way, *Yodaya thakyin* was canonized within the Burmese musical tradition. As I mentioned at the beginning of this essay, even today the training of classical musicians, either through apprenticeship or through state training at a university level, includes mastery of at least a dozen *Yodaya thakyin* compositions.

Yodaya thakyin music, named for a conquered city and its captured inhabitants, both follows and strays from our common understanding of the creolization process. It is a new art form born out of the cross-cultural interactions between captured people and a slaveholding society. In addition, this music is only one aspect of a much larger cross-cultural interaction that also generated new dance and theatrical art forms as well. It has been argued by both Thai and Western scholars that the influence of captured Thai artisans led to a creative transformation of the performing

---

11. Ibid., 159.

12. The other five genres, in addition to *Yodaya* are *Kyo* (harp music), *Bwe* (eulogies), *Thachin Kan* (eulogies), *Patpyo* (court songs), and *Mon* (the Mon are an ethnic group settled in coastal Burma whose autonomous kingdoms were subordinated in the years immediately proceeding the conquest of Ayutthaya). See the discussion in Sayuri Inouie, "The Formation of Genre Division in Burmese Classical Songs with Special Reference to Song Anthologies on Palm Leaf Manuscripts," presented at the Burma Studies Conference 2008, DeKalb, Illinois, 2008.

arts in Burma.[13] However, the creolization processes that generated Yodaya music was very different from those operating in Atlantic slavery because slave-taking elites were actively involved in projects to hybridize Burma's artistic culture. The moves to include Ayutthaya's musical traditions in the palace, to translate songs and plays, and then to create a genre of classical music based upon this music is just one small facet of the larger aim of slave-gathering warfare in the region, which was to incorporate the skills of captive peoples into the palace and the larger society. This is a marked contrast with the Atlantic slave system in which the African cultures of the enslaved were denigrated and laws and social mores were enforced to stifle the flow of cultural practices between the enslaved and the dominant societies. Creolization in the Atlantic world flourished in seeming opposition to the social forces arrayed against it. By contrast, in the Southeast Asian setting, the useful skills of war captives were targeted for incorporation into different kingdoms' labor systems. For this, and numerous other reasons, the adaptation of creolization theory to the Southeast Asian setting will likely be a controversial project.

Before dwelling too long on the incommensurability of the Southeast Asian and Atlantic World processes of creolization, we should undertake a brief analysis of a Buddhist religious ceremony innovated by Thai war captives after their forced relocation to Mandalay. Many captives were settled along the *Shwe Tachaung*, a transportation canal that runs along a north-south axis quite near Mandalay's royal palace. Two Buddhist temples located in that area conduct an unusual sand pagoda ceremony once yearly. Prominent marble inscriptions at both temples ascribe the origin of these ceremonies to resettled Thai captives, as does a rich oral history tradition in the neighborhoods around the temples. In central Thailand, sand pagoda building is a humble ceremony in which individual families gather at the riverside and build pagodas in remembrance of the Buddha's life and teachings. The river and the weather inevitably destroy these sand memorials, reinforcing Buddhist ideas regarding the impermanence of all things. In Burma, the resettled Thai captives elaborated and expanded this family ceremony. The scholar Nat Mauk Tun Shein writes that the practice

---

13. See Maung Htin Aung, *Burmese Drama: A Study with Translations of Burmese Plays* (London: Oxford University Press, 1957), chap. 2, and Noel Singer, "Ramayana at the Burmese Court," *Art of Asia* (December 1989).

involved the whole community, and each Thai captive (or descendant) was expected to bring one cup of water and one handful of sand to the pagoda on the ceremony day. The sand pagoda that results from this communal project is an impressive 25 feet tall, hardened with fixatives, and painted white with lime.[14] In the past these one-day ceremonies were capped with communal meals comprised of Thai foods, though in recent times this tradition has faded.[15]

Once again, creolization theory illuminates a curious cultural development. The participants in these sand pagoda ceremonies, which continue into the present day, believe that the ritual was transported from Ayutthaya. In fact, the ceremony was reinvented and transformed by the Thai captives themselves more than two centuries ago. We have no sources that explain the transformation of this ceremony, but aspects of the ceremony suggest some reasons for its development. In Thailand, Cambodia, and Laos sand pagoda traditions are especially popular among the poor. This is because it is a merit-building activity that is in a sense "free" and therefore distinguishable from ceremonies in which food or money are donated to a Buddhist temple.[16] Merit-building ceremonies themselves have a psychologically beneficial role because they provide spiritual protection to a community and are believed to decrease ill-luck, sickness and other misfortunes. The reinvention of the sand pagoda tradition was surely recuperative, in that it established an affordable venue for merit making among people who were likely as psychologically defeated as they were militarily defeated. Moreover, the expansion of the ceremony so that it demanded the collaboration and cooperation of each member of the community—in the hauling of sand and water and the shaping of the outsized stupa—must have aided in re-linking and rebuilding a Thai community shattered

---

14. Nat Mauk Tun Shein, *Win Twe Neh Thekheh Thi Min Ne Pyi [A Royal City Made of Many Quarters]* (Mandalay: Min Ma Haw Publisher, 2005), 282.

15. Author interviews with temple community leaders in Monti Su, Mandalay, Burma, Research Notebook, September 2009.

16. See the discussion in Ni Ni Myint, "The Tradition of Sand Pagodas in Myanmar," in *Traditions of Knowledge in Southeast Asia: Proceedings of the Traditions of Knowledge in Southeast Asia Conference, 17–19 December 2003* (Yangon: Myanmar Historical Commission, 2004), 221–57.

by war and forced relocation.[17] This reinvented sand pagoda tradition is more readily comparable to the creolized religions of African slaves in the Americas (for example Vodou, Santería, and Obeah) because it fits more comfortably into the model of religious traditions and beliefs transformed by the crucible of slavery and adapted to meet the demands of enslaved peoples in a new land.

It is also fitting to close this essay with sand pagoda building because it is linked to creolization by a remarkably similar metaphorical framework. Richard Price has described the "bittersweet" message of creolization: that the "inevitable loss of tradition" is inextricably tied to the "hope wrapped up in the creation of new [traditions]."[18] The inevitability of loss and destruction lies at the metaphorical heart of the Buddhist sand pagoda ceremony, as well. The sand pagoda ceremony calls on the community to come together and rebuild what has been destroyed. Creolization theory seeks to describe the historical processes in which communities rebuild what has been shattered by enslavement and forced relocation. Loss, destruction and rebuilding frame both our understanding of creolization and the development of the sand pagoda building tradition created by Thai war captives in Mandalay.

---

17. I summarize longer analyses available in my thesis: Bryce Beemer, *The Creole City in Southeast Asia: Slave Gathering Warfare and Cultural Exchange in Burma, Thailand, and Manipur* (Ph.D., University of Hawaii at Manoa, 2013), 184–92.

18. Richard Price, "The Concept of Creolization," in *The Cambridge World History of Slavery* (Cambridge: Cambridge University Press, 2011), 535.

The Creole Origins of the Early New World Banjo

James L. A. Webb Jr.

In the 1970s, music librarian Dena Epstein wrote the seminal article "The Folk Banjo: A Documentary History" in which she assembled a large number of historical references to plucked lutes in the plantation societies of the New World. The historical materials included references to a variety of different terms such as bania, banza, banshaw, and banjil (among others) that seemed related to the contemporary term "banjo." Epstein also collated scattered observations about the instruments, including their form and construction, some observations on the social contexts in which the instruments made music, and references to the music played on them. Her view, still strongly influential, was that the banjo was an African instrument that was introduced to the New World.[1]

In 1984, ethnomusicologist Michael Coolen investigated Senegambian archetypes for the American folk banjo. His work inspired others to search for African instruments and linguistic terms to which the form and the name of the North American banjo might be linked.

---

1. Dena Epstein, "The Folk Banjo: A Documentary History," *Ethnomusicology*, 19:3 (1975), 347–71. Epstein was not the first to assert an African origin. No less an authority than Thomas Jefferson, writing in his *Notes on the State of Virginia*, stated that "The instrument proper to them is the Banjar, which they brought hither from Africa, and which is the original of the guitar, its lower chords being precisely the four lower chords of the guitar." Thomas Jefferson, *Notes on the State of Virginia* (New York, 1964), 135. In 2013, the filmmaker Jim Carrier released a film entitled *The Librarian and the Banjo* that celebrated the seminal contribution of Dena Epstein.

This approach was based on the understanding that the North American banjo had African roots.[2]

The pioneering research of Epstein has been the basis for the elaboration of what one might think of as a general model of historical transfer. This general model holds that, early in the era of the Atlantic slave trade, African laborers brought African instruments or at least knowledge of African instruments into the South Atlantic basin and that African slaves built banjo-like instruments there from the mid-seventeenth century onward. These instruments were introduced into North America by the middle of the eighteenth century.

The research of Coolen has been the basis for a specific model of historical transfer. This specific model holds that African instruments were more directly introduced from West Africa to North America during the course of the Atlantic slave trade. It asserts that the New World banjo has its roots in the musical instruments of Senegal and the Gambia in West Africa. Some ethnomusicologists have asserted that the Wolof *xalam* is the likely West African prototype for the North American banjo. More recently, some banjo enthusiasts have hailed the *akonting*, an instrument currently played by the Jola from the Casamance region of southern Senegal and the Gambia, as the likely prototype.[3] The thrust of the specific model is to treat the North American banjo as if it were a direct import or little-modified survival from Africa.[4]

The scholarship on the African origins of the New World banjo has led to the rejection of an older interpretation that held that white minstrels—in particular, a Virginian named Joel Sweeney—made critically important changes to the banjo of North America by adding a high fifth string drone and employing a wooden hoop instead of a calabash for the resonating

---

2. Michael T. Coolen, "Senegambian Archetypes for the American Folk Banjo," *Western Folklore*, vol. 43, no. 2 (1984), 117–32.

3. Ulf Jägfors, "The African Akonting and the Origin of the Banjo," *The Old-Time Herald*, Winter 2003-04, 26–33. Jägfors suggests that the term "banjo" is linked etymologically to the Jola term for the neck of the Akonting, and that the gourd body, the short thumb string, and the down-picking style of attack are all traceable to the Akonting.

4. See Cecelia Conway, *African Banjo Echoes in Appalachia* (Knoxville: University of Tennessee Press, 1995), and Bob Carlin, *The Birth of the Banjo: Joel Walker Sweeney and Early Minstrelsy* (Jefferson, N.C.: McFarland, 2007).

chamber. Some players who have been influenced by the Afro-centric models have rejected this interpretation of the white contribution to the creation of the North American banjo as an act of cultural expropriation and a denial of the banjo's African roots.[5]

This essay advances an interpretation of the early New World banjo as an instrument with a complex cultural history. Its broad argument is that the plucked lute that became known as the banjo developed in the South Atlantic basin from South Asian, European, and African elements that were introduced though the systems of forced labor. The banjo was born in the New World. For this reason it is best understood as a "creole" instrument, rather than an instrument with exclusively "African" origins.

European and African Lutes

For musicologists, the banjo belongs to a category of instruments known as chordophones—instruments that have strings that vibrate between fixed points. One subcategory, known as composite chordophones, encompasses all instruments with a sound chamber, more-or-less straight neck, and strings that vibrate. Those composite chordophones with strings that run parallel to the sound chamber are known as lutes (from the Arabic al-'ud). The lutes encompass a wide array of instruments including, among others, guitars, mandolins, ukeleles, violins, and cellos. As the Arabic etymological root suggests, the grouping of instruments classified as lutes may be loosely associated with the diffusion of a broad Islamic cultural synthesis, and many ethnomusicologists accept the view that the lute instruments of sahelian West Africa were introduced at some point during the early expansion of Islam.[6]

---

5. One example is Otis Taylor's audio CD *Recapturing the Banjo*, released by Telarc in 2008 (ASIN: B0010VD7FS).

6. This is far from certain, however, and it may simply reflect a prejudice about the importance of the Mediterranean ecumene that underplays the originality and creativity of West African societies. One alternative interpretation is that the lute emerged in ancient Egypt and diffused into sahelian Africa, the Mediterranean, and southwest Asia. Yet another possibility is that because lutes are known to have existed in other early societies, such as those in East Asia, there may well be more than one, or even several, cultural areas that "originated" lutes. For a fascinating, broad, and insightful reflection on the relationships between the musical traditions that merged in the United States, see Peter Van Der Merwe,

It is certain that plucked lutes of West Africa were one of the major influences on the lutes that developed in the South Atlantic. Evidence from the sixteenth century onward documents the presence of plucked lutes in West Africa with either a calabash gourd resonator or a wooden box or bowl-like trough resonator. (There were also a variety of harp-lutes with either curved or straight necks on which the strings do not run parallel to the soundboard of the resonating chamber and on which individual stops are not noted.)

The African instruments that influenced the creole plucked lutes in the South Atlantic were drawn from two West African traditions. One tradition was that of hereditary professional musical artisans, or griots, who played instruments with a wooden trough for a body. The second tradition was not restricted to a hereditary professional caste, and the non-griot lutes could be made from wooden troughs, calabashes, or metal containers.[7] The musical traditions of West Central Africa have not been as thoroughly explored as those of West Africa, but scholars of West Central African instruments have documented traditions of the construction of harp-lutes (as opposed to plucked lutes) and of many non-lute-like instruments including the thumb piano and the marimba.[8]

The western European nations had their own vibrant traditions of plucked lute construction of a broad variety of instruments having single courses or double courses of strings. All European lutes, however, had wooden resonating chambers. In the ecologies of the Mediterranean and western European Atlantic regions there were no gourds that produced stiff hollow shells that might have been suitable for use as resonating chambers.

Creole Lutes Emerge in the Caribbean

In the 1640s, the most important English colony in the Americas was Barbados. It had a population of white landowners, white indentured

---

Origins of the Popular Style: The Antecedents of Twentieth-Century Popular Music (Oxford: Oxford University Press, 1989).

7. Eric Charry, "Plucked Lutes in West Africa: An Historical Overview," *Galpin Society Journal*, 49 (1996), 3–37.

8. Gerhard Kubik, *Angolan Traits in Black Music, Games and Dances of Brazil. A Study of African Cultural Extensions Overseas* (Lisbon: Centro de Estudos de Antropologia Cultural, 1979).

servants, and African slaves. The economy of the island was undergoing a transition from tobacco to sugar cultivation, which would demand large numbers of workers. Richard Ligon (c.1589–1662) visited the island between 1647 and 1650 and left a lengthy account. Ligon wrote about the music of the "Negroes" which was "of kettle drums" and noted that the musicians would be able "to do wonders in that art" if they "had the variety of tune." He recorded the astonishment of Macaw, an African plantation 'officer' (presumably an overseer) who Ligon deemed "very apt" at drumming, when he encountered Ligon playing a plucked lute, known as a theorbo:[9]

> and when I had done, he took up the theorbo in his hand and strook one string, stopping it by degrees upon every fret, and finding the notes to vary, till it came to the body of the instrument; and that the nearer the body of the instrument he stopped, the smaller or higher the sound was, which he found was by shortening the string, considered with himself, how he might make some trial of this experiment upon such an instrument as he could come by; having no hope to ever have any instrument of this kind to practice on.[10]

Ligon went on to record that Macaw built a xylophone-like instrument with blocks of wood of different lengths.[11] Ligon's account suggests that, at least to 1650, the plucked lute had not yet become part of the culture of plantation workers on Barbadoes.

By the early eighteenth century, the era of white indentured servants on Barbadoes was near its end. African slaves were the principal work force

---

9. See Filippo Bonanni, with a new introduction and captions by Frank L. Harrison and Joan Rimmer, *The Showcase of Musical Instruments* (New York, 1964 [original Italian edition, 1723]), plates 46 and 47 with captions. "The theorbo was a larger form of lute devised in the sixteenth century. It had unstopped bass strings carried off the fingerboard from a second peg-box, and normally had single strings throughout. Its development reflects the increasing importance of the bass part. It was almost exclusively an accompanying instrument for a soloist or group." "The Archlute was still larger than the theorbo and, like it, had bass strings lying off the fingerboard. . . ."

10. Frank Felsenstein, ed., *English Trader, Indian Maid: Representing Gender, Race, and Slavery in the New World. An Inkle and Yarico Reader* (Baltimore: The Johns Hopkins University Press, 1999), 66, reproducing excerpts from the second edition of Richard Ligon, *A True and Exact History of the Island of Barbadoes* (London, 1673).

11. Ibid., 67.

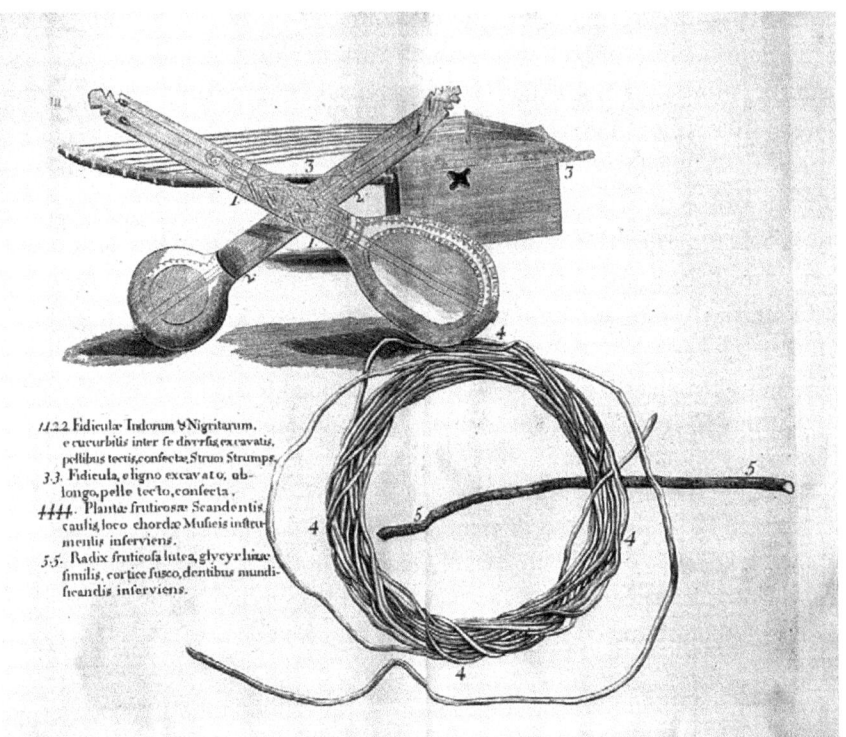

Sir Hans Sloane, *A Voyage to the Islands Madera, Barbados, Nieves, S. Christophers and Jamaica* (London, 1707-1725), II, 232.

Sloane Creole Lute

on the island. John Oldmixon, in his book *The British Empire in America*, published in 1708, noted that the African slaves had a number of instruments including the bangil, described as "not much unlike our Lute in any thing, but the Musick..."[12]

The earliest descriptive evidence for creole plucked lutes in the New World appears in Sir Hans Sloane's *A Voyage to the Islands of Madera, Barbados, Nieves, S. Christopher, and Jamaica* (London, 1707) that relates his observations of a 1687 visit to Jamaica.[13] There, he observed

---

12. John Oldmixon, *The British Empire in America* (London, 1708), vol. 1, 123; cited by Epstein, "Folk Banjo," 352.

13. Epstein found an earlier mention of an instrument known as 'banza' used by slaves on Martinique. The text from 1678 does not, however, provide any information at all about the

were "several sorts of Instruments in imitation of Lutes, made of small Gourds fitted with Necks, strung with Horse hairs, or the peeled stalks of climbing Plants or Withs. These Instruments are sometimes made of hollow'd Timber covered with Parchment or other Skin wetted, having a Bow for its Neck, the Strings ty'd longer or shorter, as they would alter their sounds."[14] Thus, the earliest evidence of lutes played by plantation laborers in the New World describes several sorts of instruments, some with wooden bodies and others with gourd bodies. Some instruments would be classed as plucked lutes and others (those having a bow for their necks) as harp-lutes. Sloane refers to the plucked lutes as "strum-strums," a descriptive pidgin term.

The image that accompanies the Sloane text shows two apparently gourd-bodied plucked lutes and a harp lute. One of the gourd-bodied lutes is said to be from "India" and the other from "Africa." The "Indian" descriptor may refer to an influence from Madagascar, in the Indian Ocean. (The Madagascan slave population is mentioned explicitly in the Sloane text, but without direct reference to musical instruments.)[15] An alternate possibility is that the Portuguese or Spaniards may have introduced a similar instrument from the Indian Ocean region during an even earlier era of the slave trade that saw the emergence of Atlantic creole culture.[16] The Portuguese

---

instrument except its name. Adrien Dessalles, *Histoire générale des Antilles* (Paris, 1847), vol. III, 297; cited by Epstein, "Folk Banjo," 351–52.

14. Sir Hans Sloane, *A Voyage to the Islands of Madera, Barbados, Nieves, S. Christopher, and Jamaica* (London, 1707), I, lix. According to the *Oxford English Dictionary*, a with is "A band, tie, or shackle consisting of a tough flexible twig or branch, or of several twisted together; such a twig or branch, as of willow or osier, used for binding or tying, and sometimes for plaiting."

15. "The Negroes are of Several sorts, from the several places of Guinea, which are reckoned the best slaves, those from the East-Indies or Madagascins, are reckoned good enough, but too choice in their Diet, but very often die. Those who are Creolians, born in the Island, or taken from the Spaniards, are reckoned more worth than the others in that they are season'd to the Island." (Sloane, *Voyage*, xlvii.)

16. Ira Berlin explains the emergence of Atlantic creole culture along the West African coast: "Atlantic creoles traced their beginnings in the historic encounter of European and Africans on the west coast of Africa. . . . some Atlantic creoles identified with their ancestral homeland (or a portion of it)—be it African or European—and served as its representatives in negotiations with others. Other Atlantic creoles had been won over by the power and largess of one party or another, so that Africans entered the employ of European trading

did introduce a South Asian lute from the Malabar Coast to Southern Africa. There the pastoral Khoi peoples embraced the instrument, and it became known as the *ramkie*.[17]

In the Sloane image, the Indian and the African plucked lutes appear to have two strings. In both instruments, the strings appear to pass through holes at the end of the neck. This may imply tuning pegs, although none are explicitly depicted. It is clear, however, that the strings are not brought to pitch by the use of ring ties, as in the West African plucked lute tradition. The fingerboard is flat, unlike the typically round

---

companies, while Europeans traded with African potentates. Yet others played fast and loose with their mixed heritage, employing whichever identity paid best. Whatever strategy they adopted, Atlantic creoles began the process of integrating the icons and beliefs of the Atlantic world into a new way of life." (Ira Berlin, *Many Thousands Gone: The First Two Centuries of Slavery in North America* (Cambridge, Mass.: Harvard University Press, 1998), 17. The path-breaking study of the mixed culture (European and African) communities in West Africa is George E. Brooks, *Eurafricans in Western Africa: Commerce, Social Status, Gender, and Religious Observance from the Sixteenth to the Eighteenth Century* (Athens, Ohio: Ohio University Press, 2003). On the Atlantic creole zones of Central Africa, see Linda M. Heywood and John K. Thornton, *Central Africans, Atlantic Creoles, and the Foundations of the Americas, 1585–1660* (Cambridge: Cambridge University Press, 2007), 169–235. On the mixing of African and other cultural musical influences in the Atlantic basin, see John K. Thornton, *A Cultural History of the Atlantic World, 1250–1820* (Cambridge: Cambridge University Press, 2013), 386–96.

17. As O.F. Mentzel, who was at the Cape between 1733 and 1741, noted of the ramkie: "The ravekinge or xguthe cannot be regarded as originally coming from the Hottentots, but as an imitated instrument which the slaves of Malabar brought with them, from whom some Hottentots copied it, and hence it is not generally found among them. . . . This instrument is not played with a fiddle bow, but the gut strings are merely plucked with the fingers in the same way as those of a lute. The Hottentots, however, who have such instruments, cannot play 'pieces,' dances or such like, upon them, and can produce nothing but the three sounds of these gut strings . . . striking them three or four times in succession. One might describe this as 3/4, 4/4, and 5/4 time." [O.F. Mentzel, *Beschreibung des Vorgebirges der Guten Hoffnung* (Glogau, 1787), vol. II: 518–19.] Cited by Percival R. Kirby, *The Musical Instruments of the Native Races of South Africa* (London: Oxford University Press, 1934), 249–50. Kirby thought that the ramkie, constructed with either a calabash body or hollowed plank, came from the Portuguese, or is a hybrid instrument. The European seaborne empires were global undertakings that facilitated the flows of all sorts of goods and cultural forms, including musical ideas and musical instruments. The best overview of the Portuguese seaborne empire is A. J. R. Russell-Wood, *The Portuguese Empire, 1415–1808: A World on the Move* (Baltimore: The Johns Hopkins University press, 1992); see particularly, the discussion of the Portuguese role in the introduction of European and African music and instruments, 193–95.

stick fingerboard of West Africa.[18] Thus, the earliest explicit textual and iconographic evidence concerning the different organological features of the plucked lutes in the seventeenth-century Caribbean suggests an amalgam, with indefinite cultural influences from West Africa, Madagascar, and perhaps South Asia.

Sloane visited a clearing on the island of Jamaica where a dozen or so African men and women were dancing to music made by two African musicians playing on handmade stringed instruments. He was accompanied by the plantation owner and by a French musician named Baptiste who transcribed the music played and the lyrics sung. (This is the earliest known transcription of music made by Africans in the New World.) Richard Cullen Rath has analyzed the three pieces of music transcribed by Baptiste and presented convincing evidence that the music and the lyrics combined elements of at least three different African regional cultures—two from the Guinea coast and one from Kongo.[19]

In the 1790s, a second iconographic representation of a New World creole lute appeared in a book by John Gabriel Stedman about the Dutch colony of Surinam, one of the core slave plantation economies in the Caribbean. It was one of several instruments depicted in the published engraving.

Numbers 3, 10, and 15 are called bania. Number 3 is "the *Ansokko bania*, which is a hard board supported on both sides like a low seat, on which are placed small blocks of different sizes, which being struck with two small sticks like a dulcimer gives different sounds that are not at all disagreeable." Number 10 is "the *Loango bania*, which I thought exceedingly curious, being a dry board on which are laced, and kept close by a transverse bar, different sized elastic splinters of the palm tree, in such a

---

18. A draft illustration for Sloane's book exists in the British Library. It was reproduced and incorrectly represented as a representation of Western sudanic musical instruments in Henry George Farmer, "Early References to Music in the Western Sudan," *Journal of the Royal Asiatic Society of Great Britain and Ireland*, 4 (1939), opp. 572.

19. For a brilliant exploration of the music heard by Sloane and his musician companion, Baptiste, see Richard Cullen Rath, "African Music in Seventeenth-Century Jamaica: Cultural Transit and Transmission," *William and Mary Quarterly*, 3rd series, 50 (1993), 700–26. For more on Sloane's text, see Kay Dian Kriz, "Curiosities, Commodities, and Transplanted Bodies in Hans Sloane's 'Natural History of Jamaica,'" *William and Mary Quarterly*, 3rd series, 57 (2000), 35–78, especially, 61–62.

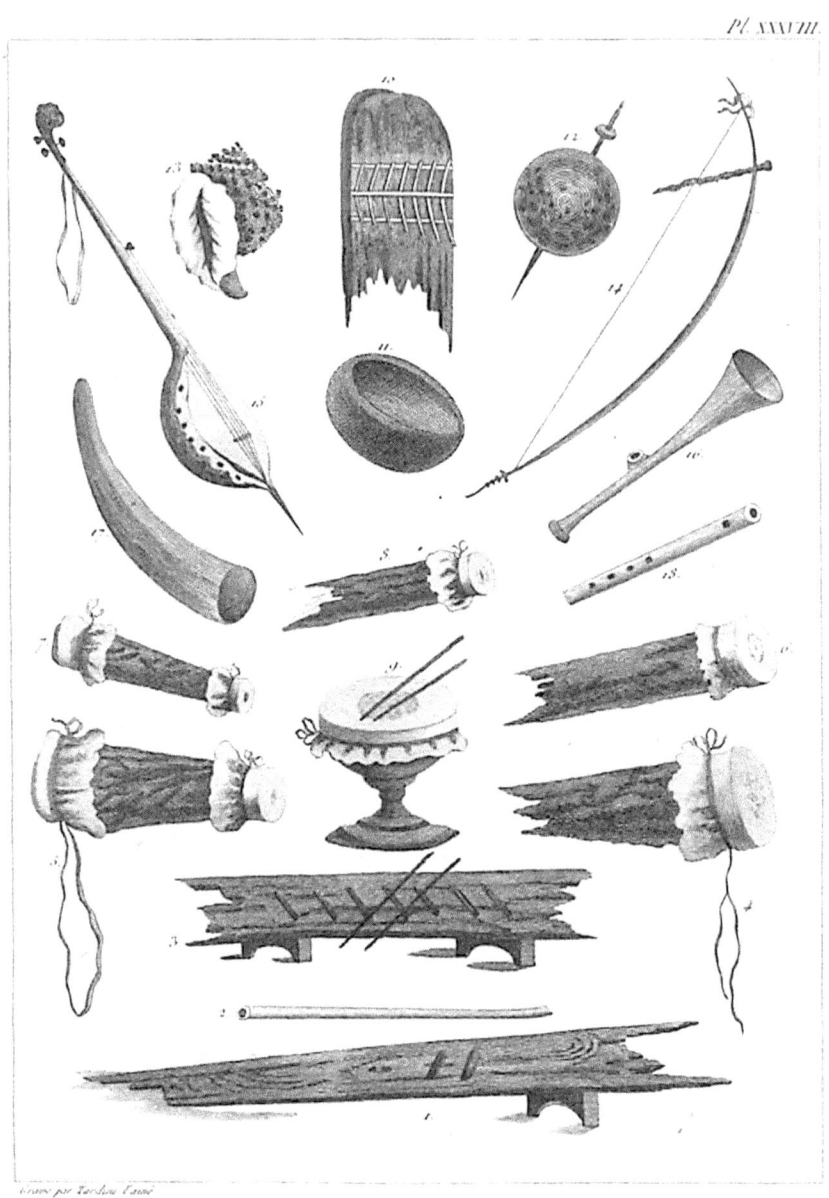

Stedman's Bania

manner that both ends are elevated by other transverse bars that are fixed under them, and the above apparatus is placed on No. 11, which is a large empty gourd to promote the sound; the extremities of the splinters are snapped by the fingers, something in the manner of a pianoforte, and have the same effect." Number 15 is "the *Creole-bania*; this is like a mandolin or guitar, being made of a gourd covered with a sheepskin, to which is attached a very long neck or handle; this instrument has but four strings, three long and one short, which is thick and serves for a bass; it is played by the fingers, and has a very agreeable sound, more so when accompanied with a song." Thus, the New World term "bania" in Surinam had a broad semantic field.[20] It covered both percussive and plucked instruments that were melodic and rhythmic.

Stedman brought back from Surinam a number of artifacts, among them the Creole-bania. This instrument is often referred to as the earliest extant "banjo" in the New World. From an organological perspective, the creole bania is an amalgam. It has a European-style carved headstock and European-style tuning pegs. Its flat fingerboard may also have reflected European influence. (Contemporary West African plucked lutes and harp lutes have round fingerboards; photographic evidence from the early twentieth century records only round fingerboards; no instruments from the eighteenth century or earlier are known to survive.) The making of a flat fingerboard requires a metal saw; and the metal saw in eighteenth-century West or Central Africa is not known to have existed outside of the coastal creole trading communities of the African Atlantic.[21]

It is certain that the early creole plucked lute was made in various forms and string configurations. Each of the two plucked lutes depicted in the Sloane book have two long strings and no short string. The creole bania depicted in Stedman's book has five strings: four long and one short. The creole bania that Stedman brought back to Europe has four strings:

---

20. Richard Price and Sally Price, eds., *Stedman's Surinam: Life in an Eighteenth-Century Slave Society* (Baltimore: The Johns Hopkins University Press, 1992), 277–78.

21. For a history of these communities, see George E. Brooks, *EurAfricans in Western Africa: Commerce, Social Status, Gender, and Religious Observance from the Sixteenth to the Eighteenth Century* (Athens, Ohio: Ohio University Press, 2003).

three long and one short.²² As mentioned above, Stedman is explicit that the short string on the creole bania is the bass string.²³

On the Etymological Roots of the Term "Banjo"

The etymology of the term "banjo" has been contested. Some scholars have asserted that the term *bania* might be traced back to Senegambia, but, as ethnomusicologist Michael Coolen has shown, *bania* is a loan word from English that had a brief career in Senegambia and has disappeared from contemporary speech.²⁴ The dictionary makers at Miriam Webster have asserted that banjo is akin to the Kimbundu *mbanza*, said to be a similar instrument.²⁵ This, however, is clearly in error. There is no tradition of plucked lutes (as opposed to harp lutes) in Central Africa, and there is no native instrument in the region that is known as either *banza* or *mbanza*. (The term *mbanza* means "capital city" in Kikongo.)²⁶

22. A photograph of Stedman's creole bania is reproduced in Robert Lloyd Webb, *Ring the Banjar!: The Banjo in America from Folklore to Factory* (Anaheim: Centerstream, 1984), plate 22. The photograph suggests that the short string attaches at the right-hand side of the neck with the fingerboard facing the observer. For a similar photograph, see Richard Price and Sally Price, "John Gabriel Stedman's Collection of 18th-Century Artefacts from Surinam," *Nieue West-Indische Gids*, vol. 53 (1979), 127.

23. The short string on the North American banjo, at least since the mid-nineteenth century, has noted the highest pitch on the left hand side of the neck. This is consonant with both European and West African traditions of lute making. Some writers about the North American banjo have held that the addition of a short string with a high pitch made the North American instrument different from its predecessors, and as noted above a controversy has taken place in American ethnomusicology over its provenience.

24. Michael T. Coolen, "Senegambian Archetypes for the American Folk Banjo," *Western Folklore*, 43:2 (1984), 131. By the time the American instrument made its appearance in Senegambia, it was classed as a European instrument. The term *banshaw*, for example, meant "European guitar" in Senegambia. The maritime banjo apparently was classed with the other European lutes, such as the guitar. It did not resonate, so to speak, with the Senegambian tradition. Michael Coolen, "The Fodet: A Senegambian Origin for the Blues," *The Black Perspective in Music*, 10:1 (1982), 74–75.

25. See http://www.merriam-webster.com/dictionary/banjo, accessed 25 August 2013.

26. Interestingly, it is possible to document the linguistic borrowing that took place in the opposite direction, from the New World to Central Africa. In the 1940s, the modern banjo diffused from southern Africa to Central Africa where the novelty took the name the 'mbanjo.' [Gerhard Kubik, "The Southern African Periphery: Banjo Traditions

The term *banjo* may have a European rather than an African etymology. According to the citations listed in the *Oxford English Dictionary*, in Western Europe a lute of three, four, or more strings was known in the sixteenth and seventeenth century as a bandore.[27] Up until the late seventeenth century, many plantation workers in the Caribbean colonies and the British North American colonies were white Europeans, either indentured servants of poor commoner backgrounds or Irish who had been enslaved and sold for their labor.[28] It is possible that the indentured whites, or their white purchasers, applied the term bandore to the creole lute of the Atlantic plantations. Jonathan Boucher, an Anglican bishop who was resident in Maryland and Virginia for many years until 1775, provided some indirect evidence on this issue. He noted in his *Glossary of Archaic and Provincial Words* (1832), that bandore was pronounced 'banjor' and that its construction was "a somewhat diversified form and make; but, generally, of great simplicity and rudeness; and in use, chiefly, if not entirely, *among people of the lower classes* [emphasis mine] . . . in Virginia and Maryland, the favourite and almost only instrument in use among the slaves there was a bandore, or, as they pronounced the word, banjer."[29]

Variants of the term banjo eventually came into common usage in the Atlantic world. The semantic fields of these variants—such as bania in eighteenth century Surinam—were broad, outside of North America.

---

in Zambia and Malawi," World of Music, 31:1 (1989), 3–29. It is likely that this mid-twentieth-century African borrowing of the Atlantic creole term is the source of the dictionary makers' confusion.

27. Etymologically, it is derived from the Greek, and finds expression in Arabic as tanbur, from which the terms bandore and ultimately mandola and other instruments are derived. The *Oxford English Dictionary* attributes the derivation of the word banjo from bandore ("a modification of the bandore").

28. The historical evidence that has survived about these "white slaves" in the Caribbean is not extensive. Hilary Beckles has written a social history of these workers on Barbadoes from the scant surviving documentation. See Hilary Beckles, *White Servitude and Black Slavery in Barbados, 1627–1715* (Knoxville: University of Tennessee Press, 1989).

29. Jonathan Boucher, *A Glossary of Obsolete and Provincial Words; Forming a Supplement to the Dictionaries of the English Language* (London, 1832), xlix and entry for bandore (unpaginated).

The Migration of the Atlantic Creole Lute to North America

The earliest evidence for the Atlantic creole lute in the North American colonies dates from the mid-eighteenth century.[30] The evidence from North American sources describes plucked lutes with different numbers of strings and with either wooden or gourd resonating chambers. The terms used in the early North American sources, however, have a much narrower semantic field than those in the Caribbean. Nothing in the historical record suggests that the various forms of the term banjo referred in North America to any other instrument than a plucked lute.[31]

The fragmentary evidence suggests that in the British North American colonies some Native Americans and poor whites, as well as African-Americans, played the banjo. The instrument became a part not only of the musical culture of the enslaved, but of the very poor generally. The banjo was used to make music in a variety of different settings. Historians have found evidence of whites dancing to slave dances that extends at least back to the years of the American Revolution.[32] These cross-cultural musical exchanges varied and must have reflected at least in part the very different demographic profiles of the colonies.[33]

---

30. n.a., "Eighteenth Century Slaves as Advertised by their Masters," *Journal of Negro History*, 1:2 (1916), 210–11, cited in Epstein, "Folk Banjo," 359.

31. Cecelia Conway, *African Banjo Echoes in Appalachia: A Study of Folk Traditions* (Knoxville: University of Tennessee Press, 1995), Appendix: Reports of Black Banjo Players and Their Instruments in the United States Before 1860, 303–11.

32. Roger D. Abrahams, *Singing the Master: The Emergence of African American Culture in the Plantation South* (New York: Penguin, 1992), *passim*. In the Caribbean, there were also slave holidays on which whites and blacks participated in revelry. Pinkster day, a holiday festival of the African-American slaves, was commented upon as early as 1755. It is clear, however, that there were multiple occasions for cross-cultural exchange in the Caribbean as well. See Dena Epstein, "African Music in British and French America," *Musical Quarterly*, 59:1 (1973), 84.

33. On the creolization of music in South Carolina and Georgia, see Richard Cullen Rath, "Drums and Power: Ways of Creolizing Music in Coastal South Carolina and Georgia, 1730–90," in David Buisseret and Steven G. Reinhardt, eds., *Creolization in the Americas* (College Station, Tex.: Texas A&M University Press, 2000), 99–130.

Conclusion

The Atlantic creole lute, known as the banjo, has a complex history that is entwined with larger processes that shaped the Atlantic world in the post-Columbian era. The early historical evidence about the instrument indicates an intertwining of cultural influences within the Atlantic basin rather than a simple unidirectional flow of musical instrument culture from the subcontinent of West Africa. For this reason, the early banjo is best understood as a creole instrument, rather than one with exclusively African origins.

Aurélie Bajeux. *Association Mamanthé, troupe Massilia Ka.*

Danse Gwoka rythme Graj

Photographer : Azedine Hsissou

Marjorie André. *Association Mamanthé, troupe Massilia Ka.*

Aurélie Bajeux. *Association Mamanthé, troupe Massilia Ka.*

Danse Gwoka, rythme Graj

Aurélie Bajeux. *Association Mamanthé, troupe Massilia Ka.*

Artiste invité : Max Diakok. *Association Mamanthé, troupe Massilia Ka.*

Danse Gwoka, rythme Graj

Artiste invité : Max Diakok. *Association Mamanthé, troupe Massilia Ka.*

Artiste invité : Max Diakok. *Association Mamanthé, troupe Massilia Ka.*

Artiste invité : Max Diakok. *Association Mamanthé, troupe Massilia Ka.*

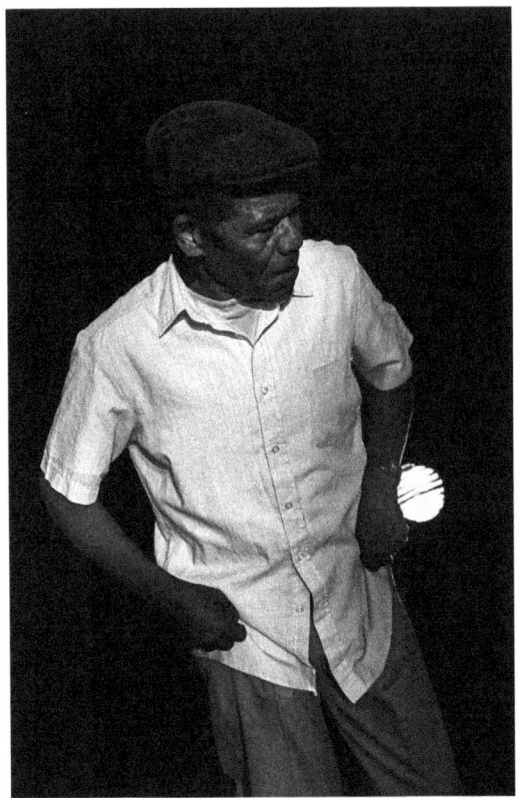

Artiste invité : Georges Janette.
*Association Mamanthé,
troupe Massilia Ka.*

Danse Gwoka, rythme Graj

Artiste invité : Georges Janette.   *Association Mamanthé, troupe Massilia Ka.*

Nathanaël Magen. *Association Mamanthé, troupe Massilia Ka.*

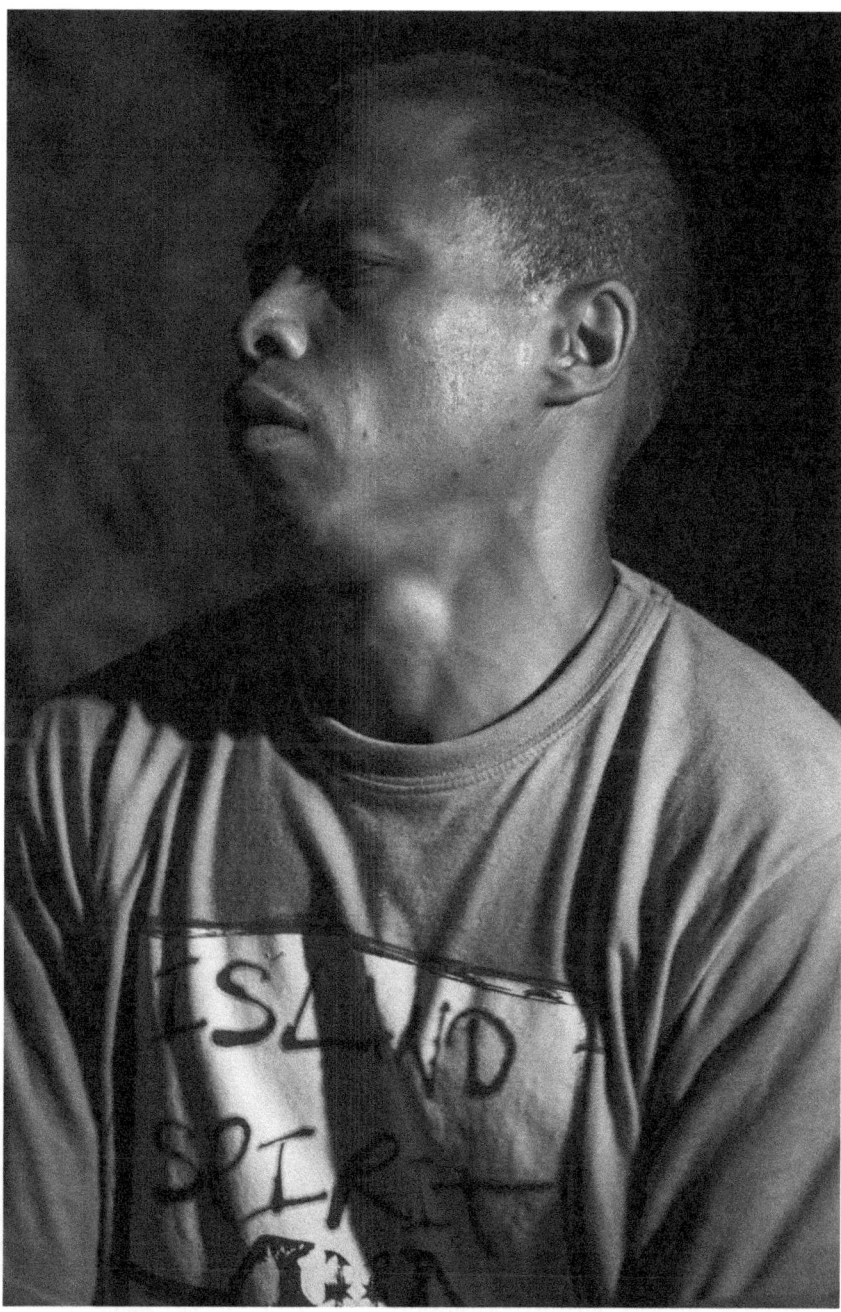

Rina Andrianaivo. *Association Mamanthé, troupe Massilia Ka.*

Artiste invité : Jan Mary Lurel avec les danseuses et les musiciens de *Massilia Ka*.

Hommage to Yolande Joseph-Noël Béhanzin (1933-2011)

Elisée Soumonni

This great and beautiful lady departed this world on December 19, 2011.
She left in the way that she lived, with courage and dignity. Conscious as she was that the end was near, she continued, despite her age, to lend her help and experience to the department of history and archeology at the University of Abomey-Calavi (Bénin). She mustered the necessary energy to meet with her students even hours before her death.

Yolande Béhanzin's professional career was devoted to research and teaching. She prepared for it through solid university training and a teaching certification in history. Her area of research and reflection was vast. It encompassed the three continents of the famous triangular trade. Afro-Martiniquais, Yolande was incontestably a link to the memory of this tragic history. The themes of her research, her publications, indeed her life, are an illustration of it. She played an active role in the inaugural conference of a UNESCO Slave Route project in Ouidah in 1994. The originality of her presentation on Africa's survival in popular culture in the Americas, was much appreciated by the participants at the conference. The Shackles of Memory, whose creation she hailed, appeared to her as an appropriate venue for research on Africa and the African diaspora, a venue in which she published articles in 1999, 2002, and 2003. She participated in the review's evolution through her contact with Jean-Marc Masseaut.

Despite her attachment to her native Martinique, Yolande could not resist the call of Africa, the continent of her origin, to which she strived to bring her contribution in the domain of education, so fundamental for the emergence of new nations born of colonial domination. This is why in 1960 she disembarked in Guinea, which had gained its independence two years earlier and was confronted with well-known decolonization difficulties. It was in Guinea that she met the person who would become her companion for life: Louis Senainon Béhanzin. It was, so to speak, a meeting of heart and historical reason. Louis was the grandson of the king Béhanzin, exiled in Martinique following a long resistance to France's conquest of his kingdom in 1892. The couple would spend nearly twenty-five years here before returning to Benin, Béhanzin's country of origin. During their long sojourn in Guinea, Yolande devoted herself to teaching and research. Her former students have wonderful memories of her, illustrated by the strong delegation that came from Conakry to participate in her memorial services in Cotonou and in Abomey. In the latter city, capital of the ancient kingdom of Dahomey, she was interred next to her husband, who died in November 2005.

In Benin, from 1984 until her death in 2011, Yolande dedicated equal energy to teaching and research. After seven years in Natitingou, in the northern part of the country, she integrated the departments of history and archeology at the National University of Benin at Abomey-Calavi. The eldest member of the department, she remained its inspiration due to her simplicity, modesty, and talent, until her death.

Memory, History, Oblivion:
The Work of History and/or of Memory
In Memory of Hugues Liborel-Pochot

Jean-Marc Masseaut

Throughout the duration of the "The Shackles of Memory" exhibition at the chateau of the Dukes of Brittany in Nantes (1992-1994), the public from Nantes and elsewhere expressed interest in the historical approach to the issues raised by slavery, the Atlantic slave trade, and their legacies.

The Shackles of Memory association decided to take on this project. But what was meant by such intent?

Could it be considered that now the page has been turned, that the accounts were now settled, and that there was nothing more to do but to bury the subject in memorials, much as we might bury someone to whose memory we ritually pay our respects?

Memory is not buried as are our dead.

Memory remains alive and sends a shock wave that does not necessarily weaken with time, but if neglected remains in constant danger of gathering new destructive energies.

The slave trade was a major collective phenomenon that contributed to the building of the Atlantic world through violence and humiliation. The dead victims of this violence, like their memories, have been silenced; but the humiliation remains. In memory it remains as trauma.

In his book *La Mémoire, l'Histoire, l'Oubli* (Editions du Seuil, 2000; translated as *Memory, History, Forgetting*, Univeristy of Chicago Press, 2006), Paul Ricoeur referred to the "collective traumas and injuries of collective memory" that may be overcome only by "the work of history whose theory remains to be completed." He proposed to thus combat using history the surprising resurgence of social conflict and political forces that seemed to be resurfacing from a bygone era. It was this same method that brought together the 1999 editorial board of the *Journal of the Shackles of Memory*. Historians first, then anthropologists, psychoanalysts, and lawyers of various nationalities rallied around the initiative of Hugues Liborel–Pochot, self-described Guadeloupian psychoanalyst, and Olivier Douville, psychoanalyst and editor of the journal *Psychologie clinique*. These therapists had acquired through clinical experience the same conviction as had Paul Ricoeur through philosophical research.

Since publication of the first issue, more than two hundred researchers have sustained this effort—especially historians of Europe, Africa, the Americas, and the Indian Ocean. By offering their work and collaboration in each edition of the *Cahiers*, they allowed the Shackles of Memory association to continue to open up unexplored territories of history and/or memory through historical research and narrative true to the complexity of historical phenomena.

Though morality, with its confessionals that select the guilty, assigns the roles of confessor or the confessed, it is insufficient for learning and understanding what really happened and why. Our European, African, and American societies that were involved with the slave trade and slavery need something else to overcome what can only be described as a trauma. And even if this was far from being the only collective crime in the history of humanity, it nevertheless had its own specificity.

There are no accounts to settle with history. However, there is much knowledge still to be gained in order to understand how the Atlantic world, built on human tragedy impossible to forget, also brought about the emergence of original societies built on the clash of not only languages but also civilizations . . . on the condition, of course, that we are willing to admit that they were civilizations in their own right.

Indeed, if the practice of the Atlantic slave trade as part of the development of the New World is one more collective crime in the history of mankind and must be accepted as such, then it was also part and parcel of the process of the creolization of Atlantic civilizations, which must be understood for the future, in its specifics and in broader theoretical terms.

This idea is not a new one. It gradually emerged among scholars and poets who were at the cutting edge of thinking based on their experience. We are beginning to understand that this development is not unique to the meeting between Europeans and Africans, but that it dates back a long time and is universal.

Up until the last weeks of his life, Hugues Liborel-Pochot endeavored to contribute to this far-reaching thinking by actively taking part in this edition of the *Journal of the Shackles of Memory,* issue number 15, entitled: *"Creolization in the French Americas."*

We have learned much from his experience and his teachings.

He can now rest in peace.

Contributors

Jordan Kellman is dean of Liberal Arts and professor of history at the University of Louisiana at Lafayette.

Jean-Marc Masseaut is editor of *Cahiers des Anneaux de la Mémoire* and vice president of the Aneaux de la Mémoire association, and a doctoral candidate at the École des hautes études en sciences sociales.

Sophie White is associate professor of American Studies, Africana Studies, and history at the University of Notre Dame, where she also holds fellowships in the Gender Studies Program and the Nanovic Insitute of European Studies.

Gordon Sayre is professor of English at the University of Oregon.

Ibrahima Seck is professor of history at the Cheikh Anta Diop University, Dakar, Senegal, and academic director of the Whitney Plantation slavery museum, Wallace, Louisiana.

Elista Istre is assistant director and on-site manager of the Historic Dyess Colony, Dyess, Arkansas.

Mona Georgelin is the founder of the Association Mamanthé, which promotes the history, culture, artists, and writers of the Caribbean and organizes the "Kadans Caraïbe" music festival in Marseilles, France. She is a dancer in the Massilia Ka group.

Max Diakok is dancer-choreographer and artistic director of the Boukoussou Company.

Josette Nonone is a doctoral student at the University of Montreal, where she is conducting research from a psychoanalytic perspective into the African diaspora, slavery, colonialism, and post-colonialism.

Rafaël Lucas is a lecturer at the Institut Ibéro-Américain and a researcher at the Centre d'Etudes de Langues et Linguistique Francophones, both of the Université de Bordeaux-3.

Jacques de Cauna holds the Chaire d'Haïti at the Université de Bordeaux, is honorary professor at l'Université de Pau and Pays de l'Adour, and is a member of the scientific council of the Centre International de Recherche sur les Esclavages.

Edouard Glissant was Distinguished Professor of French Literature at New York University and Professor of French Studies at Louisiana State University.

Olivier Douville is editor of *Clinical Psychology* and a co-founder of *Cahiers des Anneaux de la mémoire*.

Edelyn Dorismond is editor of *Recherches Haïtiano-Antillaises* and vice-president of the Centre de Recherches, Normes, Échanges et Langage.

Carlo Celius is a historian and art historian and a research fellow of the Centre national de la recherche scientifique, France, assigned to the Centre de recherche sur les pouvoirs locaux dans la Caraïbe, Université des Antilles et de la Guyane, Martinique.

Anthony Bogues is a writer, scholar, and curator. He is Lyn Cross Professor of Social Sciences and Critical Theory, professor of Africana Studies, and director of the Center for the Study of Slavery and Justice at Brown University, Providence, Rhode Island.

Bryce Beemer is Mellon Postdoctoral Fellow in History at Colby College, Waterville, Maine.

James L. A. Webb Jr. is professor of history at Colby College.

www.ingramcontent.com/pod-product-compliance
Lightning Source LLC
LaVergne TN
LVHW010400190725
816370LV00006B/21